SOCIETY FOR NEW TESTAMENT STUDIES

MONOGRAPH SERIES

GENERAL EDITOR

MATTHEW BLACK, D.D., F.B.A.

6

THE THEME OF JEWISH PERSECUTION
OF CHRISTIANS IN THE GOSPEL
ACCORDING TO ST MATTHEW

THE THEME OF
JEWISH PERSECUTION OF
CHRISTIANS IN THE
GOSPEL ACCORDING TO
ST MATTHEW

BY

DOUGLAS R.A.HARE

Assistant Professor of New Testament
Pittsburgh Theological Seminary
Pittsburgh, Pennsylvania

CAMBRIDGE
AT THE UNIVERSITY PRESS
1967

Published by the Syndics of the Cambridge University Press
Bentley House, 200 Euston Road, London, N.W. 1
American Branch: 32 East 57th Street, New York, N.Y. 10022

Library of Congress Catalogue Card Number: 67-21959

Printed in Great Britain
at the University Printing House, Cambridge
(Brooke Crutchley, University Printer)

To
W.D.DAVIES

CONTENTS

vii

CONTENTS

PREFACE

It has long been recognized that the Gospel according to St Matthew has intensified the conflict between Jesus and the Pharisees. It has frequently been suggested that this intensification reflects the continuing struggle between the Church and the synagogue, a struggle which constitutes an important part of the *Sitz im Leben* of the First Gospel. One aspect of this matter which has seldom, if ever, received sustained and thorough treatment is the theme of Jewish persecution of Christians, a theme which occurs repeatedly in Matthew's gospel. The intention of the present study is to subject this Matthean theme to careful scrutiny, with two questions primarily in mind: (1) Has Matthew exaggerated the severity of the persecution? and (2) How has the persecution influenced Matthew's theology?

The first part of the study is consequently strictly historical. In view of many exaggerated and inaccurate statements concerning the suffering imposed upon Christians by Jews, there is a great need for a reappraisal of the historical data relating to this persecution, in order to establish as accurately as possible the nature and extent of the conflict. Chapter I prepares for this historical study by examining the sociological presuppositions of persecution as related to the Jewish community. In order to evaluate properly the Matthean portrayal of persecution, we must then, in chapter II, examine the evidence found in sources other than Matthew. Here we shall be dependent primarily upon Christian sources, since they alone make explicit reference to the conflict. This is unfortunate, since the Christian accounts are clearly biased and consequently a poor foundation for an objective study. Some control, however, can be provided by rabbinic texts, which, when used with caution as regarding date, can enable us to establish to a limited extent the patterns of synagogue discipline employed in the first century. Rabbinic allusions to the Minim provide some indication of the methods used by the rabbis to control nonconformity. Employing both Christian and Jewish sources, we shall examine individually the kinds of ill-treatment attributed to Jews by Christian authors. Attention will also be paid to questions of incidence, geography and chronology, the role of Jewish religious leadership, and the role of Jews in Gentile persecution of Christians.

When a historical reconstruction of the persecution has been completed to the extent permitted by our sources, we shall then turn to the relevant passages in the Gospel according to St Matthew. Since we must be careful to distinguish between inherited traditions and the editor's own contributions to the theme, chapter III will of necessity be an essay in *Redaktionsgeschichte*. On the basis of our findings, we shall then evaluate Matthew's portrayal of the persecution by reference to the conclusions reached in the preceding chapter. This will complete the historical study.

The remaining chapters will explore the theological perspective from which Matthew views the conflict. Chapter IV will attempt to establish Matthew's answer to the question, 'Why persecution?' Chapter V will investigate the relationship between Matthew's experience of persecution and his doctrine of Israel and the Church. The Matthean emphasis upon loving one's enemies will be briefly examined. Conclusions will be drawn concerning the relationship between persecution and eschatology in Matthew's thought.

While many of the conclusions reached in this investigation are necessarily tentative because of the inadequacy of the evidence, the author hopes that the study will contribute to a clearer understanding of the conflict between the Church and the synagogue in the first century and to a firmer grasp of Matthew's theology.

Although there have been minor alterations and additions, this work is substantially a doctoral dissertation submitted to the faculty of Union Theological Seminary in New York in 1965. In its present form it is respectfully dedicated to W. D. Davies, who served as chief adviser during the preparation of the dissertation. I am indebted to Professor Davies, not only for his scholarly wisdom and tactful guidance, but also, and especially, for his gracious encouragement and support.

Helpful suggestions regarding this study were offered by Professors J. Louis Martyn and Samuel L. Terrien of Union Theological Seminary. Gratitude must also be expressed to three other teachers, F. C. Grant, George Johnston and John Knox. Although not consulted in connection with the present study, they were largely responsible for preparing the author for research in this area.

Most of the writing was done since I became employed by Pittsburgh Theological Seminary. I should like to express here my gratitude to President Donald G. Miller, Dean Gordon E. Jackson, and my colleagues in the Biblical Division, who lightened my responsibilities so that this work might be completed.

I should like to thank my typists, Mrs Audrey Jones, Mrs Claire Price and Mrs Arline Wylie for careful work cheerfully performed. Mr Charles C. Hendricks, B.D., a graduate student, has been of great assistance in the preparation of the indices. My last word of appreciation goes to my wife for her help in the tedious tasks of reading proof and preparing the bibliography.

D.R.A.H.

Pittsburgh Theological Seminary
Pittsburgh, Pennsylvania

22 September 1966

ABBREVIATIONS

Ant.	Josephus, *Antiquities of the Jews.*
Bauer	W. F. Arndt and F. W. Gingrich, *A Greek–English Lexicon of the New Testament and Other Early Literature.* Translation and adaptation of Walter Bauer's *Griechisch–Deutsches Wörterbuch,* fourth edition.
Beg.	F. J. Foakes Jackson and K. Lake, *The Beginnings of Christianity,* part I.
Bell.	Josephus, *The Wars of the Jews.*
Blass–Debrunner–Funk	F. Blass and A. Debrunner, *A Greek Grammar of the New Testament and Other Early Christian Literature.* A translation and revision of the ninth–tenth German edition by R. W. Funk.
Eccl. Hist.	Eusebius, *The Ecclesiastical History.*
E.G.T.	*The Expositor's Greek Testament,* edited by W. R. Nicoll.
H.T.R.	*Harvard Theological Review.*
J.B.L.	*Journal of Biblical Literature.*
J.B.R.	*Journal of Bible and Religion.*
J.E.	*The Jewish Encyclopaedia.*
J.E.H.	*Journal of Ecclesiastical History.*
Jos.	Josephus.
J.Q.R.	*Jewish Quarterly Review.*
J.T.S.	*Journal of Theological Studies.*
N.E.B.	*The New English Bible New Testament.*
N.T.S.	*New Testament Studies.*
par.	and parallel(s).
R.G.G.	*Religion in Geschichte und Gegenwart.*
R.S.V.	*The Holy Bible.* Revised Standard Version.
S.–B.	H. L. Strack and P. Billerbeck, *Kommentar zum Neuen Testament aus Talmud und Midrasch.*

T.D.N.T.	*Theological Dictionary of the New Testament.* A translation of Kittel's *Theologis'hes Wörterbuch zum Neuen Testament* by G. W. Bromiley.
T.L.	*Theologische Literaturzeitung.*
T.W.N.T.	*Theologisches Wörterbuch zum Neuen Testament*, edited by G. Kittel.
Z.A.W.	*Zeitschrift für die Alttestamentliche Wissenschaft.*
Z.N.W.	*Zeitschrift für die Neutestamentliche Wissenschaft.*
Z.T.K.	*Zeitschrift für Theologie und Kirche.*

Abbreviations now commonly accepted for the Dead Sea Scrolls are listed by A. Dupont-Sommer, *The Essene Writings from Qumran*, p. 421.

CHAPTER I

GENERAL REMARKS ON THE NATURE OF THE CONFLICT BETWEEN JEWS AND CHRISTIANS

In studying the early conflict between Jews and Christians one must constantly guard against a tendency to oversimplify the issues in dispute and the causes of hostility. The conflict was as many-sided as the two opposing groups.

To suppose, for example, that the Pharisees were the sole protagonists on the Jewish side is to ignore the earlier conflict with pro-Roman Sadducees and the continuing conflict with anti-Roman Zealots.[1] It further assumes that the primary opposition to Christianity was of an official nature, led by the acknowledged leaders of Jewry, and ignores the complexity of the Christian movement itself, which included a significant number of loyal Pharisees (Acts 15: 5; cf. 21: 20).

A similar inclination to oversimplification is seen in those statements which reduce the conflict to matters of orthopraxis as over against orthodoxy. It is not true to say that obedience to the requirements of Torah exempted one from conflict, regardless of one's beliefs. Whereas considerable tolerance prevailed in both areas (behaviour and belief) as far as most Jewish groups were concerned,[2] there is reason for believing that Christians met with intolerance on account of their religious beliefs as well as for failure to observe all the requirements of

---

[1] Such a view is explicitly stated by R. T. Herford, *The Pharisees* (1924), p. 213: 'If there had been no Pharisees, the Church would have met with little or no opposition.' I owe this reference to P. H. Deever, *The Anti-Judaism of the New Testament in the Light of its Biblical and Hellenistic Context* (1958), p. 138.

[2] Even the use of images was more widely tolerated than has often been assumed. Cecil Roth, 'An Ordinance against Images in Jerusalem, A.D. 66', *H.T.R.* xlix, no. 3 (1956), 170, notes that Agrippa I, who was popular with the nationalists and regarded as religiously observant, was the only Jewish ruler to circulate coins bearing his own image. Halakic disputes were frequent, yet accompanied on the whole by surprising tolerance; cf. Mish. Yeb. 1: 4.

Torah.[1] The conflict is too narrowly conceived when viewed as a series of legal disputes.

The approach of historians, both Jewish and Christian, has generally been too theological. Jewish writers tend to find the basis of the conflict in the Church's rejection of Torah.[2] Christians, on the other hand, are inclined to view the strife as due to Jewish rejection of the Messiah. This theologizing tendency is, of course, as old as the New Testament itself. In the present study we shall be particularly concerned with Matthew's theological interpretation of the struggle.[3] While a completely objective delineation of the separation of Christianity from Judaism is neither possible nor desirable, an adequate historical study must take full account of sociological factors before theological conclusions are drawn.

To a sociologist it would be obvious that certain tolerance-limits were present in the Jewish communities of Palestine and the Diaspora in the first century A.D. In any given community there is a limit to the amount of deviation which can be tolerated. In the communities with which we are concerned various types of eccentricity and religious laxity were permitted, but those deviations which challenged the community's way of life too drastically stimulated a hostile reaction which ranged in intensity from silent resentment to mob violence.

Philo's quarrel with the Allegorists of Alexandria is pertinent. His own emphasis on the reality of the unseen world inclined him to sympathy with those who subordinated the literal meaning of the laws to a spiritual understanding. He had no patience, however, with the extreme Allegorists who claimed that possession of spiritual meanings freed them from literal observance of the laws. Undoubtedly the Allegorists believed that they were carrying Philo's own approach to religion to its logical conclusion. Philo refused to follow them, because, as a man of great common sense, he realized that his beloved

[1] It is generally conceded that a primary cause of Bar Cocheba's hostility toward Jewish Christians was their persistent belief that not he but Jesus was Israel's Messiah.

[2] An extreme example is Ignaz Ziegler, *Der Kampf zwischen Judentum und Christentum* (1907). Ziegler maintains that there was no conflict with the followers of Jesus until Paul declared that the law of circumcision and the food laws were no longer binding, pp. 73 f. Cf. p. 53.

[3] See below, chapters IV and V.

Jewish community could not tolerate such a flagrant disregard for its customs.

It follows that, exactly as we have to take thought for the body, because it is the abode of the soul, so we must pay heed to the letter of the laws. If we keep and observe these, we shall gain a clearer conception of those things of which these are the symbols. *And besides that we shall not incur the censure of the many and the charges they are sure to bring against us.* [Italics added.][1]

Here Philo acknowledges the expediency of conformity. To remain within the community requires a minimal observance of the accepted *mores*.

The early Church was not as sociologically prudent as Philo. Various groups of Christians departed radically from accepted standards. In going beyond the limits of tolerance they invited anger, rejection, and, in some instances, violence. The hostility engendered by the extremism of a few could, on occasion, bring down the wrath of the community upon all known Christians. It may safely be assumed that while the more discerning would distinguish, for example, between the position of Stephen and his associates and that of the more conservative members of the Jerusalem church, the populace would tend to bulk all Christians together as undesirables and rebels.[2] To argue, therefore, that only Hellenists were under attack in 'the persecution that arose over Stephen' (Acts 11: 19) is to overemphasize the official aspect of the persecution and ignore the role of popular confusion.

From the sociological point of view it would seem that the conflict arose because of Christian disrespect for ethnic solidarity, the fundamental principle of Jewish life from the Exile to the present. Four aspects of the Christian attack may be isolated for purposes of study.

1. In the first place, *Christians questioned the central symbols of Jewish solidarity.* Symbols of first rank were Torah, Temple and Holy City; not far behind were the purity and food laws, cir-

---

[1] *Migr. Abr.* 93. All citations from Philo are from the Loeb Classical Library edition.

[2] Dom Gregory Dix, *Jew and Greek: A Study in the Primitive Church* (1953), p. 41, presents the view that popular reports of Christian antinomianism in the Diaspora were responsible for persecutions of Torah-observing Christians in Jerusalem. See also Marcel Simon, *Verus Israel* (1948), p. 304.

1-2

cumcision and Sabbath. These were symbols of Israel's distinctiveness, tokens of its separateness.

There is reason to believe that each of these prized possessions was questioned by Jewish groups other than the Church. A sceptical attitude toward these external manifestations of Israel's faith was shown by the Allegorists, as already mentioned.[1] H. J. Schoeps finds a strong anti-ritualistic strain in Palestinian Judaism of the first century.[2] The Dead Sea documents reveal at least a serious ambivalence toward the Temple and its ritual.[3] Because the Holy City was so closely identified with priestly religion, its value as a symbol for the unity of far-flung Jewry was questionable as far as many in the Diaspora were concerned.[4] Although the evidence is admittedly slender, it is probable that many individual Jews, in Palestine itself as well as in the Diaspora, were seriously tempted to spiritualize their religion and move toward closer assimilation with the dominant culture without abandoning their monotheistic faith and high moral standards. While such liberals would have aroused antagonism because of their failure to conform, and, in some instances, have been haled before the courts, the Jewish community would have regarded them otherwise than it did the Christians. Stephen, Paul and presumably many others publicly challenged the basic symbols in the name of Jesus of Nazareth. Not as non-conforming individuals alone but as members of an organized movement meeting regularly for separate acts of worship outside the synagogue (Acts 2: 42; 4: 24), Christians represented a more severe threat to the traditional way of life than even apostates, such as Tiberius Alexander, Philo's nephew. And while many Jewish Christians, including perhaps Paul himself, remained outwardly loyal to most of the customs of Judaism, there was a difference in

---

[1] Above, p. 2. See also M. Simon's identification of a 'Reform Judaism' in the Diaspora, *Verus Israel*, pp. 75 ff.

[2] *Theologie und Geschichte des Judenchristentums* (1949), pp. 219–33.

[3] See, e.g., 1QS ix. 4 f., where it is maintained that a more satisfactory atonement is wrought by obedience than by whole burnt offerings.

[4] Justin, *Dial.* 117, attributes to Trypho the Jew the opinion that 'God did not accept the sacrifices of the Israelites who then dwelt at Jerusalem, but that He has declared that the prayers of the Jews who were then in the Dispersion were pleasing to Him and that He calls their prayers sacrifices'. Cf. M. Simon, *Verus Israel*, pp. 55–7.

their attitude to these tokens of ethnic solidarity, a difference which could not fail to be noted by those who heard them preach.

Christians subordinated all symbols to the central symbol of their faith, the Christ. It must not be assumed that the dispute over Jesus was peripheral to the conflict. It is true that a good deal of tolerance existed in Jewry with respect to messianic speculation. Even the Christian claim that the crucified Nazarene was to return on the clouds of heaven as victorious Son of man may have elicited little more than derision among early opponents. It was the insistent emphasis upon the *centrality* of Jesus that excited intolerance.[1] While schismatics at Qumran might elevate their Teacher of Righteousness to a place of great honour, and proclaim the imminence of messiah(s) from Aaron and Israel, the role assigned to such figures was not crucial.[2] Torah remained supreme. Christians, however, proclaimed a Christ who transcended Torah even as he fulfilled it.[3] The followers of Jesus might disagree among themselves with regard to which precepts of Torah were still valid, but with the possible exception of the most conservative wing of the Jerusalem Church there was general agreement that the authority of Jesus transcended the authority of Torah. While moderately-conservative Jewish Christians such as the author of the First Gospel were careful to maintain that Jesus did not annul Torah (Matt. 5: 17), the contrast between their view of Torah and that of Pharisaism and Essenism was unmistakable. The focus had changed. The supreme norm for the life well-pleasing to God was no longer Torah but Jesus.

Not only Torah but also Temple and Holy City were subordinated to Jesus. It is highly probable that the prophecy of the destruction of the Temple and the Holy City attributed to Jesus in the gospels,[4] represents a genuine reminiscence, not

---

[1] G. D. Kilpatrick, *The Origins of the Gospel According to St Matthew* (1946), p. 123, declares that the distinctive character of the Matthean church 'was not due to any rejection of Judaism itself, but to its subordination to the central doctrine of Christ'.

[2] CD i. 11, xii. 23, xiv. 19; 1QS ix. 11.

[3] See W. D. Davies, *The Setting of the Sermon on the Mount* (1964), pp. 106 f.

[4] Mark 13: 2 (Matt. 24: 2; Luke 21: 6); Matt. 23: 37 f.; Luke 13: 34 f.; cf. Mark 14: 57-9 (Matt. 26: 60 f.), Mark 15: 29 (Matt. 27: 40), John 2: 19-22, Acts 6: 13 f.

a *vaticinium post eventu*.[1] The treasuring of this prophecy provides evidence that Jewish Christians were ready to surrender cherished symbols of the old faith in exchange for a place in the messianic community. Even if the 'something greater than the Temple' of Matthew 12: 6 refers not to Jesus but to the kingdom he proclaimed, there can be no doubt that for Christians Jesus was himself the central symbol of the kingdom of God. And if Jewish followers of Jesus continued to lend support to the Temple ritual (Acts 2: 46), it was with a sense of messianic freedom from cultic obligations (Matt. 17: 26 f., 'Then the sons are free. However, not to give offence to them...').

Purity and food laws, circumcision and Sabbath were likewise depreciated by Christians. It is not that Jewish Christians abandoned these symbols completely but rather that they came to be regarded as of secondary importance. Evidence for this change of attitude can be seen in the fact that the leaders of the Jerusalem church gave the right hand of fellowship to Paul, the ardent defender of Gentile freedom from such obligations (Gal. 2: 9), and in the willingness of Cephas to eat with Gentiles in Antioch with a freedom contrary to Jewish custom (Gal. 2: 12, 14). That the Sabbath continued to be an important institution is indicated by Matthew's addition of μηδὲ σαββάτῳ ('nor on the Sabbath') to Marcan material at 24: 20.[2] In view of Matthew's conservatism, his inclusion of controversy-narratives relating to the Sabbath (Matt. 12: 1–14), including the Marcan saying 'For the Son of man is lord of the Sabbath' (Matt. 12: 8), is significant evidence of the subordination of Sabbath to Son of man in primitive Christian thought.

It can hardly be doubted that such an attitude toward the basic symbols of ethnic solidarity met with hostility. Whether

[1] Accepted as genuine by R. Bultmann, *Theology of the New Testament* (1951–5), I, 21. S. G. F. Brandon, *The Fall of Jerusalem and the Christian Church* (1951), pp. 37–40, maintains that the prophecy is a post-war creation of the Church. Brandon believes that there was such a close identification of Jewish Christianity with Zealot nationalism that it is impossible that a dominical prophecy calling into question symbols cherished by the nationalists would have been preserved by Palestinian Christians. The chief weakness in Brandon's excellent work is that he underestimates the sectarian tendency in the primitive Jerusalem church which set it over against the community as a whole (see below, pp. 13–15).

[2] Cf. Kilpatrick, *Origins*, p. 116.

6

or not Christian preaching in Jerusalem following the martyrdom of Stephen was more temperate in its treatment of the accepted symbols cannot be ascertained. In the Diaspora, however, this fundamental departure from Jewish *mores* made itself increasingly apparent.

(2.) Ethnic solidarity was further challenged by Christians in their *rejection of Jewish nationalism*. Those who made Jesus the central symbol of their corporate life found that the ties of popular nationalism had been transcended. This is not to say that for Jewish Christians nationalistic feeling was completely annulled. Even Paul, presumably one of the most liberal in this respect among Jewish Christians, was not able to remove from his thought all distinctions between Jews and Gentiles, as Romans 9–11 makes abundantly clear. Apparently many believed that the coming kingdom of God would be a Jewish kingdom, to which Gentiles would belong as proselytes.[1] Acts 1: 6 suggests that there were some who looked to Jesus to 'restore the kingdom to Israel' in a this-worldly sense. The quietistic attitude of Jesus, however, militated against the development of Zealot nationalism in the Palestinian Church. Loyalty to Jesus' command to love one's enemies undoubtedly produced a sharp cleavage between Christians and political activists. While Zealots agitated for violent revolution, Christians preached spiritual repentance and called for faith in their Messiah, who would soon return to establish the kingdom by supernatural power. Their central allegiance was not to the nation and its political destiny but to Jesus, their risen Lord, who in his own person represented the real Israel.[2] Only those who confessed Jesus as Messiah and Lord could claim membership in the eschatological Israel.[3] Thus while a nationalistic

---

[1] Cf. Matt. 19: 28 (Luke 22: 30), '...You...will sit on twelve thrones, judging the twelve tribes of Israel'.

[2] The view that Jesus represents Israel is not clearly stated in the synoptic gospels, but is suggested by the corporate significance of the 'one like a son of man' in Dan. 7: 13, and by the identification of Jesus with the Elect Servant of Deutero-Isaiah (Matt. 8: 17; Acts 8: 32–5), a figure which in the LXX is more consistently identified with Israel than in the Masoretic Text (LXX Isa. 42: 1, ʼΙακὼβ ὁ παῖς μου...ʼΙσραὴλ ὁ ἐκλεκτός μου). For a discussion of Matthew's repudiation of this identification, see below, p. 159.

[3] Cf. Mark 8: 38 (Matt. 10: 32 f.; Luke 12: 8 f.); Rom. 4: 16–25.

flavour continues, it is a nationalism which is different in kind from the popular Jewish nationalism of the time.

Josephus tells us that while war with Rome was brewing he repeatedly warned his countrymen of the folly of armed revolt until he realized that his public admonitions would incur the hatred of the revolutionaries and result in his murder.[1] Undoubtedly many, like Josephus, found it prudent to remain silent or to collaborate with the Zealots. Those Christians who had not the courage to condemn violence as openly as had their Master may have elected this alternative. Others, refusing to support the Zealot cause, chose withdrawal. The extant evidence is not sufficient to indicate how much suffering was inflicted on Christian pacifists by fanatical nationalists during the first war with Rome, A.D. 66–70.[2] For our present purpose it is sufficient to say that on the issue of nationalism Christians challenged both the popular nationalism of the community as a whole and the militant nationalism of the Zealots. To the extent that this challenge was vocal and open, hostility toward the Christians would be intensified.

(3.) A third challenge to the Jewish community was present in the *Christians' attitude toward the Gentiles.*

The fundamental question of how Israel was to relate itself to the hellenistic world had remained an unsolved problem since the Antiochene period.[3] Individual Jewish response to this question ran the full gamut from complete hellenization including religious apostasy to violent treatment of Gentile intruders in the Holy Land.[4] The majority accepted the necessity of co-existing with Gentiles, and *halakoth* were issued on the use of Gentile foods and similar matters.[5]

The Mishnah indicates that it was not uncommon for Jews to share a common courtyard with Gentiles.[6] Business partnerships with Gentiles were also permitted.[7] The rabbis did not frown upon the use of Gentile baths, even those containing idols.[8] A *halakah* regulating the use of Gentile washermen is

[1] *Vita* 4–5 (17–20).
[2] Justin reports considerable suffering during the Bar Cocheba revolt, 1 *Apol.* 31.
[3] Cf. W. R. Farmer, *Maccabees, Zealots, and Josephus* (1956), p. 50.
[4] Josephus, *Vita* 23 (113).   [5] Abod. Zar. *passim.*
[6] Erub. 6: 1; 8: 5.   [7] Bekh. 1: 1; 2: 1, 4.
[8] Abod. Zar. 3: 4; cf. Maksh. 2: 5.

attributed to the School of Shammai and may be taken as indicative of the situation in Palestine in the first century A.D.[1] The Mishnah also permitted the purchase of non-Jewish bondmen or bondmaids. It is perhaps to be assumed that such slaves would eat with their Jewish owners, although this is not clearly stated. Berakoth 7: 1 allows Samaritans to be included in the quorum for the Common Grace but specifies that Gentiles may not be counted, thus indicating that at the time this *halakah* was formulated it was not uncommon to invite a Gentile to a meal. That such a practice was permissible even in the first century is suggested by a halakic dispute between the schools of Shammai and Hillel.

The School of Shammai say: An Israelite may not be numbered [in the same company] with a priest for [the consumption of] a Firstling. And the School of Hillel permit it even to a Gentile.[2]

Explicit mention of an Israelite eating with a Gentile at the same table is made in Abodah Zarah 5: 5, where the possibility of such a common meal is taken for granted and concern shown only for the ritual cleanliness of the wine to be shared.[3]

Contact with Gentiles prompted not only regulatory *halakoth* but also a vigorous proselytizing movement. The eagerness with which proselytes were sought and the success of such efforts are attested by pagan, Jewish and Christian writers of the period.[4]

---

[1] Shabb. 1: 8. [2] Bekh. 5: 2 (Danby, *The Mishnah* (1933)).

[3] The assertion of Dom Gregory Dix, p. 34, that 'the rule against "eating with men uncircumcised" (Acts 11: 3) was something which *every* practising Jew observed as an elementary act of loyalty to the covenant of his People', is as extravagant as the basis claimed therefor: 'To "eat with the uncircumcised" rendered a Jew ritually "unclean"... and so excluded any Jew *from all social and domestic intercourse with his own people*' (italics in the original). Despite the large share of attention paid to questions of cleanness and uncleanness in the Mishnah and elsewhere, the common man was little hindered by being in a state of uncleanness except when it was a question of consecrated food, the priest's portion and the second tithe, and when going on a visit to the Temple; cf. G. F. Moore, *Judaism in the First Centuries of the Christian Era* (1927), II, 76. The use of Gentile slaves is further evidence against the position maintained by Dix; cf. B. J. Bamberger, *Proselytism in the Talmudic Period* (1939), pp. 126, 289.

[4] For references by pagan authors, see Théodore Reinach, *Textes d'auteurs grecs et romains relatifs au judaïsme* (1895), pp. 155, 182, 244, 259, 263, 293, 307, 346. Examples of Christian witness to Jewish proselytism are Matt. 23: 15; Acts 2: 10; 6: 5; Justin, *Dial.* 80, 122 f. For a thorough

Josephus makes mention of a large body of 'Judaizers' in Syria.[1] Jewish congregations throughout the Diaspora were surrounded by 'God-fearers', οἱ φοβούμενοι τὸν θεόν, men and women who were inclined toward Judaism but not yet ready to become full proselytes.[2] B. J. Bamberger, who has done one of the most thorough studies of Jewish proselytism in the Talmudic era, maintains that throughout the period the rabbinic attitude toward proselytism was overwhelmingly favourable.[3] Many rabbis hoped for the ultimate conversion of all the heathen.[4] Bamberger concedes, however, that the attitude of the populace may not have been as favourable as that of their spiritual leaders, as evidenced by the strenuous support offered to the proselytizing movement by the rabbis.[5] It is probable, he suggests, that

among the people as a whole there were certain prejudices against converts. These prejudices were probably analogous to the dislike of the foreigner which we so often meet in modern nations. The few passages we have found in which the Rabbis attack converts are best explained as cases in which these popular prejudices invaded the scholarly class.[6]

The missionary zeal displayed by the Christian Church toward the Gentiles ought therefore to be viewed not as a departure from Judaism but as a continuation of a strong tendency within the parent religion.[7] If the Pharisees objected

survey of rabbinic references, see Bamberger. According to H. J. Schoeps, *Paul: The Theology of the Apostle in the Light of Jewish Religious History* (1961), pp. 27 f., the missionary zeal of the Diaspora is evidenced by specific readings in the LXX. For a discussion of the successfulness of proselytizing efforts, see E. Schürer, *A History of the Jewish People in the Time of Jesus Christ*, Div. II, vol. II, 304–11.

[1] *Bell.* ii. 18. 2 (463).
[2] Acts 10: 2, 22; 13: 16, 26; cf. Schürer, Div. II, vol. II, 304 f., 314 f.
[3] According to Bamberger, p. 161, there are only four passages in the entire literature which are unfavourable without any reservation. He finds no support for the view that while a friendly attitude toward proselytes existed in the Diaspora a negative attitude dominated Palestine, p. 277.
[4] Bamberger, p. 168.   [5] *Ibid.* p. 161.
[6] *Ibid.* pp. 277 f.
[7] The notice of Acts 11: 19 that 'those who were scattered because of the persecution that arose over Stephen travelled as far as Phoenicia and Cyprus and Antioch, speaking the word to none except the Jews' should not be taken as representing a dogmatic position. It is hardly probable that the

to the Christian treatment of the Gentiles it was not because they opposed proselytism but rather because they regarded the type of conversion accepted by Christians as incomplete. As we have already seen, for Christians Torah was subordinate to Jesus. This subordination manifested itself in the way Christians accepted as full members in the messianic community those God-fearers who confessed faith in Jesus. The convert was initiated by means of baptism in the name of Jesus, a rite comparable to Jewish proselyte-baptism, but circumcision was not required.

The importance of circumcision in Judaism should not be ignored. It was not unusual for Gentiles to retain a lifelong relationship to the synagogue without undergoing the ritual operation.[1] Despite Jewish friendliness toward such semi-proselytes, however, the annual ritual of the Passover meal demonstrated that uncircumcised adherents were still Gentiles and excluded from the People of God.[2] For Christians, on the other hand, the old Passover was no longer the distinctive festal meal of the People of God. While Jewish Christians continued to celebrate the Jewish Passover, emphasis in the Church was placed rather on the Lord's supper and the new Paschal Lamb which had been sacrificed for them (i Cor. 5: 7). Participation in the distinctive Christian meal was open to all baptized believers, regardless of their relationship to the Law of Moses.

This acceptance of Gentiles as equals without prior naturalization into the Jewish nation undoubtedly aroused a great deal of hostility among those who were diligently seeking full con-

Christian missionaries here referred to spoke publicly in the synagogues of the Diaspora without being heard by semi-proselytes. What may be meant by the author of Acts is that at this particular point in the history of the Christian mission Christians had not yet addressed their message to Gentiles who were not already adherents of the synagogue. The Gentile problem remained a real problem within the Church for many years, but the point at issue was never whether or not the Gentiles had the right to hear the message; cf. James Parkes, *The Foundations of Judaism and Christianity* (1960), p. 109, and B. S. Easton, *Christ in the Gospels* (1930), p. 125.

[1] Juvenal, *Satires* xiv, 96–106, dated after A.D. 128, speaks of the tendency for circumcision to be adopted by the second generation. Cf. also the advice of Ananias to King Izates, Jos. *Ant.* xx. 2. 4 (40–2).

[2] Cf. Moore, I, 330 and note 4, and Saul Lieberman, *Greek in Jewish Palestine* (1942), p. 79.

verts to the religion of Torah.[1] It seems probable that the hatred of Saul the Pharisee for the Christians was stimulated in part by this laxity toward the Gentiles.[2] If the free relationship with uncircumcised Gentiles, distinctively manifested in table fellowship, was a problem even within the Christian Church (Acts 11: 2; Gal. 2: 11 f.), it was surely a trying test to the tolerance of the wider Jewish community.

In assessing the sociological effect of the Christian mission to the Gentiles, full weight must be given to the attitude of Palestinian Jewry as a whole, whose prejudice against foreigners has already been mentioned. While Judeans were undoubtedly proud to behold throngs of foreign converts converging on Jerusalem for the great festivals, it seems likely that this sense of pride was balanced by in-group feelings which resented the intrusion of outsiders. The prospect of any large influx of new converts or, worse, of semi-converts such as the uncircumcised adherents of the Nazarene, could appear as a threat to Jewish solidarity. Reports of Christian missionary success in the Diaspora might easily arouse uneasiness and hostility.

Despite closer contact with the Gentiles and widespread proselytizing, a wide social gap still existed between Jews and Gentiles. The dividing wall of hostility, for Christians broken down by Christ (Eph. 2: 14), was continually reinforced by those who sensed the immensity of the threat to the traditional way of life posed by integrationists. In view of contemporary experience in race relations it is not hard to suppose that in periods of mounting tension between Jews and Gentiles violence sometimes erupted among Jews over such matters as social intercourse with the uncircumcised.[3] Liberals who showed too

---

[1] Bamberger, p. 298, speaking of the Christian mission, suggests that 'the universalism of the rabbis was perhaps more genuine than that of the daughter religion. It was expressed in policies which did not compromise the religious ideals of Judaism for the sake of missionary success'.

[2] Gal. 5: 11 suggests that Paul was at one time a preacher of circumcision like that Eleazar who persuaded King Izates that circumcision was the principal law of Torah, *Ant.* xx. 2. 4 (43–5); cf. E. Barnikol, *Die vorchristliche und frühchristliche Zeit des Paulus* (1929), pp. 18 ff.

[3] The use of ἐθνικός and ἔθνη as pejoratives in Matt. 18: 17; Gal. 2: 15 is a hint of the gulf of separation. The violent attempt to circumcise two Gentiles in Galilee reported by Josephus (*Vita* 23 [113]) is indicative of the temper of the Zealots. This zeal was probably based on the belief that God

little respect for boundary lines faced the same kind of displeasure in the ancient situation as in the modern. When nationalist feeling ran high, friendly association with Gentiles would be tantamount to treason in the eyes of extremists. Those who criticized Jesus for befriending tax agents of the foreigners (Matt. 11: 19; Luke 7: 34; 19: 7) would be far more hostile when his followers later treated uncircumcised foreigners as brothers.

That the supra-national tendency of Christianity was a distinct menace to a beleaguered Jewry is clear.[1] The attitude of Christians toward the Gentiles is simply another aspect of the wider challenge offered by Christianity to the traditional solidarity of the Jewish people.

4. A fourth aspect of this challenge was the *Christian rejection of the community-as-a-whole and its accepted religious leadership*. We may be helped in understanding the impact of this kind of rejection by considering a contemporary analogy. The Jehovah's Witnesses are a well-known example of a religious group which, like the early Church, rejects the entire community as sinful beyond measure and denounces the religious leadership as agents of the devil. While most communities are able to tolerate the outspoken criticism of the Russellites, the Province of Quebec provides an instance of a situation in which the challenge of this sect exceeded the bounds of toleration and resulted in 'persecution', mostly in the form of imprisonment.

The element of prophetic criticism in early Christianity has been minimized by those who see no marked separation between the church of Jerusalem and its Jewish environment. This is to ignore the distinctive character of the primitive Church. Christianity emerged as a conversionist movement within Judaism, proclaiming the need for universal repentance on the basis of the nearness of the Last Judgment. Baptism in the name of the Messiah Jesus distinguished those who would survive the eschatological catastrophe from those who would not (Acts 2: 38–40).[2] An 'adulterous and sinful generation' is

would not fulfil his promise regarding the Holy Land while there remained in it any who repudiated his covenant of circumcision; cf. W. R. Farmer, p. 71.   [1] Cf. Jocz, *The Jewish People and Jesus Christ* (1949), p. 44.
    [2] Ulrich Wilckens, *Die Missionsreden der Apostelgeschichte* (1961), maintains that the early speeches in Acts are the free compositions of Luke and do not

castigated in the gospels,[1] and entire communities are condemned.[2] The religious leaders of Jewry are condemned not
only for having rejected Jesus themselves but also for preventing
those under their spiritual oversight from entering the kingdom
of heaven (Matt. 23: 13). While it is probable that some of the
synoptic controversy-material comes from a date later than the
life of Jesus, this should not lead us to suppose that there was
no condemnation of religious leadership by Jesus and his
followers prior to A.D. 70. Christianity was a sectarian movement
which set itself up in opposition to the established religion and
traditional religious leadership. That rabbinic leaders who
refused to heed Jesus' call to repentance would be regarded as
hindrances to the kingdom can be assumed even without
stronger evidence than we possess. Full weight must be given to
the witness of Mark 6: 34 (Matt. 9: 36) that in the eyes of early
Christians the Jewish people were like sheep without a shep-
herd until Jesus appeared to provide genuine spiritual
leadership.[3]

The same kind of rejection of the community-as-a-whole and
its religious leadership can be seen in the Dead Sea Scrolls. The
sons of darkness are all those who do not join themselves to the
sectarian community.[4] The religious leaders who rejected
the Teacher of Righteousness and refused to be converted to
the sect's understanding of Torah are denounced.[5] While the
Essenes may have been considered a nuisance by Sadducees
and Pharisees, the sectarians' strict loyalty to Torah made
tolerance easier. The withdrawal of some groups to monastic
settlements such as the one at Qumran further reduced causes
of irritation. The Christians, on the other hand, made Jerusalem
itself their capital, and refused to be silent about the need for

presume primitive sources. Nevertheless it can hardly be doubted that the
call to repentance with the accompanying exhortation 'Save yourselves
from this crooked generation' (Acts 2: 40) represents early Jerusalem
preaching, rooted in Jesus' own call to repentance (Mark 1: 15). The
Christian promise of doom forms a notable contrast to the optimistic dictum
of the rabbis: 'All Israel has a share in the world to come' (Sanh. 10: 1).

[1] Mark 8: 38; Matt. 12: 39; 16: 4; cf. Luke 11: 29.
[2] Matt. 11: 20–4; Luke 10: 13–15.
[3] For a later denunciation of Jewish religious leadership by a Christian,
see Justin, *Dial.* 112, 140.
[4] 1QS iii. 16–25; v. 11–13.   [5] 1Qp Hab. ii. 1–4.

repentance. Strident criticism of the kind attributed to Stephen (Acts 7: 2–53) was tolerated only with difficulty. We can readily understand how in the case of Stephen the limits of tolerance were exceeded.

As the conflict between the new sect and the old religion developed, prophetic criticism became hardened into a doctrine of the rejection of 'Israel according to the flesh'.[1] It is to be noted, however, that this rejection was present from the beginning in the insistence that membership in the eschatological Israel required conversion. That this view of Israel was offensive to non-Christian Jews is obvious.[2]

Associated with the Christian rejection of traditional religious leadership was a rejection of traditional exegesis.[3] The authority of the Scribes as bearers of the tradition was denounced. To Christians alone had been revealed the real meaning of Scripture (2 Cor. 3: 14–16); to Christians alone belonged the divine promises (Acts 2: 39; Rom. 4: 16; 2 Cor. 1: 20; 7: 1; Gal. 3: 14). Whereas for rabbinic leaders Scripture was essentially Torah, that is, instruction in the way of life willed for man by God, in the hands of Christians Scripture was essentially prophecy, and was treated as a quarry for predictions which found fulfilment in Christ and the Church. This exegetical dispute is probably pre-Pauline, as indicated by Paul's use of παρέλαβον in 1 Corinthians 15: 3 in relation to events which had occurred κατὰ τὰς γραφάς.[4] That the Christian rejection of traditional exegesis was a cause of irritation to the rabbis can easily be believed by those who have attempted to dispute with Jehovah's Witnesses about the meaning of Scripture!

In addition to this fundamental attack on ethnic solidarity, other lesser causes of irritation might be cited. It is not unlikely that Jewish sensibilities were offended by the enthusiasm of the new sect, just as the Establishment in England was offended by the enthusiasm of John Wesley's societies. The experiment in economic sharing at Qumran was not as irritating to public sentiment as the parallel Christian experiment

[1] Matt. 21: 43; Rom. 9: 1–13; but cf. Rom. 11: 1 f.; see below, chapter v.
[2] Cf. James Parkes, *The Conflict of the Church and the Synagogue* (1934), p. 149; Jocz, pp. 71, 73.
[3] Cf. Jocz, p. 46: 'Indeed, the controversy between Judaism and Christianity was, to a large extent, of an exegetical nature.'
[4] Cf. Bultmann, *Theology*, 1, 41 f.

within Jerusalem itself described by Acts (2: 44–7; 4: 32–7);
according to Aboth 5: 10 only an ignorant man (*'am ha'areṣ*)
says 'What is mine is thine and what is thine is mine'. As
W. D. Davies points out, the 'enthusiasm' of Matthew 6: 34
would strike the prudential leaders of Jewry as very much
lacking in common sense.[1]

The apocalyptic enthusiasm of the Christians may likewise
have been regarded with disgust and annoyance by many of
the rabbis.[2] Because of the close relationship in Jewry between
messianic enthusiasm and political unrest, it is not at all unlikely that those charged with the maintenance of public order
thought it advisable at times to take action against Christians.

Several scholars have argued that this was the most important cause of conflict between Jews and Christians. Paul Winter
maintains that as late as Tacitus the Christian movement was
regarded by the Romans as 'a hotbed of political unrest
wherever there was a Jewish population within the Empire'.[3]

This group, which preached the impending dissolution of the natural
and social order and its replacement by a divinely ordained new
order, roused the antagonism of Rome and Jerusalem alike. The
Romans, unable as yet to distinguish between the 'Apostolic
Church' and other Jewish sects, enforced restrictive measures upon
all Jews, whether affected by messianic aspirations or not. Such
measures as the Imperial Government took were the result of
Christian agitation. Hence, induced by the Roman attitude toward
messianic propaganda, the Jewish authorities responsible for the
administration of community affairs saw fit to restrict the preaching
of the coming enthronement of Jesus of Nazareth as Christ the King
who was to replace all other kings and powers.[4]

[1] *Setting*, p. 300.
[2] The rabbinic literature ignores the apocalyptic movement. This silence
may imply either continuing opposition or, on the supposition that early
Pharisaism was as much involved in apocalyptic speculation as other contemporary Jewish groups, a suppression of such elements; cf. P. Winter,
On the Trial of Jesus (1961), pp. 132 f.; Moore, I, 127 f.; and W. D. Davies,
Paul and Rabbinic Judaism (1962), p. 353. After the failure of the Bar Cocheba
revolt there appear in rabbinic writings imprecations on those who 'cal-
culate the times'; see Sanh. 97 *b*, and Moore, II, 352.   [3] P. 59.

[4] P. 116; cf. pp. 127, 130 f. Jewish opposition to Paul and other Christian
leaders is seen as essentially political in nature by Winter, pp. 81–7, 130;
cf. S. Zeitlin, *Who Crucified Jesus?* (1942), pp. 194, 200 f.; Hugo Mantel,
Studies in the History of the Sanhedrin (1961), pp. 299 f. The view that

While this approach has much to commend it, its exponents do not give sufficient attention to the possibility that the disturbances involving Christians which resulted in political reprisals on the part of both Roman and Jewish authorities need not have been messianic in a political sense, but may have been due rather to the over-all challenge made by Christians to the Jewish way of life. The either/or of political expediency and dogmatic intolerance suggested by Winter as the basis of persecution is a false one.[1] Not only were *both* these factors present, but in addition the broader cause of conflict which we have outlined.

Against the hypothesis of dogmatic intolerance, Winter maintains that the concept of religious heresy did not exist; 'No religious party denied another party the right to propagate their teachings'.[2] This statement is probably true with respect to non-Christian Jewish sects, for the simple reason that no other Jewish sect departed so radically from traditional ways of thinking. That even a Torah-observing Jew who departed radically from monotheism was regarded as an apostate and worthy of death is demonstrated by Sanhedrin 11: 6:

He that prophesies in the name of a strange god and says, 'Thus says the god', [is culpable] even if he conformed with the *halakah* so as to declare unclean what is unclean and to declare clean what is clean.[3]

The Christological titles applied to Jesus by Christians must have been early regarded as a challenge to Jewish monotheism, and Christian adoration of their risen Lord must have provoked cries of 'Idolatry!' from many fellow Jews.[4] Only a

Christians were regarded simply as political offenders is not of recent origin. Mantel, p. 299, refers to David Hoffmann, *Der oberste Gerichtshof in der Stadt des Heiligthums* (1878).

[1] P. 130.   [2] P. 129; cf. Zeitlin, p. 210; Mantel, pp. 283 ff.

[3] In this connection it is also noteworthy that while Talmudic tradition regarding Jesus and his death is garbled, two facts are generally assumed: that Jesus was a deceiver of the people, and that he had been put to death on that account by the Jews. Cf. R. Travers Herford, *Christianity in Talmud and Midrash* (1903), pp. 89 ff.

[4] Cf. Parkes, *Foundations*, p. 161. The Fourth Gospel reports Jewish hostility to the Church's Christology (John 5: 18; 8: 58 f.; 10: 33). The Johannine statements can be used as historical evidence only with extreme caution. Nevertheless there is no plausible reason for denying this testimony that Christians who proclaimed that Jesus was the Son of God met with resistance among Jewish hearers, a resistance which presumably ranged from quiet resentment to violent antagonism.

closer examination of the data will reveal what concrete action was taken against such idolaters. Even if Winter's thesis that no official action was taken against Christians on account of their beliefs could be conclusively demonstrated, the possibility of unofficial persecution on the part of religious zealots would not be excluded. On *a priori* grounds it can be claimed that in most cases the Christological factor was only one of several which, taken together, aroused Jewish antagonism to the point of active opposition.

What has been attempted in this introductory section is the establishment of the *a priori* case for friction between Jews and Christians. We have maintained that the challenge to the traditional Jewish way of life and its fundamental conception of ethnic solidarity was so severe that conflict was inevitable. Christians, with an otherworldly allegiance that defied opposition, showed little concern for community sensibilities. The basic symbols of Judaism were subordinated to Jesus: nationalism was replaced by a supra-nationalism which included a new relationship to the uncircumcised and a rejection of the community-as-a-whole in favour of the messianic community of believers.

In view of the severity of this challenge we can only admire the restraint shown by the Jewish community toward the vociferous minority in its midst. That this restraint was at times broken as the limits of tolerance were exceeded should occasion no surprise.

CHAPTER II

SURVEY OF THE DATA OF JEWISH PERSECUTION OF CHRISTIANS IN SOURCES OTHER THAN MATTHEW

I N order to evaluate adequately the role played by the persecution theme in Matthew, it will be necessary to make a survey of the data of Jewish persecution of Christians in other sources, both Christian and non-Christian. That outbursts of violent opposition to the new religion did at times occur in Jewry seems certain.[1] What is not at all certain is the nature and extent of this hostile reaction. It has been suggested that Christian authors have greatly exaggerated the amount of persecution suffered by Christians at the hands of the Jews.[2] This is a possibility to be reckoned with. It is not at all uncommon for religious minorities who challenge a majority religion to regard any restrictions placed upon them by the community as a whole as 'persecution'.[3] We must therefore be cautious in assessing the witness of Christian authors to Jewish persecution.[4]

Apart from Christian writings, however, our sources on the subject are extremely scanty. While the New Testament writings themselves fail to give us anything approaching an adequate historical report, the rabbinic sources are even less helpful. On *a priori* grounds, however, it is to be expected that the plaintiffs will be more explicit than the defendants. The historical ac-

---

[1] C. G. Montefiore, *The Synoptic Gospels* (1927), I, ciii f., cites the opinion of Renan that had it not been for the Roman overlordship the persecution would have been more grave and more extensive.

[2] D. W. Riddle, 'Die Verfolgungslogien in formgeschichtlicher und soziologischer Beleuchtung', *Z.N.W.* xxxiii (1934), 279.

[3] Riddle, pp. 284 f., distinguishes between subjective and objective persecution.

[4] Uncritical acceptance of Christian statements regarding Jewish hostility is a weakness in the massive study recently published by W. H. C. Frend, *Martyrdom and Persecution in the Early Church* (1965). To take one example, Frend cites Justin, 1 *Apol.* 31, in favour of the view that Jews were actively involved in pagan persecution of Christians, without noting the exaggeration in Justin's statement; contrast Justin, *Dial.* 16 (see below, p. 66).

curacy of the charges made by the former can to some extent be checked by reference to the literature of the defendants, in which the problem of nonconformity is occasionally discussed. The underlying thesis of this chapter is that references in rabbinic and other Jewish literature to religious non-conformists, while they do not all allude to Jewish Christians, provide us with reliable evidence concerning the treatment of Christians by the Jewish community.

Violent death

A careful survey of the Christian sources for the period up to and including Justin Martyr yields the conclusion that there is not a single clear case of judicial execution of a Christian by Jewish religious authorities for purely religious reasons. Indeed, the number of named martyrs whose deaths are attributed to Jewish agency is exceedingly small. The author of Acts, who is certainly not hesitant to report instances of violent hostility to Christians on the part of the Jews, can produce stories of only two martyrdoms.

(a) *Stephen.* The first of these two, the martyrdom of Stephen, is given with considerable detail and constitutes a prototype for later martyrologies. Despite the scepticism of some concerning the historicity of this martyrdom, there is little reason to suppose that the author invented the story.[1] Although an analysis of the narrative reveals certain problems, there is no good reason for doubting the historical kernel; namely, the tradition that a Christian Hellenist, Stephen, publicly attacked traditional Judaism and thereby so angered his auditors that he was lynched.

The narrative as we now have it in Acts 6: 9 — 8: 2 appears to blend two traditions; according to one Stephen was lynched by an angry mob, while according to the other he was judicially executed at the order of the Sanhedrin.[2] Those who believe that

[1] H. J. Schoeps, *Theologie* (1949), p. 448 and note. The suggestion of Schoeps, p. 441, that the Stephen of Acts is not a historical person but an *Ersatz-figur* for James created by Luke is gratuitous conjecture.

[2] Cf. W. L. Knox, *The Acts of the Apostles* (1948), p. 25; F. J. Foakes Jackson and Kirsopp Lake, *Beg.* II, 148–51. Ernst Haenchen, *Die Apostel-*

Judea's Roman rulers had deprived the Sanhedrin of the right to execute capital sentences find little difficulty in the narrative. According to this view the Sanhedrin found Stephen guilty of a capital offence, but since it was incapable of executing the death sentence the mob took the law into its own hands and put him to death illegally.[1] The question of the capital competence of the Sanhedrin under Roman rule is an exceedingly difficult one; the little evidence that is available is so evenly balanced that no consensus of scholarly opinion seems possible. No attempt will be made to review the evidence in these pages. For the purposes of the present investigation it will be assumed that the Sanhedrin did possess the right to try capital cases and to execute the death penalty except in those cases in which a Roman court claimed jurisdiction on the grounds that the defendant was guilty of a political offence.[2] On this hypothesis the Sanhedrin was competent to execute Stephen had it found him guilty of a capital crime.

Which of these two traditions is historical? Was Stephen judicially executed or lynched? A careful analysis of the narra-

geschichte (1959), p. 247, suggests that the second of these two traditions is the creation of the author himself; this is also the view of Hans-Werner Surkau, *Martyrium in jüdischer und frühchristlicher Zeit* (1938), pp. 110 f.

[1] Cf. *Beg.* II, 150.

[2] For a good bibliography of the dispute, cf. Joseph Blinzler, *The Trial of Jesus* (1959), pp. 159 f. Reference to nineteenth-century literature can be found in Emil Schürer, *A History of the Jewish People in the Time of Jesus Christ* (1890), Div. II, vol. I, p. 187 n. 513.

Two items in support of the view here espoused deserve more attention than they have received. (1) Philo, *Legatio ad Gaium* 307, declares that violation of the inner shrine of the Temple by unauthorized priests is punishable by θάνατον ἀπαραίτητον, 'a death against which there can be no appeal' (this is the excellent rendering of E. Mary Smallwood, *Philonis Alexandrini Legatio ad Gaium* [1961], p. 130). Philo could not have been ignorant of the status of Jewish competence in such cases. Had the Romans reserved to themselves all rights of capital punishment, it would have been foolish indeed for Philo to insert this phrase in a letter purporting to be Agrippa's appeal to the emperor himself. (2) The author of Acts apparently wishes to give his readers the impression that the Sanhedrin possessed the right to execute those it found liable to the death penalty (Acts 7: 58). Had the Sanhedrin not possessed such a right, this fact would have been well known, and it would surely have suited the author's purposes better to note that the execution of Stephen was an illegal act not countenanced by the Romans.

tive supports the latter alternative.[1] While the author retains certain elements pertaining to a judicial execution, viz. the removal of the condemned man to a place outside the city and the initiation of the lapidation by the two witnesses (Acts 7: 58; cf. Deut. 17: 5–7; Lev. 24: 14), he fails to report a formal verdict of the court. Although the author says nothing to indicate that he regarded the execution as irregular or illegal, he none the less leaves the reader with the impression that it resulted more from the tumultuous violence of a mob than from the orderly carrying out of a legal sentence.

Paul Winter maintains that 'Stephen was executed by stoning in consequence of a regular trial and judicial verdict... The introduction of Paul into the story of Stephen's death may be unhistorical, but in other respects the procedural details mentioned in Acts 7: 58 are too exact to represent an invention by a non-Jewish writer (cf. Deut. 17: 5–7)'.[2] Against this view it must be said that, in the first place, any non-Jewish writer as deeply steeped in the Septuagint as the author of Luke–Acts could have 'invented' the narrative of Stephen's execution, and, in the second place, there is no *a priori* reason why a lynch mob, also familiar with the Mosaic requirements, should not have chosen to fulfil them. If Stephen's antagonists were as zealous for the Torah as the narrative suggests, it is to be expected that they would not wish to pollute the Holy City by spilling the blood of a sinner on its consecrated ground. Nor would it be unnatural for the instigators of the lynching to be given the privilege of casting the first stones, in accordance with the Mosaic requirement.

[1] Blinzler, p. 163, probably is correct in his estimate that the majority of scholars regard the execution of Stephen as an act of lynch law. In addition to the studies referred to by Blinzler, the following are worthy of mention: M. Dibelius, *Studies in the Acts of the Apostles* (1956), p. 208 n. 3; E. Haenchen, p. 246; Surkau, p. 111.

[2] P. 192 n. 3. See also p. 156 n. 38, where it is stated that 'incontestable evidence has survived of three actual trials', of which the trial of Stephen is first. A similar position is maintained by Hans Zucker, *Studien zur jüdischen Selbstverwaltung im Altertum* (1936), p. 81; T. A. Burkill, 'The Competence of the Sanhedrin', *Vigiliae Christianae*, x (1956), 92. S. Zeitlin, *Who Crucified Jesus?* (1942), p. 190, suggests that Stephen was sentenced to die by stoning on the charge of being a 'beguiler' and 'deceiver'. There is no justification for such a charge against Stephen, however, since the offence indicated by these words has reference to idolatry (Deut. 13: 6 ff.; Sanh. 7: 10; Tos. Sanh. 10: 11; 11: 5).

Also in favour of the view that Stephen was lynched is the notice of Acts 8: 2 that 'devout men buried Stephen and made great lamentation over him'. Mourning was forbidden for those executed by order of the court, according to the Mishnah (Sanh. 6: 6). That this was not a later invention of the Tannaim but a rule which was in force in the first century is suggested by a statement of Josephus: 'Let him that blasphemeth God be stoned, then hung for a day, and buried ignominiously and in obscurity (ἀτίμως καὶ ἀφανῶς).'[1] Since this reference to the manner of burial is not taken by the historian from his Pentateuchal sources, it must be assumed that he is here depending on contemporary custom. Furthermore, had Stephen been legally executed for blasphemy his body ought to have been hanged in public view, in accordance with Deut. 21: 22 f. and this passage from Josephus. In view of the central importance for early Christian thought of Jesus' hanging on a tree it would be difficult to explain the absence of such an important detail from the narrative of the first Christian martyrdom had this requirement been fulfilled.

Those who maintain that Stephen was convicted by the Sanhedrin on a charge of blasphemy show little concern for the legal difficulties involved in such a view. That Stephen was not guilty of reviling God in any ordinary sense is surely obvious. If 'blasphemy' in the legal sense denoted a verbal attack upon God (such as the charge of Rabshakeh that the God of Israel was impotent to save Jerusalem from the Assyrian armies, 2 Kings 18: 28–37), then the author of Acts is declaring that Stephen was convicted on a trumped-up charge, as was Naboth (1 Kings 21). This, of course, is not impossible, but it does not seem to represent the kind of charge made against Stephen before the Sanhedrin. The author informs us that while the original instigators had raised a popular cry of 'Blasphemy!' on the basis that Stephen had said ῥήματα βλάσφημα εἰς Μωϋσῆν καὶ τὸν θεόν (6: 11), the charge made by the witnesses was less closely related to the technical charge of blasphemy: Stephen had not reviled God directly but had spoken ῥήματα κατὰ τοῦ τόπου τοῦ ἁγίου τούτου καὶ τοῦ νόμου (6: 13). This is a different charge, and must not be confused with the charge

---

[1] *Ant.* iv. 8. 6 (202), translation by H. St J. Thackeray in the Loeb Classical Library edition.

of blasphemy. Undoubtedly any attack on Torah or Temple was regarded as blasphemous, but this is not to say that such attacks could be treated as blasphemy in the technical sense and punished as capital crimes.[1]

How was the capital crime of blasphemy defined by the legal practice of the half century preceding the destruction of the Temple? We may agree with Dalman that it is unlikely that the extremely narrow definition of Sanhedrin 7: 5 was in force in the time of Jesus.[2] Nevertheless it must be maintained that *some relatively narrow definition* was in existence at that time. Had the legal definition been broad enough to include such charges as are brought against Stephen in Acts 6: 13, all the Pharisees were liable to capital prosecution by the Sadducees! That Pharisaic sophistry effected material changes in the Mosaic code is well known, and it is undoubtedly true that many of these innovations were regarded as 'blasphemous' by religious conservatives, but there is no record of an attempt on the part of Sadducees to bring a capital charge of blasphemy against a Pharisee for 'changing the customs which Moses delivered to us' (Acts 6: 14).[3]

In this connection the mention by Josephus of the Essene custom of punishing any blasphemy against their law-giver with death is significant.[4] Josephus would not have mentioned this as a distinguishing characteristic of the Essenes had it been

---

[1] That the term 'blasphemer' could be used in this non-technical sense, without any thought of liability to capital punishment, is seen in a dictum attributed to Jehuda ben 'Ilai (second century A.D.): 'He who translates a verse quite literally is a liar, while he who adds anything thereto is a blasphemer' (Tos. Meg. end; Kidd. 49a). J. F. Stenning, *The Targum of Isaiah* (1949), p. ix, explains how this dictum was applied: 'Thus Ex. 24: 10, "and they saw the God of Israel", must not be rendered literally, since no man can be said to have seen God; on the other hand, to insert the word "angel" (מלאכא) would be blasphemous, since an angel would be substituted for God. The correct rendering is "and they saw the glory (יקרא) of the God of Israel".'

[2] G. Dalman, *Die Worte Jesu* (1898), I, 258.

[3] The attitude of the Sadducees is reported by Josephus, *Ant.* xiii. 10. 6 (297 f.). The use of 'blasphemous' in such a context is illustrated by the Zadokite Document: 'And with a blasphemous tongue they have opened their mouth against the ordinances of the covenant of God, saying, They are not established; and they are speaking error against them...', CDC v. 11, translation by Chaim Rabin, *The Zadokite Documents* (1954), pp. 19 f.

[4] *Bell.* ii. 8. 9 (145).

a common practice in Judaism as a whole. The conclusion is almost inescapable that Josephus was not aware of any significant number of capital cases for blasphemy in the regular courts of Jewry. Whether this was due to a definition of the crime which was intentionally narrow or to lack of enforcement cannot now be determined, but the probability would seem to lie with the former alternative, in view of the fact that the Sadducees were more severe in their punishments than the Pharisees and at the same time more conservative in their interpretation of the Mosaic code.[1]

The question remains whether the Christian proclamation of Jesus as a divine being at the right hand of God constituted blasphemy in the eyes of the judiciary. The synoptic passion narratives present the view that Jesus was sentenced to die by the Sanhedrin on the capital charge of blasphemy because he prophesied his own exaltation to the right hand of Power and his return as Son of man with the clouds of heaven (Mark 14: 62; Matt. 26: 64; Luke 22: 69). The Fourth Gospel makes no reference to the charge of blasphemy in the context of the examination by the high priest (John 18: 19–24), but later, before Pilate, 'the Jews' declare: 'We have a law, and by that law he ought to die, because he has made himself the Son of God' (19: 7). The author of the Fourth Gospel believes that the Christian faith in Jesus as divine Son is regarded as blasphemy by the Jews; earlier in his gospel he describes attempts to stone Jesus (apparently without formal legal proceedings) because of such blasphemy (10: 33; cf. 5: 18; 8: 59; 11: 8). There is no reason to doubt that the Christian claims on behalf of Jesus were regarded as blasphemous in the non-technical sense, and may have aroused such hostility that on occasion stone-throwing was the result, but it is quite another matter to assume that the legal definition was modified to include this specific violation of Jewish theology. There is no reason to suppose that the author of the Fourth Gospel was more accurately informed on this subject than we are.

It is important to note that had Jesus been condemned to death on a charge of blasphemy for having made the kind of confession contained in Mark 14: 62, then *the profession of Christianity was from the beginning a capital crime* from the point of

---

[1] *Ant.* xiii. 10. 6 (294, 297 f.), xx. 9. 1 (199).

view of the Jewish judiciary. If it was legally blasphemous for Jesus to identify himself with the apocalyptic figure of the Son of man prior to his crucifixion, then it was equally criminal for his followers to make a similar confession after Jesus had been formally cursed by being hung upon a tree. Since the basic Christian message was the proclamation of Jesus as the Messiah who had been raised from death to the right hand of God (Acts 2: 32 f.), Christian preaching on this hypothesis constituted a capital offence. Such a view, however, is not supported by the record of early Church life reported in Acts. Had the author known that to confess faith in Christ was a capital offence he must surely have made mention of it. Instead he informs us that the Sanhedrin, after hearing the confession of Peter and John, found no way to punish them 'because of the people' (4: 21). Indeed, the author can name only one Christian martyr whose death he can associate with the judiciary, namely Stephen, and he bases this capital case not on messianic preaching but on words against the Temple and Torah (6: 13 f.). If the preaching of Christ were itself a capital crime, it would be superfluous to search for other charges related to the same legal offence, namely blasphemy (6: 11). The letters of Paul, erstwhile persecutor of the Church, give no evidence in support of the hypothesis that the profession of Christianity made one liable to capital prosecution by the Jewish courts.

Just as little evidence can be found in support of the view that verbal attacks on the Temple and Torah constituted blasphemy in the legal sense. Several scholars have maintained that Jesus' statement concerning the destruction of the Temple[1] would have been regarded as blasphemy in this sense.[2] Josephus' narrative concerning Jesus the son of Ananias is adduced in

[1] The original form of the logion is disputed, but it seems clear that the report of the 'false witnesses' in the trial narratives of Mark and Matthew (Mark 14: 58; Matt. 26: 61) is a reminiscence of a genuine word of Jesus, of which John 2: 19 and Mark 13: 2 provide further evidence.

[2] Julius Wellhausen, *Das Evangelium Marci* (1903), p. 132; U. Holzmeister, 'Zur Frage der Blutgerichtsbarkeit des Synhedriums', *Biblica*, XIX (1938), 163; Kilpatrick, *The Trial of Jesus* (1953), pp. 11 f.; Blinzler, p. 162. In Blinzler's opinion the words of Jesus concerning the Temple did not form the basis of the final sentence, pp. 100 f. For reference to those who maintain that this was the crime for which Jesus was given a capital sentence by the Sanhedrin, cf. *ibid*. note 26.

support of this thesis.[1] It is claimed that this unfortunate prophet of woe, who prophesied the destruction of the Temple four years before the war began, was tried as a blasphemer by the Sanhedrin and handed over to the procurator, Albinus, for execution. This conclusion is far-fetched. It must be noticed, in the first place, that there had been no universal cry against this Jesus. Josephus reports that it was 'certain of the most eminent among the populace'[2] who objected so strongly to his behaviour. Had prophesying against the Temple been generally recognized as a capital offence a more general indignation among the populace would surely have been forthcoming. In the second place, it must be noted that according to Josephus this prophet was flogged and released. If he was tried on a capital charge, why was he released to resume his heinous activity?[3] Holzmeister and Blinzler assume that it was because the court which tried the case lacked the competence to execute a capital sentence. This hypothesis, however, fails to explain why the accused was handed over to the procurator for execution after having first been released following flogging. If the Sanhedrin had found the defendant guilty of a capital offence, and if the normal procedure was to transfer such capital cases to the procurator for execution, there would have been no release. The only possible explanation is that Jesus son of Ananias was tried for a serious breach of the peace, punished by flogging and released. At the time of his second arrest the Jewish authorities responsible for public order handed him over to Roman law, which conceivably provided more stringent punishment for such an offence, especially when possible political repercussions were involved as in this instance.[4]

[1] *Bell.* vi. 5. 3 (300–5) is so employed by Holzmeister, pp. 161–4, and Blinzler, p. 162.

[2] τῶν δὲ ἐπισήμων τινὲς δημοτῶν. The English rendering is that of William Whiston, *The Complete Works of Flavius Josephus* (n.d.), *ad loc.*

[3] Whereas Jesus of Nazareth was acquitted of the charge because of insufficient evidence (Mark 14: 58; Matt. 26: 61), this cannot have been the reason for the release of the second Jesus, whose words concerning the Temple were repeated 'day and night' in 'all the alleys'.

[4] Holzmeister, p. 163, maintains that even in the Old Testament era threats against the Temple were treated as capital offences, citing as evidence Jer. 26: 11. This very passage, however, refutes the hypothesis it is adduced to prove. The whole point of the narrative is that a prophecy

27

The source of the Marcan tradition that Jesus was found guilty by the Sanhedrin of the capital offence of blasphemy must presumably be found elsewhere than in Jewish criminal law, of which the author of our earliest gospel may have had very little knowledge. It may be tentatively suggested that the evangelist (or the tradition before him) felt that it was incongruous that the Son of God should be sentenced to die on a purely political charge.[1] The theological facts of the matter were that the religious claims of Jesus (whether implicit or explicit) had been rejected by the religious leaders of his people; the *essential* charge against Jesus thus concerned not revolutionary political ambitions but his unacceptable claim to a unique role in the divine economy. Since Christian claims on behalf of Jesus were undoubtedly denounced as blasphemous in the non-legal sense, it was not difficult for Mark to transfer the charge of blasphemy from a non-legal situation to a legal one. Whether or not Mark believed that the charge that Jesus had prophesied against the Temple would have been sufficient to justify a death penalty had the testimony of the witnesses been in agreement (14: 57–9) cannot be determined. It is possible that this item is introduced as a reminiscence from the martyrdom of Stephen. In any event it is omitted from the trial narrative by Luke, who apparently regarded the matter as irrelevant to the trial of Jesus but of central importance to the trial of Stephen.

We must therefore reject Burkill's suggestion that the Marcan narrative of the trial before the Sanhedrin 'is basically a reflection of the fact that certain Christians had been put to death at the order of the Jewish authorities for committing blasphemy in identifying the crucified Jesus with the promised Messiah'.[2]

against the Temple and Holy City is not *ipso facto* an offence, but only if it is spoken without divine authorization. That is to say, the offence for which Jeremiah is on trial is not blasphemy *per se* but false prophecy (cf. Deut. 18: 20). On the latter count the court finds Jeremiah innocent. It could not find him innocent on the postulated charge of speaking against the Temple, since the evidence was clear. Cf. Josephus' understanding of this indictment against Jeremiah, *Ant.* x. 6. 2 (88–93): the charge is that of using divination against the king. Cf. also the Martyrdom of Isaiah 3: 6 f.

[1] Note that Mark, without any attempt to prepare his readers for the political charge, abruptly introduces Pilate's examination of Jesus with the question, 'Are you the king of the Jews?' (15: 2).

[2] T. A. Burkill, 'The Competence of the Sanhedrin', *Vigiliae Christianae*, x (1956), 80. Acts 26: 10 f. assumes that the profession of Christianity was

The attempt on the part of Bar Cocheba to compel Christians to deny the Messiahship of Jesus is not to be construed as evidence that 'the assertion of the Messiahship of Jesus was frequently held to be blasphemous in a strict sense among Jewish authorities'.[1] Bar Cocheba's aim was surely as much political as religious: there was not sufficient room in Israel for two Messiahs! The refusal of Christians to recognize Bar Cocheba's Messiahship constituted treason, *lèse majesté*, and was punished accordingly.

We have no means of determining the legal definition of blasphemy which was in force in the Jewish courts of the first century A.D. It seems to this writer that a grave injustice is done to those courts by statements of Christian writers to the effect that blasphemy 'was a very elastic conception'.[2] A legal definition cannot be expanded to cover a certain case and thereafter be retracted to its former dimensions. In the Jewish judiciary of Jesus' day, as in modern judicial systems, laws were defined to a large extent by precedent. No responsible court could declare that the things said by Jesus or Stephen constituted blasphemy without realizing that a dangerous precedent was thereby established whose application might prove far wider than desirable.

In the absence of positive evidence from non-Christians concerning the legal definition of blasphemy, it is to be presumed that even when Sadducaic influence was strong the tendency in the courts was toward precision in the definition of laws, especially those involving capital punishment. In view of Sadducaic conservatism it is probable that blasphemy was narrowly defined on the basis of Lev. 24: 14 and Exod. 22: 28. This is supported by Josephus' reference to the use of capital punishment for blasphemy by the Essenes, a reference which is best understood as indicating that the law of blasphemy was seldom if ever invoked in the Jewish judiciary. Finally, it is presumed that the purpose of the law of blasphemy was not to enforce orthodoxy, which itself was not clearly defined, but to

a capital offence in the eyes of the Jewish authorities, and associates the punishment with blasphemy, but the passage is open to various objections, including that of gross exaggeration ('I punished them *often* in *all* the synagogues'), so that it cannot be treated as serious evidence.

[1] Burkill, p. 83. [2] Blinzler, p. 105.

maintain 'public decency' by providing severe sanctions against the public use of language insulting to the God of Israel.

[The conclusion to be drawn from this examination of the legal definition of blasphemy is that neither Jesus himself, nor Stephen, nor any other Christian, was condemned to death by a Jewish court on the charge of blasphemy.]

(b) *James son of Zebedee.* It is apparent that the second Christian martyrdom named by Acts cannot be treated as an instance of religious persecution in the ordinary sense, since, according to our source, it was Herod Agrippa I who was responsible (Acts 12: 2). There is no suggestion in the text that the action was suggested to the king by the Sanhedrin or by the high priest. In view of the fact that Acts has already presented the Jewish religious authorities as generally hostile to Christians, it is to be expected that if these authorities had played any significant role in the martyrdom of James the author would not have been averse to including mention of this fact in his report. From the form of execution it may be inferred that the charge made against James was not a religious one. Decapitation was reserved by the Mishnah for murderers and members of an apostate city (Sanh. 9: 1), and although such evidence is later than our period there is good reason for believing that stoning was more generally acceptable than decapitation for religious offences.[1] If we may accept the report of Josephus that Agrippa was anxious to appear a loyal Jew, it will follow that he would have permitted religious offenders to be tried by the Sanhedrin and to be executed in the prescribed manner.[2]

It is sometimes assumed that no legal charge was necessary in such an instance: the king, with power of life and death, was able, it is suggested, to execute arbitrarily anyone who was *persona non grata.* Even if this were possible, however, it is unlikely that the king would have employed such power except in rare cases, in view of Jewish insistence on legal justice.[3] It is

---

[1] Cf. R. J. Knowling, *E.G.T.* II *ad loc.*

[2] *Ant.* xix. 7. 3 (331).

[3] Cf. the angry reaction to the summary execution of robbers by Herod the Great while governor of Galilee, *Ant.* xiv. 9. 3 (167), *Bell.* i. 10. 6 (209). Josephus further reports that the charge against Herod in this instance was a capital one, *Bell.* i. 10. 7 (211), *Ant.* xiv. 9. 4 (173), 5 (177). Note the similar reaction to the unwarranted execution of James the brother of Jesus by Ananus, *Ant.* xx. 9. 1 (201).

therefore probable that a charge was made by Agrippa against James, and that this charge was of a political nature. In view of the fact that both John the Baptist and Jesus had been regarded as dangerous to the political stability of Palestinian Jewry, it is not surprising that other members of the Baptist–Christian movement were regarded with similar suspicion.[1] King Agrippa may well have regarded the vociferous proclamation of 'another king, Jesus' as a case of *lèse majesté* or as anti-Roman sedition. A verdict of guilty on either charge normally resulted in a death sentence. That the execution of a leader of the Christian movement was 'pleasing to the Jews' (Acts 12: 3) is not surprising in view of the various causes of tension which have been examined in the preceding chapter. It is improbable, however, that the king would have arbitrarily executed a Christian leader simply to please public opinion. While it is entirely possible that public hostility had at this time risen to a new peak on account of reports of the Gentile mission in Antioch and elsewhere in the Diaspora,[2] it is not safe to assume that a public outcry against the Christians would have induced Agrippa to execute a Christian leader without a justified capital charge; such behaviour would have made him liable to the charge of misgovernment.

There is good reason to assume that if any important section of the Jewish people, whether the Sanhedrin or an angry mob, had instigated this brief persecution against the Christians, the source of the Acts account would have remembered this fact and the author himself would have recorded it. All responsibility, however, is placed by Acts upon the king himself. The very terseness with which the second Christian martyrdom is

---

[1] For a careful study of the political implications of the ministry of John the Baptist, see J. B. Tyson, *The Execution of Jesus*, unpublished Th.D. dissertation, Union Theological Seminary (New York, 1959), ch. VI, 'The Career of John the Baptist'. Tyson's conclusion is that Jesus was viewed by the people and by Herod Antipas as John's successor in a religio-political movement, and for this reason Herod attempted to arrest Jesus (p. 275). Cf. also Paul Winter, p. 135: it was the effect of Jesus' teaching on certain political elements that induced the authorities to take action against him. Similarly O. Cullmann, *The State in the New Testament* (1956), pp. 11 f.

[2] E. Schwartz, 'Noch einmal der Tod der Söhne Zebedaei', *Z.N.W.* XI (1910), 100; A. Loisy, *Les Actes des Apôtres* (1920), p. 481; M. Goguel, *The Birth of Christianity* (1953), p. 108.

reported strongly suggests that the author knows but does not wish to cite the charge laid against James and Peter.[1]

We have no way of knowing why this political persecution of Christians by Agrippa was of such short duration and of such limited extent.[2] What is certain is that this was not a wholesale attack on the Church as such. Perhaps this 'son of thunder' (Mark 3: 17) had, like John the Baptist, publicly criticized royal policy beyond the limit of royal indulgence. A public speech which combined prophetic criticism of the contemporary king with proclamation of Jesus as the king to whom allegiance was properly due could well be regarded as treasonous.

(c) *James the Brother of Jesus*. The martyrdom of James the brother of our Lord is reported by Josephus and Hegesippus.[3] Since the two reports differ in almost all details except the name of the martyr, they must be used with extreme caution. Considerable disagreement exists among scholars as to which narrative is to be preferred. The Josephan account is regarded as a Christian interpolation by von Dobschütz, Juster, Schürer and Zahn, while its genuineness is upheld by Büchsel, Dibelius, Goguel, Kittel and Lietzmann.[4] To the present writer the

---

[1] That the charge against Peter was also a capital one is indicated by the execution of his guards; 'the guards would answer for the escape of the prisoner by suffering a like penalty, cf. Cod. Just. ix. 4. 4', Knowling, *E.G.T. ad loc.* O. Cullmann, *State in N.T.*, pp. 16 f., suggests the possibility that Peter and the 'sons of thunder' had had associations with the Zealot movement prior to becoming disciples of Jesus. The policy of Agrippa toward the Zealots is not clear. It is not impossible, however, that the majority of the fourteen hundred condemned men whom Agrippa contributed as gladiators were political revolutionaries, *Ant.* xix. 7. 5 (336–7).

[2] The author does not ascribe to this persecution the extent he has previously attributed to that which arose at the time of Stephen's martyrdom. With reference to the earlier persecution he says that all, πάντες, were scattered except the apostles (8: 1), whereas the Herodian attack is directed only against τινας, some members of the Church (12: 1).

[3] *Ant.* xx. 9. 1 (200); Hegesippus' Fifth Memoir is quoted by Eusebius, *Eccl. Hist.* II. 23. 4–18.

[4] E. von Dobschütz, *Die urchristlichen Gemeinden* (1902), p. 274; J. Juster, *Les Juifs dans l'Empire romain* (1914), II, 140 f.; Schürer, Div. I, vol. II, pp. 186–8; Theodor Zahn, *Forschungen zur Geschichte des neutestamentlichen Kanons und der altkirchlichen Literatur*, VI. Teil (1900), pp. 301–5.

F. Büchsel, *Z.N.W.* xxx (1931), 203; M. Dibelius, *Der Brief des Jakobus* (1921), p. 13; M. Goguel, *The Birth of Christianity* (1953), pp. 126 f.; G. Kittel, *Z.N.W.* xxx (1931), 146; H. Lietzmann, *Z.N.W.* xxxi (1932), 79.

arguments presented by S. G. F. Brandon in favour of the authenticity of the passage are convincing.[1] Brandon points out how unlikely it is that a Christian scribe, intent on making Josephus a witness to the truth of Christianity, would have been content with such a bare mention of the martyrdom, without any edifying details whatsoever.[2] Furthermore, Origen witnesses to the fact that in his text of Josephus the righteousness of James was acknowledged while the messiahship of Jesus was denied.[3] It is hardly possible that a Christian scribe would have interpolated the reference to James in the passage under consideration and have failed to amend the depreciatory treatment of Jesus which was extant in Origen's text of Josephus.[4] The unadorned report of Josephus has a far greater claim to credence than the legendary narrative of Hegesippus.[5]

From Josephus' account, then, we learn that the high priest Ananus, shortly after his appointment by Agrippa II, took advantage of the interregnum between the death of Festus and the arrival of Albinus to convene a court, συνέδριον κριτῶν, and summon before it James the brother of Jesus and some others, τινας ἑτέρους, whom he charged with being law-breakers, παρανομησάντων. The trial seems to have been highly irregular, not only because Ananus neglected to obtain approval from the procurator before convening the court,[6] but also because of the proceedings themselves. This is indicated by the indignation of 'all those who in Jerusalem were reputed to be men of good sense and strict in their observance of the Law'.[7] It is probable that the people so described were Pharisees.[8] As

---

[1] Brandon, pp. 96–114.   [2] P. 96.   [3] P. 111.

[4] The description of James as τὸν ἀδελφὸν Ἰησοῦ, τοῦ λεγομένου Χριστοῦ, is by no means proof of an interpolation. An interpolator who presented Josephus as a convinced witness to the messiahship of Jesus, *Ant.* xviii. 3. 3 (63), would hardly have been satisfied with λεγομένου, which, like the English expression 'so-called', may convey a note of scepticism. Since Jesus was publicly crucified under the titulus 'King of the Jews', and his messiahship loudly proclaimed by Christians, it is not surprising that Josephus, although an unbeliever, should refer to Jesus in this way.

[5] It must be remembered that Hegesippus flourished a century after the death of James whereas Josephus was a contemporary.

[6] *Ant.* xx. 9. 1 (202).

[7] Brandon's rendering, p. 95. The text reads: ὅσοι δὲ ἐδόκουν ἐπιεικέστατοι τῶν κατὰ τὴν πόλιν εἶναι καὶ τὰ περὶ τοὺς νόμους ἀκριβεῖς.

[8] Cf. Brandon, p. 97, and authors there cited.

Pharisees they would have opposed the over-zealous use of the death penalty even for those capital offences enumerated in the Torah, but the intensity of opposition aroused in this instance surely indicates that they were convinced that the executed persons had not been guilty of a capital offence.[1] The vagueness of the accusation reported by Josephus certainly suggests a trumped-up charge. The trial is reminiscent of similar proceedings under Herod the Great.[2] There is no indication of why Ananus wished to have James and 'certain others' put to death. The haste with which the matter was effected—apparently soon after his appointment—suggests that it was a case of personal animosity.[3] It cannot be maintained that this was a religious persecution, or that Ananus was expressing the popular hostility toward Christians in general by this judicial murder. Indeed, the evidence suggests that his action was unpopular. In view of the legendary tradition preserved by Hegesippus that James was a solitary martyr, it is possible that the 'certain others' who were put to death at the same time according to the Josephan report were not Christians but other personal enemies of the new high priest.[4]

Returning, then, to the proposition stated at the beginning of this section, we repeat that the number of named martyrs whose deaths can be attributed to Jewish agency is extremely small (three), and in no instance is it clearly a matter of judicial execution by Jewish religious authorities for purely religious reasons.[5]

---

[1] This is surely a more natural interpretation of the text than the supposition that the protests were based primarily on the fact that Ananus had exceeded his competence in executing condemned criminals, as suggested by Blinzler, p. 162. Had the verdict of the court been regarded as just by the standards of Torah, few Jews of patriotic persuasion would have been so base as to inform against the high priest.

[2] *Ant.* xvi. 10. 5 (320), 11. 7 (393); *Bell.* i. 27. 6 (550).

[3] Cf. Brandon, p. 96; Goguel, pp. 127, 131.

[4] Cf. Goguel, *ibid.*; Brandon, pp. 96 f., assumes that these others were Christians.

[5] James Parkes, *The Conflict of the Church and the Synagogue* (1934), Appendix 5 (pp. 402–4), lists the martyrdoms of the first century ascribed to Jews, collected from the martyrologies. It is interesting that in only one instance, a variant report of the death of Matthew (*Acta Sanctorum*, Feb. 22), is the death attributed to a Jewish judiciary. While there is much that is legendary in these martyrologies, they illustrate, as Parkes maintains, p. 402, 'that

Let us consider now the evidence for non-judicial killing of Christians in the pre-war period. The Book of Acts reports two mob attacks on Paul (14: 19; 21: 31), neither of which resulted in death. Neither of these narratives is in itself improbable, and in one instance, the stoning at Lystra (14: 19), a measure of corroboration is provided by Paul's own testimony in 2 Corinthians 11: 25 that he had once been stoned. It might be argued that the author of Acts could easily have informed us of other early attacks upon Christians, some of them resulting in death, had this been his purpose. Against this supposition, however, must be placed those statements in Acts which report the peace of the Church. In sharp contrast to his narrative concerning the attempt of the Hellenists in Jerusalem to kill Paul, the author announces in 9: 31 'So the Church throughout all Judea and Galilee and Samaria had peace and was built up...'. Although this is a general summary, and although the author is eager to show that Christians found favour with the Jewish people at large (2: 47), it is hardly likely that he would have ignored a situation of violent persecution had he known of it.[1]

The *argumentum a silentio* is notoriously weak, but surely this is a situation in which the burden of proof lies with those who would maintain that Christians frequently suffered martyrdom at the hands of the Jews between the death of Jesus and the revolt against Rome in A.D. 66. Apart from Acts our best witness to the historical situation is the Pauline correspondence. It is noteworthy that although Paul on several occasions mentions that he had formerly been a persecutor of the Church, he never suggests that he had been responsible for the death of any Christian. Since his purpose in 1 Corinthians 15: 9 is to contrast his unworthiness with the saving grace of God, one would expect him to mention such heinous deeds had they occurred. In Galatians 1: 13 f. and Philippians 3: 5 f., Paul relates that his zeal for Judaism had been so great that he had become a persecutor of the Church. Here again one might expect Paul

there was a *common tradition* of Jewish responsibility in the persecution of individual Christians during the first century of Christianity, but that there was no *precise knowledge* of the actual fate of the individual concerned'. It is therefore significant that in this 'common tradition' so little guilt is attributed to Jewish courts. Frequently the victim is attacked by a mob of Jews or of Jews and Gentiles.

[1] Cf. Brandon, pp. 90 f.

3-2

to illustrate the extent of his zeal by citing the martyrdoms for which he had been responsible (in the same fashion as the confession attributed to him in Acts 26: 9–11). On the basis of Paul's letters, therefore, one must conclude that although Paul had indeed zealously opposed the new sect and attempted to destroy it, his zeal had not led him to commit murder. We may assume that many other early opponents of the new sect likewise shrank back from defending Torah by committing so great an offence against Torah.

It must further be observed that Paul, in summoning his churches to contribute money for the relief of the saints at Jerusalem, makes no reference to notable sufferings of that congregation as a basis for his appeal, as one might expect had the situation warranted it.[1] In Romans 15: 30 f. Paul suggests that his life or liberty may be threatened by unbelievers in Judea, but this is best understood as a matter which concerns Paul, not Christians in general.[2] The polemic against the Jews in 1 Thessalonians 2: 14–16, whether written by Paul or by a later interpolator, attributes to the Jews the death of Jesus and the prophets but makes no mention of the lynching of ordinary Christians. Had this been a widespread practice it would surely not have been omitted from the indictment.

One would likewise expect the Revelation of John to make mention of any relevant martyrdoms which could be attributed to the 'Synagogue of Satan' (Rev. 2: 9; 3: 9). Only one martyr is mentioned (2: 13), and the agents of his death are not specified.

In the absence of assured evidence to the contrary, therefore, we must incline to the conclusion that up to the beginning of the revolt in A.D. 66 there were few Christian martyrdoms attributable to Jewish agency.[3] That violence occasionally erupted against Christians is not improbable, but the fact that Paul himself was able to persist in his controversial ministry for so many years witnesses to the restraint with which the Jewish community dealt with the 'Christian problem'.

---

[1] This suggestion is made by Brandon, p. 91.

[2] The same sentence shows that Paul is not certain of the reception he will receive from the *Christians* of Jerusalem.

[3] A similar conclusion is reached by Brandon, p. 100, and M. Simon, *Verus Israel*, p. 306.

We possess no positive evidence concerning the violent persecution of Christians during the first war against Rome. There
are several items, however, which suggest that there was an
increase in the amount of suffering imposed upon Christians.
One is the tradition that the church of Jerusalem migrated to
Pella before the war.[1] If this tradition has any basis in history,
there is good reason for believing that the flight of Jewish
Christians to a Gentile city beyond the Jordan was induced by
a serious outbreak of persecution. The possibility of such distress
is also suggested by the reports of Josephus. The Jewish historian
provides ample material for a demonstration of the chaotic
situation in Palestine during these troubled years. He mentions,
for example, that the Galileans, apparently without due process,
had punished one suspected of being a forger by cutting off his
hand.[2] Even the barest suspicion of a tendency to accept Roman
rule was sufficient at times to jeopardize a man's life, again
without benefit of trial.[3] Zeal for the Torah led on one occasion
to the destruction of the Herodian palace at Tiberias because
it was ornamented with figures of living creatures, and on
another occasion stimulated an attempt to circumcise forcibly
two Gentile refugees.[4] Gentile inhabitants of Jewish towns were
liable to meet with violent death.[5] In such a situation of
aroused passions the ambivalence of Jewish Christians toward
the popular cause against Rome would surely bring them
into odium with the nationalists. The generous attitude of
Christians toward the Gentiles would readily be regarded by
many as a form of treason. Christians who dared to be outspoken in their declarations concerning the fate prophesied for
Jerusalem by Jesus and the necessity of loving one's enemies
undoubtedly attracted violent attack at the hands of mobs
inflamed with hatred for the Romans and zeal for the symbols of
Jewish nationalism. How many Christians suffered violent death
during this period cannot be determined. The martyrologies

[1] Eusebius, *Eccl. Hist.* III. 5. 3, and Epiphanius, *Adversus Haereses* xxxix.
7; both authors probably derive the tradition from Hegesippus: cf. Lawlor
and Oulton, in Eusebius, *The Ecclesiastical History and the Martyrs of Palestine*
(1927), II, 82. Brandon, pp. 168–73, argues against the authenticity of the
tradition, but concedes that some Jewish Christians, possibly from Galilee,
may have found refuge in Pella during the war.

[2] *Vita* 35 (177).   [3] *Vita* 28 (136).

[4] *Vita* 12 (65), 23 (113).   [5] *Vita* 12 (67).

provide no evidence that Christians were lynched as traitors during the war.[1] We possess no reliable sources depicting the condition of the Palestinian churches during the war. It is possible that the Gospel according to St Matthew witnesses to the suffering experienced at this time, but a full discussion of this possibility must be delayed until the next chapter.[2]

The treatment of Christians during the Bar Cocheba revolt, as witnessed by Justin Martyr, suggests that the same fate may have befallen Christians during the earlier war against Rome. In his *Dialogue* with Trypho, Justin makes frequent mention of the suffering imposed on Christians by Jews.[3] In the *First Apology*, he writes:

But these Jews, though they read the books [the Septuagint], fail to grasp their meaning, and they consider us as their enemies and adversaries, killing and punishing us, just as you do, whenever they are able to do so, as you can readily imagine. In the recent Jewish War, Bar Cocheba, the leader of the Jewish uprising, ordered that only the Christians should be subjected to dreadful torments, unless they renounced and blasphemed Jesus Christ.[4]

There is little reason to doubt this testimony. Bar Cocheba was regarded as the Messiah by as important a leader as Rabbi Akiba.[5] Since it was impossible for Christians to acknowledge any other Messiah than Jesus, they were liable to the capital charge of *lèse majesté*. The Bar Cocheba revolt, therefore, does not provide an identical situation with that of the first Jewish War, since no messianic leader demanded Christian allegiance in the earlier episode. The similarity lies in the fact that in both wars the Christians were less than enthusiastic in their support of the revolutionaries. This could easily have been regarded as treason in the first as in the second revolt, and have resulted in death for many who were unable to evade nationalist attention.

For the period between the wars we are again without adequate sources for the condition of Jewish Christianity. That this

[1] This statement is based solely on the martyrological evidence collected by Parkes, *Conflict*, pp. 402–4.

[2] This position is argued by Brandon, pp. 173 f.

[3] Chs. 16, 95, 110, 122, 133.

[4] 1 *Apol.* 31; translation by Thomas B. Falls, *The Writings of Saint Justin Martyr* (1948), p. 67.   [5] Jer. Taanith 68 d.

was a period of increasing tension between rabbinic Judaism and Jewish Christianity is indicated by the insertion of the *Birkath ha-Minim* in the Eighteen Benedictions as a means of identifying Christians and discouraging them from participation in synagogue worship.[1] Assuming, however, that the Romans were able to restore law and order and that the rabbis encouraged the people to take their grievances to the proper judiciaries, there is little reason to suppose that violent death was frequently inflicted on Christians during this period.[2] It is possible that the Christian claim that the destruction of Jerusalem was a divine punishment for the Jewish rejection of Jesus at times provoked violence on the part of Jewish hearers, but

[1] See below, pp. 49, 54–7.

[2] G. D. Kilpatrick, *Trial* (1953), p. 13, maintains that severe persecution, including the use of the death penalty, was practised after A.D. 70. 'Where Rabbinic authorities had the power, they executed sectaries, Minim, if they did not conform...Certain kinds of religious sectaries at least were liable to be put to death.' Cf. also Kilpatrick, *Origins*, p. 115. Unfortunately, Kilpatrick does not cite his evidence. The present writer has found none to support such a thesis. Nowhere, to my knowledge, in its many discussions of the Minim, does the rabbinic literature indicate that Minim are liable to capital punishment. The most extreme treatment that the rabbis will countenance is that the lives of Minim may be endangered and not saved, Tos. B. Mezia 2:33: 'The Minim and the apostates and the betrayers are cast in[to a pit] and not helped out' (translation by R. Travers Herford, *Christianity in Talmud and Midrash* [1903], p. 94). Kilpatrick's hypothesis that attacks on the Temple and the Law were treated as capital crimes in the period before A.D. 135 must be rejected in view of the fact that laws of such severity cannot be derived directly from Sadducaic law (conservatively based on Old Testament legislation), nor can their existence be inferred from later rabbinic *halakoth* in Tractate Sanhedrin. The severity of the Tosefta toward the Minim would lead us to expect some trace to remain in this compilation of rabbinic tradition of those laws postulated by Kilpatrick. In view of the loyal respect with which the Pharisees regarded their own traditions, how does Kilpatrick explain such a complete reversal of policy, from severity to leniency, without any rabbinic tradition being preserved to explain how the change was effected? Josephus' testimony that the Pharisees were inclined to be lenient in their punishments is also not to be ignored. Unless Kilpatrick can produce evidence to the contrary, it is best to assume that this Pharisaic leniency was a constant factor in developing rabbinism throughout the period under consideration.

A late passage reporting the execution of five disciples of Jesus (Sanhedrin 43a) may very well reflect the persecution of the Bar Cocheba period, as Herford suggests, p. 94. In any event it cannot be construed as serious evidence in support of Kilpatrick's hypothesis.

no thoroughgoing persecution of a violent kind is likely during this period.[1]

In dealing with references to persecution 'to the death' one must constantly be aware of the tendency to exaggeration in both Christian and Jewish writers. An obvious example is 1 Clement 4: 9, where it is stated that envy made Joseph to be persecuted to the death and come into slavery. Both the author and his readers know that Joseph had not in fact suffered martyrdom; the phrase 'persecuted unto death' simply conveys the thought that the will-to-kill had been present although not actualized.[2] A similar kind of exaggeration is seen in statements of Philo and Josephus affirming the rigorousness with which the death penalty was applied in Judaism.[3] There is good reason to believe that, despite such statements, there was considerable leniency in the punishment of capital offences in the first century A.D. This is illustrated by the treatment of Sabbath-profanation. The gospels reflect controversy between Jesus and the Pharisees concerning Sabbath-observance. In Mark 2: 24 the Pharisees ask Jesus why his disciples are doing on the Sabbath that which is not lawful, ὃ οὐκ ἔξεστιν. Whether or not this pericope accurately reflects the *halakah* accepted by the Pharisees in the period of Jesus' ministry or at the time when the gospel was written, the passage indicates that Mark did not have any knowledge of a court action against Jesus' disciples on the capital charge of Sabbath-profanation. The sectarians who produced the Damascus Document were even

---

[1] We may assume that Christians were frequently 'stoned' without being killed. Stone-throwing was a characteristic way of expressing disapproval in ancient Jewry. Cf. Acts 5: 26; *Bell.* ii. 17. 1 (406); Kiddushin 70 *b*.

[2] According to Pesahim 49 *b*, R. Eleazar declared that it was permissible to stab an '*am ha'areṣ* on a Day of Atonement which coincided with Sabbath. His disciples asked if he meant 'slaughter' (as in the ritual slaughter of clean animals for food). He replied that ritual slaughter required a benediction, whereas stabbing did not. This and similar hyperboles cannot be accepted as evidence that '*amme ha'areṣ* frequently met violent death at the hands of the *haberim*.

[3] Josephus, *Contra Apionem* ii. 24 (201), 27 (207), 30 (215–17). Philo, *De Josepho* 42–3, *Spec. Leg.* ii. 28, *Hypothetica* (Eusebius, *Praep. Evang.*) 7: 1 ff. Both the *Contra Apionem* and the *Hypothetica* are apologetic works, as Belkin notes, *Philo and the Oral Law* (1940), pp. 24 f. In both we find statements regarding punishments which are in conflict with non-apologetic statements by the same authors.

more rigorous in their observance of the Sabbath than the Pharisees, yet, according to the Damascus Document, imprisonment, not capital punishment, is prescribed for Sabbath-breaking.[1] Another example of this kind of exaggeration is the case of the apostate. In the Diaspora apostasy must have been a continual temptation, and, on the basis of the threats made against apostates, we may assume that the number of renegades was not insignificant. Philo advocates that Jewish idolaters be summarily executed without benefit of trial.[2] Tos. Sanh. 11: 11 reports that R. Eleazar ben Zadok (fl. *c*. A.D. 80–120) taught that one who worshipped idols might be saved from the transgression at the cost of his life.[3] The popularity of this idea is further witnessed by 3 Maccabees 7, which jubilantly narrates a slaughter of Jewish apostates. There is very little likelihood, however, that Rome would have tolerated habitual lynching among the Jews. The political success of one notable apostate, Tiberius Alexander, son of Philo's brother,[4] suggests that Jewish anger over apostasy did not always find violent expression. In view of the available evidence it would seem safer to assume that apostasy was seldom avenged, either by judicial or non-judicial execution.

In view of this tendency to exaggeration concerning the application of the death penalty, one must treat the New Testament evidence concerning 'persecution to the death' with great caution. Such a statement as John 16: 2, 'Indeed the hour is coming when whoever kills you will think he is offering service to God', may be nothing more than a Christian reflection of Jewish declarations that Christians *ought* to be lynched.[5] This by no means proves that the wish was translated into deed.[6]

In dealing with predictions of persecution in the gospels we must always remember that such predictions need not have been

---

[1] CD 12: 4. From Tos. Sanh. 11: 2 and Mish. Sanh. 7: 8 (cf. Kerithoth 1: 1) we gather that although Sabbath-profanation was technically a capital offence it was seldom prosecuted as such in the Tannaitic period.

[2] *Spec. Leg.* i. 54 f.

[3] This view is specifically repudiated by Mish. Sanh. 8: 7.

[4] *Ant.* xx. 5. 2 (100).

[5] This is perhaps the best explanation of John 19: 7.

[6] Even in our own day there are people in the United States who talk about lynching the Chief Justice of the Supreme Court, presumably without the slightest intention of attempting it!

41

fulfilled in order to be meaningful to those who preserved and transmitted them in the oral tradition. Mark 13: 12 predicts: 'And brother will deliver up brother to death, and the father his child, and children will rise against parents and have them put to death.' This oracle reflects in part Micah 7: 6, but exceeds the latter in terms of the woe it predicts. It is best interpreted as simply one more conception of what will take place during the messianic woes.[1] While the verse in question may have been cherished by Roman Christians because of an experience of the demoralizing effect on family relationships of the Neronic persecution, its original *Sitz im Leben* may well have been the Palestinian church. Even though the number of martyrs may not have been large, there was among the Christians a clear sense of separation from the community-as-a-whole and an awareness of the continuing hostility of the wider community, including the hostility of unconverted relatives. Each expression of this hostility reminded Christians that the bounds of tolerance might some day be broken and unrestricted violence ensue. To what extent the prediction was fulfilled during the chaotic days of the two wars with Rome we cannot say. The point that must be stressed is that this prediction need not be regarded as a *vaticinium ex eventu* and cannot therefore be used as proof of its fulfilment.[2] It is not unusual for a persecuted group to anticipate worse treatment than it actually receives. The likelihood of such an anticipation is heightened by the treasuring of an apocalyptic tradition concerning the woes of the 'last days'.[3]

Summary. We have discovered no clear instance of execution of Christians by Jewish religious authorities for purely religious reasons. There is no evidence of a systematic effort to eliminate Christianity by treating it as a capital crime. There was no

---

[1] Internecine strife is prophesied for the 'last days' in a number of apocalyptic passages, e.g. Zech. 14: 14; Enoch 100: 2; Jub. 23: 16–20; 4 Ezra 5: 9; 2 Baruch 48: 37; 70: 7.

[2] *Contra* D. W. Riddle, *Z.N.W.* xxxiii (1934), 287.

[3] Cf. Mark 13: 19 f. Luke 21: 16 provides a parallel to Mark 13: 12, although the saying here assumes a quite different form and the effect is less severe. It is impossible to determine whether the variant form derives from a non-Marcan tradition or from Lucan editing. It is conceivable that the author of the Third Gospel moderated the severity of the prediction to bring it into closer accord with the facts of historical persecution as he knew them.

Jewish forerunner of the Spanish Inquisition! There were probably instances of lynching not known to us, especially during
the first war with Rome, as indicated perhaps by the Pella-
tradition. Even more severe was the persecution during the
Bar Cocheba revolt, as witnessed by Justin, but the latter was as
much a political as a religious persecution, and was conducted
presumably by military, not religious, authorities. In the
earlier period, A.D. 35–66, public hostility may have frequently
resulted in instances of near-lynching. Paul, for example, may
have been more than once *in danger* of death from Jewish
enemies. Mobs may have attacked Christians without intend-
ing to do more than inflict insulting blows; in some instances
the results may have been none the less fatal. It cannot, however,
be maintained on the basis of available evidence that violent
death was frequently inflicted on Christians by Jews.[1]

We must conclude, therefore, that despite Christian expectation of martyrdom, the Jewish community showed considerable
restraint in the expression of hostility toward Christians. Violent
deaths did occur, but the number must not be exaggerated.

Judicial flogging

According to the Mishnah a flogging of thirty-nine stripes could
be administered by a judiciary of three judges for the violation
of a negative precept of the Mosaic law not coupled with a
positive precept.[2] Condemnation by the court required the
evidence of two witnesses and proof that proper warning had
been made and acknowledged.[3]

If these regulations were in force in the period in which Paul
received the thirty-nine stripes five times (2 Cor. 11: 24), it
would be difficult to understand how Paul could have been so
treated. We have no positive evidence that Paul ever flagrantly
disregarded the Mosaic requirements or that he encouraged

---

[1] There is not a single instance in the latter part of the New Testament,
i.e. 1 Timothy to Revelation, or in the Apostolic Fathers, of a Christian
being put to death by Jews. In the Martyrdom of Polycarp the Jews gladly
assist but are clearly not responsible for the execution (13: 1). Among the
apocryphal Christian writings, the Acts of Philip is exceptional in its portrayal of Jewish violence toward converts to Christianity; cf. M. R. James,
The Apocryphal New Testament (1924), pp. 439–53.

[2] Sanh. 1: 2; Makk. 3: 4; Hull. 12: 4.

[3] Sanh. 3: 6; 4: 1; Makk. 3: 7 f.; cf. Makk. 16a.

other Jewish Christians to abandon their observance of Torah (1 Cor. 9: 20).[1]

In Mark 13: 9, the followers of Jesus are warned that they will be beaten in synagogues (εἰς συναγωγὰς δαρήσεσθε; cf. Matt. 10: 17, μαστιγώσουσιν). The implication surely is that Christians will be punished not for ordinary violations of the Mosaic code, for which not only Christians but all Jews were liable to flogging, but for their specifically Christian activities.

The Mishnah provides no legal support for the suppression of heresy by the application of corporal punishment. Assuming that Paul was not found guilty of a wilful violation of Torah, what possible legal grounds could there have been for the punishment administered to him?

It is possible that the officials responsible for public order were permitted to employ the sanction of corporal punishment in ways not defined by the Mosaic code or by rabbinic *halakah*. The prophet Jeremiah was beaten by Pashur the priest, chief officer in the house of the Lord (Jer. 20: 1 f.; cf. 37: 15). A close parallel to this treatment of Jeremiah is offered by the narrative concerning the prophet Jesus son of Ananias, who was given 'a great number of severe stripes' at the instigation of certain Jewish leaders.[2] Apparently in both cases the civil authorities (who might, of course, be identical with the religious authorities) felt that the uttering of woes against Jerusalem was endangering public order and must be halted by the employment of severe punishment.

S. Zeitlin maintains that there was no established rule about punishment for an offence against the State.[3] Although Hebrew law did not make any sharp distinction between civil and religious legislation, it must be postulated that the civil government of Israel, especially during the monarchy, involved a great many civil laws which have not been preserved for us in Scripture. It may be assumed that such laws were not regarded as part of Israel's holy constitution but as 'executive orders'.

---

[1] Paul's habit of eating with Gentiles did not in itself constitute a breach of Torah; see above, p. 9. It is possible, of course, that Paul was not always scrupulous in his observance of the Mosaic food laws when eating with Gentiles, but we have no evidence of this. Paul nowhere suggests that his opponents accuse him of transgressing the Mosaic code.

[2] *Bell.* vi. 5. 3 (302).   [3] P. 196.

Among such would be rules concerning public order, private assembly, and the collection of taxes, and regulations defining the division of authority between the central government and local city government. It can be further argued that even under the Roman procurators many such civil laws were needed, since it is likely that the Romans left local authorities responsible for the maintenance of public order except in cases of anti-Roman activity.[1]

It can be maintained, therefore, that the flogging of the apostles in Acts 5: 40 was not for a religious offence *per se* but for a breach of the peace. Jesus of Nazareth had been executed by the Romans on a charge of seditious activity; those who were so soon proclaiming publicly the continuing messiahship of this condemned man were endangering public order and ought to be silenced.

This hypothesis, however, leaves unexplained the prediction of Mark 13: 9 (Matt. 10: 17) that Jesus' followers were to be beaten in the *synagogues*: εἰς συναγωγὰς δαρήσεσθε. Nor is it likely that Paul, who spent most of his life in the Diaspora, should have received all five floggings in localities where Jewish authorities were in charge of civil government. Paul's testimony, combined with the evidence of Mark 13: 9, strongly suggests that Christians were flogged in synagogues upon the authority of the local council of elders. It would seem to follow that such local councils were in the Diaspora as in Palestine empowered to employ various sanctions, including corporal punishment, for the maintenance of public order among the members of the synagogue. The Mishnah provides evidence that the synagogue authorities could impose a 'punishment for disobedience' in certain instances not involving the violation of a Mosaic commandment.[2] Since the Mishnah nowhere defines the nature and

---

[1] Cf. Acts 19: 35–41. It is instructive to note that the sectarian community which produced the *Manual of Discipline* did not feel compelled to derive all its communal regulations from Torah. Although a strict application of Torah was required, an extensive code was enacted for the direction of communal behaviour. This code specified the penalties to be imposed for infractions. It is possible that local synagogues had similar codes of behaviour and means of enforcing them.

[2] Nazir 4: 3; cf. Shabb. 40*b*, and K. Kohler, article 'Synagogue', *Dictionary of the Apostolic Church*, ed. J. Hastings (1918), II, 545; article 'Malkut' in *Jüdisches Lexicon*, ed. G. Herlitz and B. Kirschner (1929), III,

application of this non-Mosaic punishment we must assume that considerable freedom was permitted in its use.[1]

It need not be assumed that the profession of Christianity was defined as a crime punishable by flogging. Active missionaries such as Paul, however, would on occasion attract the hostile attention of the authorities because of the divisive effect of their activities. In situations where Paul's preaching produced a sharp cleavage within the synagogue community (cf. Acts 18: 5-8) the local authorities may well have regarded him as a 'pestilent fellow' (Acts 24: 5) and have sentenced him to flogging for having disturbed the peace. On the other hand, other missionaries in other localities may have quietly persisted in their task of preaching Christ without being adjudged worthy of stripes by the elders. We have no reason for believing that even the preaching of Christianity was universally treated as a criminal act by the synagogues of Palestine and the Diaspora.[2] In making reference to the floggings he had received, Paul's purpose was to show that he had suffered far more for Christ than had the 'superlative apostles' (2 Cor. 11: 5) who were wooing his Corinthian converts. Since these rivals were also Jewish missionaries (11: 22), we must assume that not all were flogged on account of their Christian preaching, or Paul could not have made his boast.

We must conclude, therefore, that flogging was not a penalty which confronted all Jewish Christians on account of their faith. While it may be said that flogging was a method of religious persecution among the Jews, such a statement would have to be carefully qualified. There was no determined effort on the part of Jewry to stamp out Christianity by punishing with flogging all who professed faith in Christ.

col. 1349; article 'Stripes', *J.E.* xi, 570; Maimonides, Sanh. 18: 5. Such punishment may have sometimes employed rods rather than leather thongs. 2 Cor. 11: 25 is interpreted in this light by Kohler; cf. Sanh. 7b.

[1] Sanh. 46a attributes to R. Eliezer ben Jacob (fl. A.D. 80-120) the tradition that the *Beth din* may impose flagellation and pronounce capital sentence even when not warranted by Torah. The principle invoked for such extraordinary punishment: 'The times required it.' Such a principle may have been invoked by synagogue authorities when confronted by the threat of Christianity. Extreme caution, however, must be used in the employment of this passage when more positive evidence is lacking.

[2] Acts 22: 19 cannot be regarded as trustworthy evidence.

Imprisonment

According to S. Zeitlin, there is no law in the Bible or in the Tannaitic literature authorizing imprisonment for a religious offence.[1] This is not entirely accurate, since Sanh. 9: 5 (Tos. Sanh. 12: 7) authorizes imprisonment for those who have incurred flogging a third time for the same offence.[2] We must agree with Zeitlin, however, that there was no Tannaitic legislation authorizing imprisonment for religious offences of the kind presupposed by Acts 8: 3. The profession of Christianity was not a religious offence punishable by imprisonment.[3]

A distinction must be made between imprisonment as detention pending trial and imprisonment as punishment. It is possible that Acts 8: 3; 22: 19 refer to the former. Most references to Jewish imprisonment in Acts clearly allude to detention (4: 3; 5: 18; 12: 4; cf. 9: 2, 14, 21).

As in the case of flagellation, the punishment of imprisonment was employed by the civil authorities in ways not defined by Torah. It was possible for Herod Antipas to detain John the Baptist in prison for an indefinite period pending a final settlement of the case.[4] According to Josephus, the Pharisees suggested to Hyrcanus that a suitable punishment for one who had openly challenged the king's right to the high priesthood would be stripes and imprisonment.[5] E. Schürer believes that local Jewish tribunals sentenced men to imprisonment for robbery in the years preceding the first revolt, citing as evidence *Bell.* ii. 14. 1 (273): καὶ τοὺς ἐπὶ λῃστείᾳ δεδεμένους ὑπὸ τῆς παρ' ἑκάστοις βουλῆς...[6] It is possible, therefore, that the local Jewish councils

---

[1] P. 196.

[2] CD 12: 4 substitutes imprisonment (seven years) for the death penalty in cases of Sabbath violation. Other transgressions may be punished by a term of one year in prison, according to CD 15: 14 f. (Rabin, p. 74).

[3] Juster, II, 161, states that imprisonment was used as a punishment for 'religious delinquents', but cites as evidence only Acts 22: 19 and the Zadokite Document.

[4] The evidence of Mark 1: 14 (cf. Matt. 4: 12) and Matt. 11: 2 that John was imprisoned for an extended period prior to execution is apparently supported by Josephus, *Ant.* xviii. 5. 2 (119), who reports that John was sent as a prisoner to Macherus and there put to death. An immediate execution would not have required such a transfer. Cf. also the imprisonment of Jeremiah, Jer. 37: 15.

[5] *Ant.* xiii. 10. 6 (294).   [6] Div. II, vol. I, p. 151.

sometimes thought it wise to place certain Christians, whose activities were regarded as obnoxious, in indefinite detention. Apart from the uncertain testimony of Acts 8: 3; 22: 19, however, we have no evidence in support of such a hypothesis.[1] As far as Diaspora synagogues are concerned, it remains to be proved that they possessed the legal competence and the facilities for executing such a punishment. On the whole it seems more likely that even in Palestine the local councils would employ other sanctions than imprisonment in dealing with Christian propagandists.[2]

Exclusion from the synagogues

It has been frequently asserted on the basis of certain New Testament passages (Luke 6: 22; John 9: 22; 12: 42; 16: 2) that Jewish Christians of the first century were permanently excluded from the synagogues by means of a formal sentence of excommunication.[3]

The Jewish practice of excommunication during the period under consideration is shrouded in mystery. Despite all that has been written on the subject the fact remains that the extant materials which can be safely dated to the period directly preceding and following the first war with Rome are too scanty to provide a clear picture.[4]

---

[1] While it is possible that Paul's pre-Christian activities as persecutor of the Church involved arranging for the trial of Christians who publicly attacked traditional Judaism, we have no supporting evidence in the Pauline letters. The clear testimony of Gal. 1: 22, however, makes it impossible for us to accept 8: 3 as historical evidence. This, in turn, raises serious doubts about 22: 19, which appears to refer back to 8: 3.

[2] The eschatological discourse in the Third Gospel promises Christian believers, 'But before all this they will lay their hands on you and persecute you, delivering you up to the synagogues and prisons (εἰς τὰς συναγωγὰς καὶ φυλακάς), and you will be brought before kings and governors for my name's sake. This will be a time for you to bear testimony' (Luke 21: 12 f.). The passage is apparently based on Mark 13: 9, but contains a number of changes, including the addition of the reference to prisons. In the light of the author's second volume, it is best to take this as an advance reference to the various imprisonments recorded in Acts, both Jewish and Roman.

[3] Most recently by R. E. Brown, *The Gospel according to St John (i–xii)* (1966), p. 380; Frend, *Martyrdom*, pp. 185 f. and note.

[4] For older studies on the subject, see the bibliography provided by Schürer, Div. II, vol. II, p. 61 n. 52.

One of the classical studies on the subject is the excursus by Paul Billerbeck in his *Kommentar*.[1] Billerbeck's conclusion is that the purpose of the ban was to increase obedience to Torah and its representatives and thus hold the guilty one close to the synagogue, not to exclude therefrom: '... Die Aufgabe, aus der Synagoge auszuschliessen, wird ihm nirgends zugewiesen.'[2] The Minim, including Jewish Christians, were indeed excluded from the synagogue, but by other means than the *cherem* or *niddui*: all personal and business contact with them was forbidden, and they were formally cursed in the *Shemoneh Esreh*.[3] The New Testament passages which are commonly taken to refer to synagogal excommunication (Luke 6: 22; John 9: 22; 12: 42; 16: 2) can therefore not be taken as references to the ban but must be understood as referring to an exclusion accomplished by other means.

These conclusions are contested by Claus-Hunno Hunzinger's Göttingen dissertation, *Die jüdische Bannpraxis im neutestamentlichen Zeitalter*.[4] Hunzinger maintains that by leaving questions of chronology out of account Billerbeck (and those who follow him) has left unclear the pre-war situation. A historical study of the material yields the conclusion that in the first century there was only one type of ban, the *niddui*, which was imposed by the Sanhedrin for a period whose lower limit was ordinarily thirty days but which could be lifted by the Sanhedrin on its own initiative either before or after the thirty days. In an excursus on the pertinent New Testament passages, Hunzinger argues that the Johannine ἀποσυνάγωγος-passages refer to the *Birkath ha-Minim*, while the verb ἀφορίζειν in Luke 6: 22 refers to the *niddui*. He concludes that even before the destruction of the Temple the Jewish Christian community was persecuted by the Sanhedrin by means of the ban.

Hunzinger notes that no one found occasion to use the *niddui* in the first century except for the protection of the halakic tradition. As a general rule this may stand, but certain possible exceptions must be considered. A quite different use of the ban is suggested by the narrative concerning the protest made by

---

[1] 'Der Synagogenbann', *S.–B.* IV, part I, 293–333.
[2] *S.–B.* IV, part I, 330.　　　　　　　　[3] P. 331.
[4] Unpublished, 1954. A summary is given in *T.L.* LXXX (1955), cols. 114 f. The following statements are based on this review.

Simeon ben Shetah (c. 80 B.C.) to Onias the Circle-Maker, who had commanded the Almighty to produce rain.

Hadst thou not been Onias I had pronounced a ban against thee! (גּוֹזְרַנִּי עָלֶיךָ נִידּוּי). But what shall I do to thee?—thou importunest God and he performeth thy will, like a son that importuneth his father and he performeth his will; and of thee Scripture saith, 'Let thy father and mother be glad, and let her that bare thee rejoice'.[1]

If taking undue familiarity with God was considered a sin worthy of the ban in the time of Simeon ben Shetah, it is not impossible that Jesus and his disciples were regarded as guilty of a similar offence for their claim to possess the Holy Spirit.[2]

If Hunzinger is correct in his conclusion that the ban was used largely to protect the halakic tradition, its use must have been severely limited prior to the destruction of the Temple, for during that period there was no halakic uniformity. The Sadducees rejected the oral tradition *in toto*, the sectarians cherished their separate traditions, the Pharisaic schools of Hillel and Shammai strove among themselves, and the 'amme ha'areṣ who belonged to none of these groups were happy to ignore many of the traditions regarded as important by the Pharisees. We have no record of a wide use of the ban to secure halakic uniformity in this period. It might be suggested that this failure to use the ban was due to the fact that the Pharisaic party was not yet strong enough politically to dominate either the Great Sanhedrin in Jerusalem or the local councils in the towns. While this is probably true, it must also be noted that in the later period when the Pharisees became the dominant party the ban was used primarily for the censure of those who opposed halakic decisions orally or insulted a

---

[1] Taanith 3: 8; Hebrew text as given by P. Blackman, *Mishnayoth* (1963), II, 426. Cf. Berakoth 19a. It is not clear whether Simeon b. Shetah had authority to pronounce a ban as an individual or whether he meant that through his position of leadership in the Sanhedrin he would obtain the sentence from that body.

[2] Antipathy toward Christian Spirit-enthusiasm is perhaps reflected in the rabbinic dogma that with the passing of Haggai, Zechariah and Malachi, the Holy Spirit had ceased from Israel, Yoma 9b; cf. W. D. Davies, *Paul*, p. 216. This antipathy may also be reflected in the Beelzebul controversy of the synoptic tradition, Mark 3: 22–30 par.

rabbi.[1] That is to say, punishment for offences against established *halakoth* was probably by other means, such as 'flagellation for disobedience', not the ban.[2] It was not ordinary laymen who were the recipients of the ban but rather rabbis and laymen who exerted religious leadership.[3]

The possibility that in the period prior to A.D. 70 cases of flagrant disobedience to unwritten custom were punished by means of a ban imposed by the Sanhedrin is indicated by Ezra 10: 8, but we have no other evidence in Jewish sources.[4] This hypothetical ban imposed by the Great Sanhedrin or by the local council of elders must be carefully distinguished from the Pharisaic ban which was extant in the same period.

It seems probable to the present writer that a close parallel to the Pharisaic ban is provided by sectarian practice as evidenced by the Dead Sea Scrolls. The separatist groups which produced the Manual of Discipline and the Damascus Document maintained their own halakic traditions. Those outsiders who failed to be convinced of the truth of the sectarian position remained outsiders, and there was no question of employing a ban against them. Within the sectarian community, however, excommunication was employed as a means of preserving the tradition against the attacks of dissident members.[5] The exclusion could be partial and temporary or complete and permanent.[6] It is reasonable to suppose that the *haberim*, the Pharisaic 'Associates', employed the ban in like fashion to remove from their intimate fellowship those who refused to accept the halakic decisions of the party.

A clear example of this is the case of Akabya ben Mahalaleel,

---

[1] For the twenty-four offences punishable by the ban in later rabbinic usage, see *J.E.* v, 285–7, article 'Excommunication'.

[2] See above, p. 45.

[3] Thaddeus of Rome was liable to a ban in the eyes of Simeon ben Shetah because he had accustomed Roman Jews to eat kids roasted whole on the eve of Passover, Berakoth 19 a. There is no suggestion that the Roman Jews who followed his leadership were equally liable to the ban.

[4] E. Schürer, Div. II, vol. II, pp. 60–2, maintains on the basis of Ezra 10: 8 that it was the elders of each synagogue who possessed the right of excommunication. Only after the dissolution of the old political organization did the professional scribe obtain the authority to excommunicate from the synagogue.

[5] 1QS vi. 24 — vii. 25; CD ix. 23, xx. 3 (MS *B* ii. 3).

[6] Cf. 1QS vi. 25 with ix. 1; see also *Bell.* ii. 8. 8 (143–4).

whose activity is dated as pre-Tannaitic.[1] According to Eduyoth
5: 6 Akabya was placed under a ban by his colleagues because
he refused to retract four opinions which he maintained represented majority opinion at the time he received them.[2] Akabya
died while still under the ban, but before his death warned his
son to yield to the majority. There is no reason for assuming
that this early ban in Pharisaic circles necessarily involved
exclusion from the synagogue.[3] It need not have meant that the
one so disciplined was necessarily excluded from fellowship
with non-Pharisees. While no Pharisee would come within the
four-cubit limit, it may be assumed that Sadducees and 'amme
ha'areṣ would feel no such restriction. The wearing of mourning by the one banned was entirely dependent upon his willingness to co-operate in performing this penance, motivated by
a desire for reinstatement. Those individuals who refused to
conform to majority opinion may have in many instances re-
turned to the ranks of the ordinary members of the synagogue.
Only in synagogues dominated by Pharisees would a Pharisaic
ban be equivalent to a ban from synagogue fellowship. We
cannot assume that this was often the case until the period
of reorganization following the destruction of the Temple.
The crisis of national defeat provided the climate of public
opinion necessary for a Pharisaic domination of the synagogues.
Even then, however, the rabbis did not immediately succeed
in taking full control of the local councils and courts, as witnessed by rabbinic complaints concerning 'amme ha'areṣ who
were judges.[4] Such complaints would have been unnecessary

[1] Before A.D. 10; cf. Danby, *The Mishnah* (1933) p. 799. The Mishnah
places Akabya's separation after Shemaiah and Abtalion; cf. Eduyoth 5: 6.

[2] Berakoth 9a attributes the ban to derogatory remarks about scholars
after their death, but the Mishnaic tradition seems more probable.

[3] Apparently even in later days the ban did not exclude from the synagogue services but rather from the intimate fellowship of common meals
and scholarly discussion. Billerbeck, *S.–B.* IV, part I, 330, maintains that
Raba (and with him the entire Old Synagogue) was not conscious of the
fact that the ban could serve to exclude from the synagogue. He notes that
this was in fact the result in many instances, but as a result of the free
decision of the one banned. According to Tannaitic tradition, those under
a ban were not prevented from visiting the Temple, Middoth 2: 2. For the
view that one under a ban was permitted to attend synagogue services,
see *J.E.* I, 559–62, article 'Anathema'.

[4] Cf. A. Büchler, *The Political and Social Leaders of the Jewish Community of
Sepphoris in the Second and Third Centuries*, p. 21.

had the rabbis been able to remove these men from office by placing them under an effective ban.

It must be maintained, therefore, *contra* Billerbeck and Hunzinger, that the purpose of the ban in the earliest period was not to discipline ordinary members of the synagogue and thus hold erring sons of the covenant close to Torah and synagogue, but rather to obtain, to whatever extent was possible, a larger measure of uniformity among the Pharisees and their scholars.[1] At a later date the ban might be employed to secure popular respect for established *halakoth* and for the rabbis who were responsible for new legislation,[2] but conditions necessary for an effective ban on non-Pharisees were not present in the pre-war situation.[3]

It is unlikely, therefore, that ἀφορίζειν in Luke 6: 22 has reference to the *niddui*, as Hunzinger suggests. A more likely frame of reference for Luke 6: 22 is the informal ban employed by every community, ancient and modern, toward individuals it despises. Social ostracism is a kind of excommunication which could well inspire the words of the Lucan beatitude. The gospels reveal a situation in which friendliness toward tax collectors, Samaritans and other social outcasts invited severe public disapproval (cf. Luke 19: 7). It is unlikely that Zacchaeus had been formally excluded from the synagogue, but it is just as improbable that the chief tax collector of Jericho would have found anyone willing to sit near him had he attended a synagogue service. Wherever the followers of Jesus became the objects of public disapproval they would receive the same kind of treatment. That Jewish Christians and other Minim were actually so treated is witnessed by the Tosefta:

[1] Particularly to be noted is the *apologia* of Rabbi Gamaliel in connection with the banning of R. Eliezer ben Hyrcanus: '...That strife may not multiply in Israel', Baba Mezia 59 *b*.

[2] Berakoth 19 *a*.

[3] To be effective the ban required the co-operation of the one banned and of the community. The community concerned might vary from the well-defined fellowship of the 'Associates' to the more amorphous community of synagogue-adherents and the wider Jewish community including the *'amme ha'areṣ*. While the public ban of a leper would be universally respected, it cannot be assumed that the same effectiveness pertained to rabbinic bans until the later decades of the Tannaitic period. At that time the ban became an instrument of community discipline which might be exercised even by a layman or a woman; cf. Moed Katan 17 *a*.

One does not sell to them or receive from them or take from them or give to them. One does not teach their sons a trade, and does not obtain healing from them...[1]

Trypho tells Justin, 'Our teachers laid down a law that we should have no intercourse with you'.[2] The accuracy of this statement has been challenged, but there can be no doubt that an unwritten law to this effect was in force in many communities. The Aboth Rabbi Nathan declares:

'*Remove thy way far from her*' refers to sectarianism [*minuth*]. When a man is told, 'Go not among the sectarians and enter not into their midst, lest thou stumble through them', he might retort, 'I have confidence in myself that, although I enter into their midst, I shall not stumble through them'. (Or) perhaps thou mightest say, 'I will listen to their talk and then retire'. Therefore the verse says, *None that go unto her return, neither do they attain unto the paths of life*.[3]

In another chapter of the same work the reader is advised to hate the Minim while loving the '*am ha'areṣ*.[4]

This kind of exclusion was practised by the Dead Sea covenanters. In the *Manual of Discipline* we read: 'For all who are not reckoned in His covenant are to be separated, both they and all they have.'[5] This is a generalized ban, not a specific exclusion aimed at the discipline of an individual.

Social ostracism, however, does not suffice to explain the testimony of the Fourth Gospel concerning being put out of the synagogue, ἀποσυνάγωγον ποιεῖν (John 16: 2; with γενέσθαι, 9: 22; 12: 42). It is suggested by Hunzinger that these passages refer to the *Birkath ha-Minim*.[6] This is doubtful. The effect of the twelfth benediction, inserted into the daily prayer by Samuel the Small approximately fifteen years after the destruction of the Temple, was to prevent sectarians from taking a leading role in synagogue worship.[7] Any who stumbled in the recitation

---

[1] Tos. Hullin 2: 20 f., as rendered by Herford, *Christianity in Tal. and Midr.* p. 177; cf. the case of Ben Damah, cited by Herford, pp. 103 f. See also Tos. B. Mezia 2: 33, quoted above, p. 39 n. 2.

[2] *Dial.* 138. 1; cf. W. D. Davies, *Setting*, p. 279.

[3] Ab. R. Nath. ch. 2; translation by J. Goldin, *The Fathers According to Rabbi Nathan* (1955), p. 25.   [4] Ch. 16; Goldin, p. 86.

[5] 1QS v. 18; cf. v. 14 ff.   [6] *T.L.* LXXX, col. 115.

[7] A convenient bibliography of the study of the *Birkath ha-Minim* is given by Jos. Bonsirven, *Le Judaïsme palestinien au temps de Jésus-Christ* (1934–5), II, 145 n. 1. See also W. D. Davies, *Setting*, p. 275.

of this 'test' benediction were suspected of *minuth*. It has been assumed that this was an effective way of excluding Jewish Christians from the synagogue. While this was undoubtedly the result, it must be noted that the *Birkath ha-Minim* involves self-exclusion only and does not constitute excommunication from the synagogue. Those detected by this means were subject to social ostracism, but this was not strictly equivalent to formal exclusion. The Johannine passages, however, suggest a positive exclusion of Christians by the Pharisees. In 12: 42 we are told that many of the rulers, ἄρχοντες, believed in Jesus but did not confess openly on account of the Pharisees, lest they should be excluded from the synagogue. This agrees with 9: 22, where it is stated that the 'Jews' had decided that if anyone should confess that Jesus was Christ he should be ἀποσυνάγωγος. The impression given by these passages is not that those who confess Christ are to be made so uncomfortable in the synagogue services that they will choose not to attend but rather that they will be given no choice in the matter and will be excluded against their will. The import of 16: 2 is that Jewish Christians will be tempted to fall away from their faith in Christ when they are put out of the synagogue on account of it.

We have no other evidence that Christians were individually and formally excluded from the synagogues. John's peculiar hostility toward the Jews makes it difficult for us to know whether these passages represent historical facts or unfulfilled predictions on the part of the author.[1] That certain ardent missionaries such as Paul were excluded from individual synagogues at certain times on various charges can readily be believed. The hypothesis that *all* Christians were individually excluded by action of the local council of elders associated with each synagogue has little to commend it. Nowhere else in the New Testament, Apostolic Fathers or non-Christian Jewish literature, do we find evidence that the confession of Jesus as the Christ was defined as a crime punishable by formal exclusion from the synagogues of Jewry.

Let us recapitulate. There is little reason to believe that the *niddui* or *cherem* was widely employed against Jewish Christians in the first century. It seems likely that a sentence of formal

---

[1] Many scholars believe that John's anti-Judaism has led him to contradict historical fact in 18: 31; cf. Winter, pp. 88–90, and literature there noted.

exclusion from a synagogue was exceptional and directed not so much against faith in Christ *per se* as against those activities of Christians which were regarded as objectionable by the synagogue-community involved (cf. Acts 18: 5–7, 13). More common was the informal exclusion of Christians by the pressure of public disapproval and social ostracism (cf. Acts 18: 8 f.). As the struggle between Christianity and Rabbinism grew in intensity in the synagogues of Palestine and the Diaspora, this public disapproval was crystallized into a formal denunciation by means of the *Birkath ha-Minim*. Those who maintained supreme allegiance to the Nazarene could not with good conscience continue to participate in the daily services after this addition to the *Shemoneh Esreh*. While it cannot be said on the basis of available evidence that the Jewish Christians were excommunicated, it is most probable that the exclusion effected by social ostracism and the *Birkath ha-Minim* was fully as effective as any formal act of excommunication. The separation of Church and synagogue was probably complete by the end of the first century.

Economic reprisals

The history of religious persecution exhibits frequent use of economic pressure. Fines, confiscation of property and economic boycott are not uncommon as attempts of a majority group to contain the influence of a minority which threatens the old order.

The use of an economic boycott by Jews against Minim has already been mentioned.[1] The application of this kind of persecution was, of course, individual and voluntary. No specific mention of such action has been found in Christian literature by the present writer.

The imposition of fines is a remote possibility suggested by a number of ancient Jewish inscriptions (in the Greek language) found in various cities of the Diaspora, which mention fines to be paid to the Jewish community or synagogue treasury for the violation of Jewish religious statutes.[2] No evidence has been found that Christian Jews were penalized for their faith by means of fines.

[1] Above, p. 53.

[2] Cf. Ralph Marcus, Loeb Classical Library edition of Josephus, vol. vii, p. 76 note b.

The question of confiscation of goods is more complex. Justin, in his *Dialogue* with Trypho the Jew, suggests that Christians have been deprived of their property by Jews.

For the expression, 'He that is afflicted [and driven out]', i.e. from the world, [implies] that, so far as you and all other men have it in your power, each Christian has been driven out not only from his own property, but even from the whole world; for you permit no Christian to live.[1]

Since this statement is clearly an exaggeration, it cannot be depended upon as evidence of the confiscation of goods by Jews.

The plundering of property mentioned in Hebrews 10: 34 may be due to Jewish persecution, but the circumstances referred to in this writing are so uncertain that this evidence cannot be used with any assurance.[2] The conjecture of Charles that the poverty of the Christians in Smyrna, mentioned in Rev. 2: 9, is due to Jewish persecution is not supported by any certain evidence.[3] Other statements in the New Testament concerning loss of property are too vague to be useful.[4]

It is possible that under certain circumstances one formally banned by the Jewish community suffered the confiscation of his property to the Temple.[5] We have already drawn a negative conclusion concerning the hypothesis that the ban was widely employed against Christians. It is unlikely, therefore, that Jewish Christians frequently suffered this kind of confiscation.

We must conclude that while voluntary economic boycotts against Christians may have been common there is little reason to believe that more severe economic sanctions were imposed. Nor is there sufficient evidence to support the view that there was widespread plundering of Christian property by Jewish mobs.

---

[1] *Dial.* 110. Translation by George Reith in the Ante-Nicene Christian Library, vol. II, *Justin Martyr and Athenagoras* (1874).

[2] The hypothesis that Hebrews was addressed to Jewish readers is one which the present writer can no longer accept. Even if the hypothesis were demonstrable, however, it would remain to be proved that the persecutors here referred to were Jews rather than pagans.

[3] R. H. Charles, *A Critical and Exegetical Commentary on the Revelation of St John* (1920), I, 56.

[4] Luke 6: 30; Phil. 3: 8.

[5] Ezra 10: 8; *Ant.* xi. 5. 4 (148); Moed Katan 16*a*.

Social reprisals

Social ostracism as a means of expressing hostility toward Christians has already been mentioned.[1] Under the present heading attention will be given briefly to public insults, both physical and oral.

It is well known that ancient Jewish culture considered public insults a serious matter. David Daube has reminded us that a slap in the face, such as is contemplated in Matthew 5: 39 and Luke 6: 29, was treated as an injury for which legal recourse could be had.[2] More frequent, however, were the verbal insults for which no such recourse was possible. The author of Psalm 69 indicates how heavily such insults weighed upon him. The hymns of the Dead Sea sect manifest a similar concern.[3]

The New Testament has a good deal to say about how Christians are to respond to the verbally expressed hatred of opponents, but for the most part this is generalized advice which does not point to Jewish adversaries in particular. An exception is the beatitude concerning the happiness of those who are reviled on account of Jesus, where Jewish opponents are clearly implied.[4] The author of the Apocalypse complains about the βλασφημία of those who say that they are Jews but who are really a Synagogue of Satan (2: 9). The author of Acts uses the verb βλασφημέω twice to describe Jewish reviling of Paul (13: 45; 18: 6). In 14: 2 he testifies that unbelieving Jews 'poisoned the minds' (ἐκάκωσαν τὰς ψυχάς) of Gentiles against the brethren. The verb κακολογέω is similarly employed in 19: 9. Paul, for his part, does not identify the slander and insults of which he has been the object as specifically Jewish. We must assume that he had received this kind of treatment from Gentiles as well as Jews.[5]

It is clear that this aspect of Jewish persecution does not receive widespread attention in our sources. Whether the

---

[1] Above, pp. 53 f.

[2] D. Daube, *The New Testament and Rabbinic Judaism* (1956), p. 257.

[3] Hodayoth ix. 2 — x. 12; T. H. Gaster, *The Dead Sea Scriptures* (1956), p. 171.

[4] Matt. 5: 11 f.; Luke 6: 22 f. See below, pp. 114–21.

[5] 1 Cor. 4: 12 f.; 2 Cor. 6: 8, 12: 10; cf. 2 Cor. 11: 26.

absence of specific reference to verbal hostility is due to Jewish restraint or to Christian indifference cannot be determined.[1]

Unspecified persecution

We have now examined data concerned with the major kinds of persecution employed by Jews in their opposition to Christianity. Attention must now be paid briefly to those evidences of persecution which do not specify the kind of activity involved.

We may conveniently begin with St Paul's testimony concerning his anti-Christian activity. In 1 Corinthians 15:9 he tells us that he is not worthy to be called an apostle, 'because I persecuted, ἐδίωξα, the church of God'. This testimony is intensified in Galatians 1: 13, where he declares that his persecuting was καθ' ὑπερβολήν, 'excessively' or 'to an extraordinary degree', and that his object was to destroy the Church.[2] In 1: 23 he informs us that Christians who had never met him learned that 'he who once persecuted us is now preaching the faith he once tried to destroy'. The fourth reference to his anti-Christian activity occurs in Philippians 3: 6, where Paul states that the extent of his zeal on behalf of the Jewish religion was indicated by the fact that he had been a persecutor of the Church.[3]

On the basis of these statements alone it might be said that Paul's purpose as a persecutor of Christianity was to destroy the Church and its faith, not to destroy individuals who belonged to the Church and professed its faith. That is to say, on the basis of the Pauline evidence, there is no ground for the view that Paul conducted an inquisition of the Spanish type.

Paul gives us no indication of the kind of action he employed as persecutor of the Church. From what we know of his character and abilities it seems highly probable that this activity was primarily verbal. Convinced that the doctrines of Christi-

[1] Justin makes frequent mention of Jewish cursing of Christians, but since many of his complaints specifically mention the synagogue as the *locus* of the cursing, we may assume that he is referring to the *Birkath ha-Minim* rather than to the violent outbursts of individuals; *Dial.* 16, 47, 93, 95, 96, 108, 123, 133.

[2] The Revised Standard Version is probably correct in understanding the imperfect of πορθέω here and in 1: 23 as conative; cf. Bauer, p. 699, *sub* πορθέω.

[3] κατὰ ζῆλος διώκων τὴν ἐκκλησίαν.

anity were inimical to the Judaism upon which the national life of Israel was based, Paul the zealous Pharisee vigorously denounced those who preached Christ to Jews and Gentiles in the Diaspora. We can picture him presenting stinging rebuttals to unsophisticated presentations of the Christian gospel. It is probable that he employed strong language to warn his co-religionists against the folly of being deceived by the Christian message. We can imagine him saying, 'If any man gives ear to this foolishness, let him be anathema!' He may also have organized community opposition by persuading Jewish leaders to ostracize known Christians. It is further possible that in some communities Paul may have instigated legal action against out-spoken missionaries of the gospel on a charge of disturbing the peace, although our evidence is insufficient to substantiate such a hypothesis. Nor can we rule out the possibility that on occasion Jewish crowds, fired by the impassioned oratory of this dedicated Pharisee, may have become abusive in their treatment of Christian preachers. On the basis of the extant evidence, however, we cannot say that Paul was either directly or in-directly responsible for the death of any Christian.

In dealing with references to persecution in the New Testa-ment one must remember that the verb διώκω, rendered in English by 'pursue' or 'persecute', need mean nothing more than 'annoy' or 'harass verbally'. It is used in John 5: 16 to denote a hostile attitude toward Jesus on the part of his Jewish opponents, whose activity does not warrant the term 'persecution' as we use it.[1] When Paul asks, 'But if I, brethren, still preach circumcision, why am I still persecuted?' (Gal. 5: 11), he does not thereby suggest that he is being mistreated daily by Jewish opponents. The hostility toward Paul was a continuing one, and was expressed in a variety of ways, but, as has already been noted, the very fact that Paul was able to persist in his controversial ministry for so many years is our best evidence that Jewish opponents employed considerable restraint in dealing with the Apostle to the Gentiles. Those Jewish Christians whom Paul castigates for seeking to have Gentile converts circumcised 'only in order that they may not be persecuted for the cross of Christ' are therefore not to be thought of as fearing mortal danger; the persecution feared

[1] Cf. also Matt. 5: 11; see below, p. 119.

may be nothing more than the hostility which destroys fellow-ship and ostracizes from the Jewish community.[1] D. W. Riddle suggests that a 'loose' use is made of διώκω in this passage.[2] To the present writer it seems more accurate to say that διώκω itself contains a wide range of possible applications. The basic meaning would seem to be 'pursue aggressively'. The context alone determines more specifically the type of action con-templated.

With respect to some of the vague references to persecution in Christian literature, it must be said that their orientation may well be more theological than historical. A basic article in early Christian theology, stimulated by the conflict with non-Christian Judaism but probably older than Christianity, was the conviction that the Jews had always persecuted the messengers of God.[3] Numerous statements concerning Israel's persecution of the prophets are found in the New Testament, Apostolic Fathers, Justin Martyr and Christian additions to Jewish apocryphal writings.[4] As possessors of the prophetic

[1] Gal. 6: 12. According to Johannes Munck, *Paul and the Salvation of Mankind* (1959), pp. 87–90, the 'Judaizers' of Galatians are not Jewish Christians but rather Gentile Christians who have independently adopted the view that circumcision is essential to salvation. *Contra* Munck, it must be urged that there is little evidence that Gentile Christians had cause to fear persecution on account of uncircumcision. In 5: 11 Paul asserts that he would not still be persecuted if he were yet preaching circumcision. It seems clear that the persecutors here alluded to are Jews. While Paul, a Jew, was continually liable to synagogue discipline, Gentiles were not. It must also be remembered that Gentile adherents of the synagogue were not com-pelled to be circumcised (see above, p. 11). Those who procrastinated were not regarded with hostility. Jewish Christians who preached that circum-cision was unnecessary, however, undoubtedly aroused great antagonism.

[2] *Z.N.W.* xxxiii, 283.

[3] R. H. Charles regards the Martyrdom of Isaiah as a Jewish work of the first century A.D. (*Apocrypha and Pseudepigrapha*, II, 157 f.). H. J. Schoeps, *Die jüdischen Prophetenmorde* (1943), p. 7 n. 7, finds in Josephus' reference to Manasseh's daily slaughter of prophets (*Ant.* x. 3. 1 [38]) an indication of the pervasiveness of the theme of prophetic martyrdom. Schoeps postulates prophetic-apocryphal works in addition to those of which we have certain knowledge, and believes that these *Vitae Prophetarum* were very popular among Jews at the time Christianity arose. See below, pp. 137–41.

[4] The following list is not exhaustive, but will serve to indicate how widespread was the theme: Matt. 5: 12; 23: 29–37; Luke 6: 23; 11: 47–51; Acts 7: 52; Rom. 11: 2 f.; 1 Thess. 2: 15; Ignatius Magn. 8: 2; Barnabas

Spirit in the Last Days, Christians *expected* to be persecuted by unbelieving Jews. Indefinite references to future persecutions, such as Mark 4: 17 and 10: 30, may reflect this anticipation rather than any actual persecution by Jews or Gentiles.

INCIDENCE, GEOGRAPHICAL DISTRIBUTION AND CHRONOLOGY

In the period before the first war with Rome it would seem that anti-Christian activity was more common in the Jewish communities of the Diaspora than in Palestine. The view of Acts seems to be that, despite occasional outbursts, the Church in the Holy Land was not a persecuted church whereas Diaspora missionaries who broke down the dividing wall between Jew and Gentile were continually confronted by Jewish hostility.[1] It must be assumed that most if not all of the beatings, floggings, imprisonments and other hardships mentioned by Paul in 2 Corinthians 11: 23–7 took place in the Diaspora. His own persecuting activity had likewise taken place outside of Palestine.[2]

The testimony of 1 Thessalonians 2: 14–16 has been adduced in support of a Palestinian persecution.

5: 11; Justin, *Dial.* 16, 73, 95 (cf. 93), 112, 120; 4 Ezra 1: 32; cf. Mark 12: 5 (Matt. 21: 35 f.; Luke 20: 10–12). It is probable that the Martyrdom of Isaiah is alluded to in Heb. 11: 37.

[1] Acts 9: 31; 21: 20. The view of J. Munck, pp. 216 f., that the Judean church was widely persecuted is dependent on inferences drawn from Acts 1–12. If by this Munck means only that from the beginning the Christian movement was widely disapproved, we must concur. When he introduces the concept of 'Märtyrer-geschichte', however, we must point out that his historical source, Acts, can produce evidence of only two Christian martyrdoms. 'Constant persecution' (p. 217) is not an accurate description of the situation as it is known to us from the available evidence.

[2] Gal. 1: 22 f. The sketch of Paul's career based on data from Paul's own writings which is presented by John Knox in *Chapters in a Life of Paul* (1950), is here presupposed. While few subsequent Pauline biographies show the same primary regard for the Pauline data, it seems to the present writer that the main arguments of John Knox stand unrefuted. These arguments have often been ignored, but they have not been answered! Munck, pp. 78–81, expresses general agreement with Knox, although differing with respect to the value of data in Acts not contradicted by Paul. For an even more sceptical view of the data of Acts than that of Knox, cf. H. L. Ramsey, *The Place of Galatians in the Career of Paul*, unpublished Ph.D. dissertation (Columbia University, 1960).

For you, brethren, became imitators of the churches of God in Christ Jesus which are in Judea; for you suffered (ἐπάθετε) the same things from your own countrymen as they did from the Jews, who killed both the Lord Jesus and the prophets, and drove us out, and displease God and oppose all men by hindering us from speaking to the Gentiles that they may be saved—so as always to fill up the measure of their sins.

There are many problems in the exegesis of this passage. A number of scholars have urged that it is an intrusion into the context and that it is to be regarded in whole or in part as a later interpolation because of its intense anti-Judaism which cannot be paralleled elsewhere in Paul's writings.[1] Commentators have noted that Paul never accuses the Jews of killing Jesus except in this passage; in 1 Corinthians 2: 8 he attributes the death to 'the rulers of this age'.[2] For our purposes, however, the question of authenticity is secondary; more important is the interpretation of the 'suffering' here alluded to. We have already seen that the Pauline epistles as a whole yield very little evidence of Jewish persecution of Christians in Judea. Brandon points out that

in all his care to collect an impressive sum from his converts for the 'saints' at Jerusalem he never uses as an incentive to their generosity the fact of any notable sufferings by 'the saints' in defence of the faith.[3]

The same scholar notes that Paul was able to visit the Jerusalem church at widely scattered intervals and find a stable, continuing organization.[4] It is therefore not wise to exaggerate the meaning of ἐπάθετε, which may refer to public insults, social ostracism and other kinds of non-violent opposition. This understanding fits well with what the letter as a whole suggests is the current experience of the Christians in Thessalonica. These converts had originally received the word 'in much affliction' (ἐν θλίψει πολλῇ, 1 Thess. 1: 6); Paul had declared to them the gospel 'in the face of much opposition' (ἐν πολλῷ

---

[1] For a review of scholarly opinion, see J. E. Frame, *A Critical and Exegetical Commentary on the Epistles of St Paul to the Thessalonians* (1912), pp. 108–16. Cf. also Brandon, pp. 92 f.

[2] οἱ ἄρχοντες τοῦ αἰῶνος τούτου. Cf. Deever, p. 127.

[3] P. 91.   [4] *Ibid.*

ἀγῶνι, 2: 2). Now in Paul's absence they are experiencing certain afflictions (θλίψεσιν, 3: 3). Paul reminds them that while still with them he had forewarned them concerning affliction (μέλλομεν θλίβεσθαι, 3: 4). It is impossible to know what kinds of θλῖψις and ἀγών are referred to in these passages. What is certain, however, is that these words do not here designate a thoroughgoing, systematic persecution. The letter is not addressed to a suppressed group meeting surreptitiously; if such were the case, the exhortations of 4: 11 f.; 5: 14 would be pointless. It may be assumed, therefore, that the Thessalonian Christians, like those in Judea, are experiencing various kinds of abuse, some of it perhaps physical, but there is not sufficient evidence to support the view that the reference in 1 Thessalonians 2: 14–16 is to a serious outbreak of violent persecution.

Although evidence is lacking, it is probable that during the first war with Rome the situation in Palestine became so chaotic that Christians there suffered far more from Jewish hostility than their brethren in the Diaspora. This was certainly the case during the Bar Cocheba revolt. In the period between the wars there was a gradual process of separation which succeeded in isolating Jewish Christians from the synagogues of Palestine and the Diaspora. It seems probable that hostile measures employed by the synagogues against Christians in this period were as common in the Diaspora as in the Holy Land, but on the basis of available evidence no certainty is possible.

ORGANIZATION AND SPONTANEITY

Our examination of the data of Jewish persecution leads to the conclusion that in the period before A.D. 70 there was little in the way of organized opposition to the new sect. Martyrdoms were due to the spontaneous fury of a mob or to the arbitrary action of a king or high priest. Less drastic forms of punishment, such as floggings, were probably meted out by individual synagogues, and represented a local response to a local problem. There is no reliable evidence that any religious authority in Jerusalem—Sanhedrin, high priest or rabbinic leader—undertook to organize a world-wide suppression of Christianity during this period. Over against the suggestion of Acts 9: 1 f. (22: 5; 26: 12) that the Jewish religious authorities undertook such action must be placed a later statement by the same author, attributed to leaders of Roman Jewry:

We received no letters from Judea about you, and none of the brethren coming here has reported or spoken any evil about you. But we desire to hear from you what your views are, for with regard to this sect we know that everywhere it is spoken against (28: 21 f.).

While the report of Acts 9: 1 f. is otherwise unsupported and is suspect on internal grounds, the situation described in 28: 21 f. is precisely what we have been led to expect.[1]

It is probable that this situation changed after the first war. The insertion of the *Birkath ha-Minim* into the Eighteen Benedictions is clear proof that the rabbinic authorities regarded Christianity as a threat to a beleaguered Jewry. Even without further evidence it should be assumed that notice of this liturgical innovation was transmitted to synagogues throughout the Diaspora. We are not limited to assumptions, however. We have the testimony of Justin that selected men were sent out from Jerusalem 'into all the world' (εἰς πᾶσαν τὴν γῆν) to report the outbreak of the Christian heresy.[2] In addition we have the evidence of Tos. Sanh. 2: 6 that letters were on at least one other occasion sent out to all the Diaspora communities on the subject of liturgical matters.[3]

There is no indication that rabbinic authorities at Jamnia undertook to organize a more violent persecution than this. Organized violence did occur during the second war with Rome, but this persecution was undoubtedly limited to Palestine and was more political than religious in its motivation.[4] If flogging and imprisonment of Christians continued to take

---

[1] The extradition contemplated in 9: 2 would require letters to the secular power in Damascus, which at that time was an ethnarch representing the Nabataean monarch, Aretas (2 Cor. 11: 32). In view of the antipathy between Aretas and Herod Antipas (*Ant.* xviii. 5. 1 [109]) it seems improbable that an extradition treaty would be in force. It seems even more unlikely that such a treaty would allow for the extradition of refugees from religious persecution. The story of Paul's commission is likewise rendered suspect by its association with the narrative of his activity as a persecutor in Judea, a narrative which is flatly contradicted by Gal. 1: 22.

[2] *Dial.* 17. The reference to Jerusalem appears to be anachronistic.

[3] Cf. also Rosh ha-Shanah 1: 4.

[4] Above, p. 38.

place in the period between the wars, such punishments were probably still local and sporadic rather than the expressions of a universal policy dictated by rabbinic authorities in Jamnia.

THE RELATIONSHIP BETWEEN JEWISH AND GENTILE PERSECUTION OF CHRISTIANS

A number of modern scholars have maintained that the Roman persecution of Christians was due in no small measure to the active hostility of Jews. Harnack's statement has given weighty support to this thesis.

Unless the evidence is misleading, they [the Jews] instigated the Neronic outburst against the Christians; and as a rule whenever bloody persecutions are afoot in later days, the Jews are either in the background or the foreground.[1]

The evidence on which this judgment is based is slim indeed. It must be examined in detail.

The primary source is Justin Martyr. In chapter 16 of the *Dialogue* Justin absolves the Jews of contemporary violence against Christians while charging them with violent persecution in the past: 'Now indeed you cannot use violence against us Christians, because of those who are in power, but as often as you could you did employ force against us.'[2] In the following chapter he accuses the Jews of spreading calumnies against the Christians and thus inspiring heathen hostility toward Christians.

For other nations have not inflicted on us and on Christ this wrong to such an extent as you have, who in very deed are the authors of the wicked prejudice against the Just One, and us who hold by Him. For after you had crucified Him, the only blameless and righteous Man—through whose stripes those who approach the Father by Him are healed—when you knew that He had risen from the dead and ascended to heaven, as the prophets foretold He would, you not only did not repent of the wickedness which you had committed, but at that time you selected and sent out from Jerusalem chosen men through all the land (γῆν) to tell that the godless heresy

---

[1] Adolf Harnack, *The Expansion of Christianity in the First Three Centuries* (1904), I, 66.

[2] Translation by G. Reith, in Ante-Nicene Christian Library, vol. II (1874), p. 108.

of the Christians had sprung up, and to publish those things which all they who knew us not speak against us. So that you are the cause not only of your own unrighteousness, but in fact of that of all other men.[1]

Justin's use of τότε, 'at that time', suggests that he believes that these apostles of calumny were dispatched soon after the death and resurrection of Jesus. There is reason to believe that the testimony of Acts is to be accepted that no such organized and international attack had been made at the time Paul reached Rome (Acts 28: 21 f.). The emissaries to whom Justin refers are more probably the messengers of the reconstituted Sanhedrin meeting at Jamnia. It is not at all unlikely that the *Birkath ha-Minim* was communicated to the congregations of the Diaspora by such apostles.[2] Since one purpose of this 'benediction' was to effect the separation of the Church from the synagogue, those who brought information concerning it were inevitably regarded by Jewish Christians as enemies. It is to be doubted that these apostles were also guilty of spreading the rumours that charged Christians with infanticide, cannibalism, incest and other sexual perversions.[3] In all fairness it should be observed that since the purpose of the emissaries was to effect a separation which apparently had not yet been completed they would hardly attempt to propagate rumours which their Jewish hearers would know to be false because of their continuing contact with Christians.[4] Justin himself does not clearly indicate that he regarded Jews as responsible for such rumours. Origen is more explicit:

He appears to me, indeed, to have acted like those Jews who, when Christianity began to be first preached, scattered abroad false reports of the gospel, such as that 'Christians offered up an infant in sacrifice, and partook of its flesh'; and again, 'that the professors of Christianity, wishing to do the "works of darkness", used to extinguish the lights [in their meetings], and each one to have sexual intercourse with any woman whom he chanced to meet'. These calumnies have long exercised, although unreasonably, an influence over the minds of very many, leading those who are aliens to the gospel to believe that Christians are men of such a character; and

---

[1] *Dial.* 108 repeats the charge and clarifies the meaning of γῆ by substituting οἰκουμένη.   [2] See above, p. 65.
[3] These rumours are not elaborated by Tacitus, but they clearly underlie his use of *flagitia*, *Annals*, xv. 44.   [4] See Appendix 1.

even at the present day they [the calumnies] mislead some, and prevent them from entering into the simple intercourse of conversation with those who are Christians.[1]

It is this later testimony that inclines modern readers to interpret Justin's vague reference as an allusion to such calumnies.

In any event neither Justin nor Origen maintains that *contemporary* Jews are spreading these rumours. Each knows that the stories have been in existence for a long time. It is notoriously difficult to discover the originator of a false rumour. One would be tempted to ask these fathers of the Church how they can be so certain that the slanderous stories were invariably invented by Jews. Underlying the charge would seem to be the hypothesis that Jews are the source and origin of all the evil which comes upon Christians. According to this hypothesis the enmity of Gentiles can be due only to ignorance, whereas the Jews' hatred is deliberate.[2] Apparently it was difficult for Christians to recognize that their behaviour was likely to arouse antagonism among their fellow Gentiles without any inspiration from Jewish calumny. The following remarks of E. T. Merrill are apposite:

The poor were by the inevitable conditions of their existence herded closely together. There was among them a necessary community of life, an intimacy of acquaintance bred of their close contact, a prying curiosity about the affairs of their neighbours. Ostentatious reserve on the part of next-door residents aroused resentment, as if it were an affectation of superiority. Notorious withdrawal from free social intercourse, or abstention from popular religious festivals... was interpreted as due to gloomy moroseness. Preaching of asceticism was a robbery of the joy of life. Secrecy about religious rites, when almost all worship was as open as the day, created a suspicion that there was something in them that needed to be concealed, something that violated the ordinary moralities and decencies of life.[3]

No Jewish agency was needed to arouse antagonism in pagans toward the Christians in their midst. Luke–Acts habitually

---

[1] *Contra Celsum* vi. 27. Translation by F. Crombie, in Ante-Nicene Christian Library, vol. xxxiii, p. 366.

[2] Cf. Simon, *Verus Israel*, p. 147; Jas. Parkes, *Conflict*, p. 426; P. Winter, pp. 51–61.

[3] E. T. Merrill, *Essays in Early Christian History* (1924), p. 91. The truth of Merrill's statement is supported by 1 Peter 4: 4.

demonstrates that Jews are responsible for Gentile opposition to Paul, yet even in this work we have the story of the Ephesian riot (in which Jews are more closely associated with those attacked than with the attackers; cf. Acts 19: 33 f.) and the Philippian incident (16: 16–24). That some Jews were guilty of circulating calumnies concerning the Christians need not be doubted (cf. Rev. 2: 9), but there is not sufficient evidence to support the view that the Jews were the only rumour-mongers or that they were primarily responsible for the hatred which the Gentile community held toward the Church.

We must now examine two other passages from Justin which have been cited as evidence that Gentile persecution of Christians is to be attributed to Jewish instigation.

For you curse in your synagogues all those who are called from Him Christians; and other nations effectively carry out the curse, putting to death those who simply confess themselves to be Christians.[1]

...Punishments even to death have been inflicted on us by demons, and by the host of the devil, through the aid ministered to them by you.[2]

It must be clear to any impartial reader that there is no causal link in the first passage between the uttering of the curse and the persecution which fulfils the intention of the curse.[3] It is, of course, possible that Justin and many of his contemporaries believed that curses of this kind had an objective effect. Whether or not Justin here manifests such a belief, we cannot hold the Jewish synagogues responsible for Gentile persecution of Christians on this basis. The brief reference to Jewish agency in the second passage may well belong to the same kind of thinking; the assistance offered the host of the devil may be nothing more substantial than imprecations and other expressions of hatred. In any event the allusion is too vague to justify a general indictment.

Another source frequently cited in this connection is the Martyrdom of Polycarp, in which Jewish participation is specifically mentioned.

[1] *Dial.* 96. [2] *Dial.* 131.

[3] Frend, *Martyrdom*, p. 192 and note 123, apparently sees a causal relationship between Jewish hostility (expressed in synagogue cursing) and pagan persecution.

These things then happened with so great speed, quicker than it takes to tell, and the crowd came together immediately, and prepared wood and faggots from the work-shops and baths and the Jews were extremely zealous, as is their custom, in assisting at this.[1]

The Jews are again mentioned in connection with the disposition of the corpse, anxious lest its disappearance might give rise to another resurrection-myth (17: 2 — 18: 1). Although the Jews are singled out for special mention, however, it is clear that their role is secondary rather than primary. The Martyrdom of Polycarp nowhere accuses the Jews of instigating the persecution; responsibility is placed entirely on the pagan authorities. Since the Jews were themselves so frequently the objects of persecution in the Hellenistic East, they must have been relieved to see public antipathy directed toward another minority group. On account of religious rivalry they had more cause for hostility toward Christians than the general populace, and it is therefore not surprising that they should assist in the persecution of Christians. This kind of role, however, falls far short of meriting the indictment offered by Harnack.[2]

It has been argued by a number of scholars that Jews were the instigators of the Neronic persecution.[3] It must be stated at the outset that there is not a shred of positive evidence in support of this view. Those who postulate Jewish instigation do so for the most part because they assume that prior to this time

[1] Mart. Poly. 13: 1. Translation by K. Lake, *The Apostolic Fathers* (1952), II, 329. The reference to Jewish participation in 12: 2 is clearly inaccurate, and by its very inaccuracy indicates that the role played by the Jews was a subordinate one.

[2] The suggestion of Kilpatrick, *Origins*, p. 114, that the police agent Herod may have been a Jew is unwarranted. The name was common among pagans. Had this official been a Jew, it is not unlikely that his nationality would have been specified for the benefit of the readers in Philomelium, in view of the other references to Jewish participation. Cf. Mart. Poly. 8: 2; 17: 2.

[3] A. Harnack, *Expansion of Christianity*, I, 66; II, 116; L. H. Canfield, *The Early Persecutions of the Christians* (1913), pp. 47–9; Frend, *Martyrdom*, pp. 164 f.; F. Huidekoper, *Judaism at Rome: B.C. 76 to A.D. 140* (1877), p. 245; Merrill, pp. 111 f.; Simon, *Verus Israel*, p. 146; H. B. Workman, *Persecution in the Early Church* (1906), p. 57. P. Allard supports this view in *Histoire des persécutions pendant les deux premiers siècles* (1903), pp. 42 f. In another work, however, he can describe the Neronic persecution without resort to the theory of Jewish instigation: *Le Christianisme et l'Empire romain de Néron à Théodose* (1925), p. 10.

the Christians were so closely associated with the Jewish community as to be indistinguishable as far as outsiders were concerned. On the basis of this assumption it is maintained that only because of Jewish informers did the Roman government become aware of the Christian church as a religious community essentially independent of Judaism.

The assumption is at best a questionable one; in the opinion of the present writer it is indefensible. There is reason to believe that the Roman church was even at this time composed largely of Gentiles, and was therefore by no means so closely associated with the synagogue-community as to be indistinguishable from it.[1] There is no reason to question Merrill's supposition that the lower-class neighbours of Christians in Rome were aware of their semi-secret associations.[2] Nor do we have any reason to assume that prior to this first great outbreak against Christianity in the capital there was any reticence on the part of Christian missionaries. With no evidence to the contrary, it must be assumed that Christian evangelists proclaimed their faith openly on the streets of Rome as elsewhere. We must also take seriously the statement of Tacitus that the Christians were hated by the Roman mob on account of their enormities.[3] Many proponents of the hypothesis of Jewish instigation suppose that Tacitus, writing at a later date, was at this point guilty of anachronism in ascribing to the time of Nero a public awareness of Christianity that was actually a result of the Neronic persecution, not its precondition. While this is not impossible in view of other inaccuracies in the account given us by Tacitus, we have no reason to deny that Christians were already the object of public intolerance in Rome prior to Nero's action. What had happened in Philippi and Ephesus could easily occur in Rome.

The hypothesis of Jewish instigation is therefore superfluous. Even if we accept the statement of Tacitus that the Christians

[1] See Appendix II.

[2] Cited above, p. 68; cf. 1 Peter 4: 4. This well-founded observation is strangely ignored by Merrill on a later page (p. 107), when he interprets the testimony of Acts 28: 22 as indicating that Jewish leaders in Rome were unaware of the Christian movement in their midst.

[3] *Annals* xv. 44, '. . . quos per flagitia invisos vulgus Christianos appellabat'. For a careful discussion of the passage in Tacitus, including a good bibliography, cf. Harald Fuchs, 'Tacitus über die Christen', *Vigiliae Christianae*, IV (1950), 65–93.

were punished by Nero as arsonists, there is no need to surmise that such a charge would not have occurred to pagan minds except by Jewish suggestion. It is not at all impossible that some Christian preachers were so outspoken in their apocalyptic discourses concerning imminent judgment by fire that pagan antagonists actually suspected them of arson at the time of the fire and reported them to the government. If, on the other hand, we follow those scholars who maintain that Tacitus was completely in error in associating Nero's persecution of Christians with the fire, there is still no need to suppose that Jews proposed government action against the Christians.[1] On the basis of the brief account of the persecution given by Suetonius,[2] Canfield concludes that

the Christians were suppressed for the same reason that the worshippers of Bacchus and Isis had been suppressed before them. They fell under the ordinary rule of Roman intolerance, and as a result their suppression became the duty of the Roman officials.[3]

Canfield's argument in favour of the hypothesis of Jewish instigation is based upon 1 Clement. In this sub-apostolic work the Roman author warns Corinthian Christians against the dangers of envy and jealousy, φθόνος and ζῆλος. He illustrates his theme by citing the sufferings of Old Testament worthies, each of whom had suffered persecution at the hands of his own brothers or fellow countrymen (Abel, Joseph, Moses and David; 1 Clem. 4). He then transfers his attention to examples taken from 'our own generation', naming specifically Peter and Paul, who also suffered on account of jealousy (1 Clem. 5). The author continues:

[1] For a survey of works sceptical of Tacitus at this point, see Canfield, pp. 44 f. Canfield himself presents an impressive case against Tacitus, pp. 43–69. He points out that Suetonius, a contemporary of Tacitus, makes reference to the persecution of Christians by Nero, but mentions the event in connection with other police actions of a similar nature, without any hint that the charge laid against the Christians was incendiarism. The account of the fire, occurring several chapters later in Suetonius' *Vita Neronis*, makes no mention of Nero's use of a scapegoat. Canfield further notes that early Christian comment on the Neronic persecution even as late as Eusebius betrays no knowledge of the charge of arson. Not until the fifth century do we find a Christian writer who connects the persecution with the fire, and this is by no means an independent testimony but one slavishly dependent upon the *Annals* of Tacitus (Sulpicius Severus, *Chronicon* ii. 29).

[2] *Vita Neronis* 16.   [3] P. 50.

To these men with their holy lives was gathered a great multitude of the chosen, who were the victims of jealousy and offered among us the fairest example in their endurance under many indignities and tortures. Through jealousy women were persecuted as Danaids and Dircae, suffering terrible and unholy indignities; they steadfastly finished the course of faith, and received a noble reward, weak in the body though they were (1 Clem. 6).

In view of the account in Acts, we have no difficulty in agreeing with Canfield that Clement regarded the martyrdom of Paul as due to the ill-will of his fellow countrymen. It is further possible that Peter's sufferings likewise involved the hostility of fellow Jews, although we have no other evidence in early Christian tradition to this effect.[1] But must we agree with Canfield that in the light of the context it must be assumed that the 'great multitude' also suffered as a result of Jewish jealousy?[2]

Cullmann argues convincingly against such a conclusion: 'The Jews cannot be meant here as authors of jealousy, for in the time of Clement they were no longer regarded as belonging to the same fellowship.'[3] This argument is strengthened if we are correct in the view that the Roman church was even at this time predominantly Gentile.[4] In Cullmann's view the context requires that we understand the ruinous jealousy as arising within the Christian fellowship itself. He suggests the possibility that it was strife between divergent factions in the Church which brought the Christian movement to the attention of the authorities, possibly through the agency of informers.[5] Cullmann cites Paul's reference to φθόνος and ἔρις in Philippians 1: 15–17 as evidence of such dissension in the Roman church.[6]

---

[1] In the legendary Acts of Peter it is maintained that Peter was executed because he persuaded certain Roman ladies to desist from marital relations with their husbands (the Vercelli Acts of Peter 33 ff.; cf. M. R. James, *Apoc. N.T.* pp. 332 f.).

[2] Canfield, pp. 48, 69. Cf. Frend, *Martyrdom*, p. 164.

[3] Oscar Cullmann, *Peter: Disciple—Apostle—Martyr* (1953), p. 102 n. 22.

[4] See Appendix II.

[5] P. 102.

[6] P. 104. Frend, in another context, suggests that pagan persecution of Christians was sometimes instigated by heretical Christians (*Martyrdom*, pp. 188, 199). It is regrettable that Frend chooses to describe these heretics with the adjective 'Jewish', which suggests to the reader non-Christian Jews.

Whether or not we agree with Cullmann's interpretation of I Clement in all respects, it is clear that Canfield's argument is not as strong as might appear at first glance. In view of the strong tendency to assimilate later martyrdoms to the prototype of the Passion of Jesus, it is highly unlikely that Jewish agency would be left unmentioned if known to the author of I Clement.[1] Since Jewish persecution of Christians is nowhere directly mentioned in this writing, there is little justification for inferring Jewish jealousy in this passage.

We must conclude therefore that since the Neronic persecution is nowhere attributed to Jewish instigation in pagan or early Christian literature, and since the government action can be just as well explained on other grounds, the hypothesis of Jewish instigation must be rejected.

It is clear, however, that Jews were on occasion the instigators of Gentile persecution of Christians, as evidenced by the Acts of the Apostles. The first mention of such activity occurs in the narrative of the Pauline mission in Pisidian Antioch. The Jews, who at first were receptive to Paul's message, became filled with jealousy at the sight of the crowds of Gentiles who gathered to hear the Christian missionary (13: 45). They attempted to thwart Paul's work by publicly reviling him, and, when this failed, they 'incited the devout women of high standing and the leading men of the city, and stirred up persecution against Paul and Barnabas, and drove them out of their district' (13: 50). This pattern is repeated at Iconium, where unbelieving Jews 'stirred up the Gentiles and poisoned their minds against the brethren' (14: 2), with the result that eventually a joint attempt was made by Jews and Gentiles 'to molest and to stone them' (14: 5). Up to this point the Jewish agitation was indigenous. At Lystra, however, trouble developed only when Jews from Antioch and Iconium arrived; these 'persuaded the people' and stoned Paul (14: 19). At Thessalonica we meet a situation closely parallel to the first in the series. As at Pisidian Antioch, the Jews here became jealous, 'and taking some wicked fellows of the rabble, they gathered a crowd, set the city in an

[1] Clement's silence concerning the source of the jealousy is better explained by Cullmann's suggestion (p. 104) that the matter was an embarrassment to Christians everywhere than by the inference that the role played by jealous Jews was well known to the Corinthian Christians.

uproar, and attacked the house of Jason, seeking to bring them out to the people' (17: 5). Not finding the chief culprits, they dragged Jason and some others before the city authorities, charging 'These men who have turned the world upside down have come here also, and Jason has received them; and they are all acting against the decrees of Caesar, saying that there is another king, Jesus' (17: 6f.). The Lystran situation is repeated in Beroea; the local Jews received Paul happily, but Jews from Thessalonica appeared, 'stirring up and inciting the crowds' (17: 13).

At Corinth another attempt was made by Jews to have Gentile authorities deal with the Christian problem. The charge presented at Gallio's tribunal was that Paul was 'persuading men to worship God contrary to the law' (18: 13). Conzelmann is probably correct in interpreting this as a deliberately ambiguous charge; the author of Acts suggests that Paul's antagonists had hoped to deceive Gallio into believing that the law which Paul had violated was Roman, but Gallio perceived that it was the Jewish law, not the Roman, which was their chief concern.[1]

In Paul's trial before Felix, Tertullus charged that Paul was 'a pestilent fellow, an agitator among all the Jews throughout the world, and a ringleader of the sect of the Nazarenes' (24: 5).[2]

Reviewing the evidence of Acts, we find that Jews are reported as instigating action against Christians by (1) poisoning the mind of the populace, (2) stirring up the rabble to attack the Christians, (3) bringing Christians before Gentile tribunals on charges of having broken Gentile law, and (4) inciting Gentiles to hale Christians into court on such charges.

There is no reason to doubt that Jews were involved in each of these kinds of action. This does not mean, however, that wherever Christians went Jews invariably aroused Gentile action against the proponents of the new sect. We have already seen that the author of Acts acknowledges two incidents in which hostile action is undertaken by Gentiles without any Jewish instigation (16: 19–24; 19: 23–41).

[1] H. Conzelmann, *The Theology of St Luke* (1960), p. 143.

[2] Conzelmann, *ibid.*, notes that the question of Paul's transgression of Jewish law is raised by Jews only among Jews; a different approach is made when Paul's case is presented to Gentiles, at which times political unrest and public scandal are cited.

From Paul's letters we learn that he was frequently in danger from Gentiles as well as from his fellow Jews, but although these two dangers can be mentioned in the same breath (2 Cor. 11: 26), the stormy missionary nowhere suggests that any causal relation existed between them—not even in 1 Thessalonians 2: 14–16! The same situation prevails in the Apocalypse. Although the author speaks scathingly of the Synagogue of Satan (2: 9; 3: 9), he makes no clear connection between Jewish opposition and the great persecution which he foresees for the Church, of which Antipas is the firstfruits (2: 13).

Apart from the Book of Acts, the New Testament provides scanty evidence indeed of Jewish incitement of Gentile persecution. The same situation prevails in the writings of the Apostolic Fathers and in the Christian apocrypha. Of special significance is the paucity of evidence in the martyrologies. The exhaustive study made by James Parkes has placed us all in his debt. Parkes reports that

> *Acta* attributed to the first century contain a very high proportion of stories ascribing definite hostility to Jews, culminating sometimes in the death of the saint. From the beginning of the second century onwards there is almost complete silence as to any Jewish responsibility for, or even interest in, the fate of the heroes of the Church.[1]

In the light of this evidence, the unsubstantiated charge of Tertullian, *Synagogas Iudaeorum fontes persecutionum*, can hardly be taken seriously.[2] Marcel Simon justly remarks: 'Est-il

[1] J. Parkes, *Conflict*, p. 132. In Appendix v of the same work are collected references to all the martyrdoms of the first century ascribed to Jews.

[2] 'Synagogues of the Jews, fountains of persecution', *Scorp.* x; cf. *Ad Nationes* i. 14. Frend, *J.E.H.* ix, 157, maintains that the evidence justifies Tertullian's dictum. That the synagogues were sources of hostility is not under dispute, but that they were *primarily responsible* for the great persecutions can hardly be entertained. Much of the evidence cited by Frend has been dealt with above. Another datum adduced by Frend (*Martyrdom*, p. 288) is the reference in an anti-Montanist writer, Apolinarius, as quoted by Eusebius, *Eccl. Hist.* v. 16. 12: 'Or was any one of the women ever scourged in the synagogues of the Jews or stoned?' Those who see in this rhetorical question evidence that Catholic contemporaries of Apolinarius are receiving this kind of treatment from Jews—in their synagogues, no less!—have missed the point of the passage. Apolinarius seeks to demonstrate that the Montanists are not real prophets, since it has been the lot of genuine prophets to suffer persecution by the Jews; see above, p. 61 n. Exception must also be taken to Frend's reference to the 'bitter hostility of the Jews towards the Christians, which

vraiment besoin de recourir aux Juifs pour expliquer des mesures voulues, décidées et appliquées par l'autorité romaine?'[1]

That Jews did in fact have a role in Gentile persecution need not be denied. That this was a role of primary importance, at least with respect to official persecution by the Roman government, cannot be demonstrated on the basis of available evidence. While the data from Justin, Origen and Tertullian are not to be entirely disregarded, they must be used with great caution.[2] It is probable that by the time of Justin a theology of the role of the Jews had been developed which required that the Jews be held primarily responsible for the sufferings of the Church. F. W. Beare has suggested that this idea is present as an apologetic motif in Acts 17: 5–10.[3] The motif does not seem to be present in other New Testament books, but there are passages in which it may have been 'discovered' by second-century readers (e.g. Matt. 10: 17 f., 27: 25; 1 Thess. 2: 14–16; Rev. 2: 9 f.). After Justin this theological tradition required little or no evidence in its support. The continuing influence of this theological attitude is reflected in Harnack's uncritical acceptance of the traditional charge against the Jews.[4]

SUMMARY

In this chapter we have dealt with the evidence of Jewish persecution of Christians found in sources other than Matthew.

ensured that there would lack neither accusers nor mobs to shout "down with the atheists" at the appropriate moment' (*J.E.H.* ix, 153). Such a generalization is indefensible in view of the evidence. Can Frend produce *one instance* in which such a cry was made by Jews? For the Jewish use of ἄθεος, see Appendix 1.

[1] *Verus Israel*, p. 148.

[2] Frend displays far too little caution in dealing with the fragmentary evidence which is available, ignoring the fact that the theme of Jewish persecution had become in Christian circles a *theological tradition*. The evidence adduced from the variant readings in Codex Bezae, for example (*Martyrdom*, p. 259), should not be used to support Frend's lamentable generalizations concerning the Jewish role in pagan persecution (pp. 154, 184, 192, 193).

[3] F. W. Beare, 'Thessalonians, First', *Interpreter's Dictionary of the Bible* (1962), iv, 623 a.

[4] For a carefully documented response to Harnack's statement on the part of a Jewish scholar, see Israel Abrahams, *Studies in Pharisaism and the Gospels* (Second Series, 1924), pp. 58 ff.

No clear instance of execution of Christians by Jewish religious authorities for purely religious reasons was found, nor did the evidence indicate any systematic effort to eliminate Christianity by treating it as a capital crime. Apart from the Bar Cocheba revolt, when many Christians suffered death on account of their faith, Christian martyrdoms at the hands of Jewish antagonists were probably few in number, and probably for the most part due to the unpremeditated violence of a mob.

Flogging was employed as a punishment against certain Christian missionaries such as Paul, but was apparently by no means universally applied, and was not employed against rank-and-file Christians. There is no evidence of a determined effort on the part of Jewry to suppress the Christian movement by flogging all who believed in Christ. Imprisonment seems not to have been used as a punishment for faith in Christ, although certain Christians may have been held in temporary detention by Jewish authorities in Palestine. Formal exclusion from the synagogue was perhaps employed against individual Christian missionaries who threatened the peace of the Jewish community, but there is no evidence that faith in Christ was defined as a crime punishable by formal exclusion from the synagogues of Jewry. More common was the exclusion of Christians by the pressure of social ostracism, as indicated by the insertion into the daily prayer of the *Birkath ha-Minim*. Social ostracism was undoubtedly accompanied by economic boycotts, which may have led to financial hardship for some Christians. In all probability Christians were the objects of various kinds of insults at the hands of hostile Jews, but little mention is made of this kind of treatment in our sources. Many of the vague references to Jewish persecution found in the New Testament may indicate that Christians *expected* to be persecuted by unbelieving Jews rather than actual experiences of persecution.

With respect to the distribution of the phenomena of persecution it was concluded that prior to the first war with Rome the church in Judea was on the whole not a persecuted church. During this period the Jewish Christian missionaries in the Diaspora who proclaimed the gospel to the Gentiles were more likely to be persecuted than Christians in Judea. Although evidence is lacking, it seems likely that during the war this situation changed, giving way to more frequent expressions of violence against the Christians in Palestine.

No evidence of organized opposition to the Christian movement was found prior to the destruction of the Temple. The insertion of the *Birkath ha-Minim* indicates that the rabbinic authorities found it necessary to oppose all minority sects in an attempt to consolidate their position. There is no evidence, however, of any attempt on their part to initiate an organized campaign of violence against the Christians. When organized violence did occur it was during the Bar Cocheba revolt, and was more political than religious in character.

The charge that Jews were largely responsible for the Gentile persecution of Christians was found to be without foundation. No evidence exists to support the hypothesis that Jews instigated the persecution by Nero. Our primary evidence for Jewish instigation of Gentile persecution comes from the Acts of the Apostles, and even this source indicates that pagan persecution of Christians could occur spontaneously, without outside suggestion.

CHAPTER III

REFERENCES TO JEWISH PERSECUTION OF CHRISTIANS IN THE GOSPEL ACCORDING TO ST MATTHEW

EXEGESIS OF THE RELEVANT PASSAGES

HAVING now examined the non-Matthean data pertaining to persecution, we will turn to the relevant passages in the First Gospel. By comparing the Matthean with the non-Matthean data we will attempt to assess the accuracy with which Matthew reflects the conflict.

Matthew 23: 29–39

In Matthew 23: 34 it is predicted that messengers of Jesus will suffer violent persecution at the hands of the scribes and Pharisees. This passage will serve as a point of departure because of its unambiguous reference to Jewish persecutors and because of its occurrence in a chapter in which Matthew's hand is particularly evident.[1]

Matthew's great discourse against the scribes and Pharisees is set within the Marcan framework, occasioned by the brief denunciation of the scribes which Mark includes at the conclusion of the disputes conducted in the Temple (Mark 12: 38–40). While Luke has here followed Mark closely, Matthew has greatly expanded the denunciation, combining material from the double tradition (Q) found in other contexts in Luke with material from his special source or sources.[2]

---

[1] The name 'Matthew' will serve to designate the author, but the unknown writer so designated must not be confused with the tax-collector to whom the gospel has traditionally been ascribed.

[2] Of the various attempts to demonstrate that the double tradition is due simply to the fact that Luke copied Matthew, none has proved convincing to the present writer. For the purposes of this study it will be assumed that the double tradition represents material used independently by the two evangelists.

Serious questions have been raised concerning the existence of Q as a literary document; cf. T. R. Rosché, 'The Words of Jesus and the Future of the "Q" Hypothesis', *J.B.L.* LXXIX (1960), 210–20. It seems to the present

In the Lucan version of the woes against the Pharisees, separate woes are enunciated against the lawyers, νομικοί (Luke 11: 37–52). It is instructive to note that two of the three woes in the second group are appropriate for religious leaders (Luke 11: 46, 52), while the three woes directed against the Pharisees (Luke 11: 42–4) are pertinent to rank-and-file members. This careful distinction between ordinary members of the Pharisaic party and their rabbinic leaders disappears in Matthew's version of the woes. In six of the seven Matthean woes the scribes and Pharisees are addressed together.[1] Matthew's fusion of the two groups is especially obvious in the prologue of the discourse, where it is stated that the scribes *and Pharisees* sit on Moses' seat (23: 2), as if the lay members of the Pharisaic party were all authoritative exegetes of the Torah! The conclusion seems inescapable that Matthew's fusion of the two groups represents a later stage of the tradition than Luke's version of the woes.

It has been suggested that the combining of Q material with material from sources peculiar to Matthew (M) was accomplished not by the author of the gospel but by those who moulded the version of Q which was used by Matthew (Q^{Mt}).[2] While this may be true in many passages, and may indeed be true of some elements in chapter 23, the chapter as a whole clearly betrays the hand of the editor who combined Q with Mark.

The use of pejorative vocatives addressed to the Pharisaic opponents is particularly characteristic of the editor of the First Gospel. The primary example is ὑποκριταί, 'Hypocrites!' (*vv.* 13, 15, 23, 25, 27, 29). This term could have been derived

writer that Rosché underestimates the significance of the agreements in order and sequence, admittedly few, of the Q materials; it is improbable that these agreements are due solely to oral transmission. It is entirely possible, however, that certain pericopes common to Matthew and Luke were received by the evangelists from oral tradition rather than from a literary document. In this study the letter Q will stand for the double tradition, whether written or oral. For a well-balanced introduction to Q, cf. G. Bornkamm, 'Evangelien, synoptische', *R.G.G.*[3], II, cols. 753–66.

[1] By implication both groups are subsumed under ὁδηγοὶ τυφλοί in *vv.* 16–22, the only woe in which they are not explicitly mentioned.

[2] John Pairman Brown, 'The Form of "Q" Known to Matthew', *N.T.S.* VIII (1961–2), 32, argues that most of the 'M' elements in Matthew, apart from the parables, had been combined with Q in a much-expanded Q^{Mt} before the latter reached the final editor.

from Q^{Mt}, but in favour of the view that Matthew himself is responsible is the fact that in 15: 7 and 22: 18 the same vocative represents an editorial alteration of the Marcan source (Mark 7: 6; 12: 15). The pejorative γεννήματα ἐχιδνῶν, 'Offspring of vipers!' (v. 33), is taken from Q in an earlier passage (3: 7; cf. Luke 3: 7), but its presence in 12: 34 is probably editorial (cf. Luke 6: 45), and consequently the editor may likewise be held responsible here.[1] In the latter instance he has expanded the epithet by prefixing ὄφεις, 'Serpents!' Twice in chapter 23 we find the epithet ὁδηγοὶ τυφλοί, 'Blind guides!' (vv. 16, 24). The use of this epithet in 15: 14 seems to be inspired by the Q-saying concerning the blind leading the blind (Luke 6: 39). Whether or not Matthew was the first to apply the epithet to the Pharisees, its use in chapter 23 would seem to reflect his fondness for pejorative vocatives. The same could be said of τυφλοί, 'You blind!' (vv. 17, 19), and Φαρισαῖε τυφλέ, 'Blind Pharisee!' (v. 26). The vocative use of μωροί, 'Fools!' (v. 17), is in curious contradiction to the prohibition of the term in 5: 22.[2]

Although the evidence in favour of editorial addition with respect to each instance is by no means conclusive, the cumulative effect is compelling. Since these epithets are not simple insertions but form a part of the context, it is highly probable that the discourse as it now stands is the creation of Matthew himself.[3]

Assuming, then, that the hand of Matthew can be traced in 23: 29–39, we will now attempt to identify the redactional elements, in the expectation that they will shed some light on the historical context in which the gospel was written.

The logic of the seventh woe (vv. 29–31) is strained, to say

[1] It must also be noted that in the Q passage from which the epithet is derived it is applied to the crowds generally (Luke 3: 7), while Matthew alters the context in order to apply the epithet to Pharisees and Sadducees.

[2] The currency of two other pejoratives is perhaps implied by the text: 'Ye sons of Gehenna!' (cf. vv. 15, 33) and 'You whitewashed tombs!' (cf. v. 27). The currency of the latter is urged by E. Hirsch, who adduces Acts 23: 3; cf. his *Frühgeschichte des Evangeliums* (1941), II, 112.

[3] Ernst Haenchen, whose careful literary analysis of Matthew 23 is worthy of highest praise, argues that it is Matthew's skill as an author that is reflected in this composition; cf. 'Matthäus 23', *Z.T.K.* XLVIII (1951), 57 f. He examines the author's combination of disparate materials and notes the impressive climax achieved in the concluding verses.

the least. This is as true of the Lucan form (Luke 11 : 47 f.) as of the Matthean. It is the logic of polemic, not of reasoned argument. The underlying idea, however, is clear. Those addressed are accused of manifesting the same negative attitude toward contemporary prophecy as those who killed the prophets of earlier ages, and therefore are to be regarded as the spiritual children of the prophet-slayers even though they profess respect for the murdered prophets by constructing elaborate memorials.

If Jeremias is correct in his conclusion that the building of tombs for the prophets occurred at a date as early as the time of Jesus, it may well be that a genuine word of Jesus lies behind this seventh woe, occasioned, perhaps, by an expression of hostility toward his prophetic ministry.[1] It may be assumed that the original context of the saying was not clearly remembered during the period of oral transmission. It seems most probable that the opponents to whom the woe was originally directed were not specified in the earliest form of the tradition.[2]

In the Lucan context the woe is directed against the νομικοί, 'lawyers' (Luke 11 : 45–8). This term is preferred by Luke as a designation for the legal experts of the Pharisaic party, commonly referred to as γραμματεῖς, 'scribes', by Matthew and Mark, and later known as 'rabbis'. Unlike the preceding woe in Luke, this woe does not intrinsically involve religious leadership. There is no *a priori* reason for assuming that the rabbis played a major role in the construction of memorials for the prophets. Jeremias suggests that the practice of erecting monuments to mark the graves of Israel's heroes was a new and unfamiliar one at the time this woe originated.[3] He maintains that as far as our knowledge will permit any opinion, it was Herod the Great who initiated this custom by erecting a monument of white stones at the entrance to the tomb of David.[4] Because this monument is explicitly denominated a ἱλαστήριον μνῆμα

---

[1] Joachim Jeremias, *Heiligengräber in Jesu Umwelt* (1958), pp. 118–21. In any event the woe must be dated before the destruction of Jerusalem; as Haenchen points out, p. 51, there was not the means for building and decorating the tombs of the prophets in the early post-war period. For an excellent study of the post-war situation, cf. A. Büchler, *The Economic Conditions of Judea after the Destruction of the Second Temple* (1912).

[2] R. Bultmann, *The History of the Synoptic Tradition* (1963), p. 52.

[3] P. 118.

[4] P. 121, referring to Josephus, *Ant.* xvi. 7. 1 (182).

by Josephus, Jeremias sees here a precedent for the erection of expiatory monuments for the murdered prophets mentioned in Matthew 23: 29.[1] Expiation, he points out, was not the only motive, however; the motive of honouring the dead must have been fully as important.[2] Neither of these motives proposed by Jeremias presupposes that it was the rabbis who were especially interested in the construction of monuments for murdered prophets or the adorning of the graves of the righteous. Indeed, to the extent that a superstitious desire to atone for innocent blood was present in such projects, we can imagine that the rabbis were very reluctant supporters if not active opponents.

There is no good reason, therefore, for supposing that this woe was originally addressed by Jesus to the Pharisaic scribes. We are on safer ground if we assume that it was addressed to a heterogeneous group of opponents of Jesus regarded as representatives of the eschatological generation (cf. Luke 11: 15 f., 29), a generation characterized by a rejection of the prophetic message while ostentatiously honouring dead prophets with newly built monuments.

Since this woe in both Matthew and Luke is directed against the Pharisees and/or scribes, it would appear that the identification of the opponents is as early as the Greek version of Q which served as the archetype for Q^{Mt} and Q^{Lk}. It is possible, however, that the earliest form of Q did not contain this identification. In both gospels this woe is closely associated with the saying ascribed to the Wisdom of God by Luke (Luke 11: 49 f.). In each case the Wisdom-saying is introduced by διὰ τοῦτο, which serves to make the Wisdom-saying a commentary on the situation inveighed against in the woe. The Wisdom-saying, however, seems not to have in mind any particular religious group (the Pharisees or their scribes) but rather the eschatological generation (τῆς γενεᾶς ταύτης, *bis* Luke 11: 50 f.). The Matthean form of the Wisdom-saying differs widely from the Lucan, but a reference to 'this generation' persists (23: 36), suggesting a wider application than the one now found in Matthew.[3]

[1] P. 121.   [2] *Ibid.*
[3] Although the Jerusalem-saying (23: 37–9; Luke 13: 34 f.) probably occurred in a different context in Q (see below, pp. 94 f.), it none the less serves as indirect evidence that the opposition to Jesus was viewed in more general terms by the earliest form of Q.

It has long been recognized that the later strata of the gospels manifest an interest in the identification of the opponents of Jesus which is practically absent from the earliest strata.[1] This tendency was probably at work within the history of the transmission of Q. The woe against those who erect monuments over the graves of murdered prophets seems not to have been originally directed against the scribes and Pharisees. The later identification seems also to have been lacking at the stage of the tradition when the woe was coupled with the Wisdom-saying. The identification was undoubtedly introduced when this independent woe was combined with others to form a series of woes against the Pharisees and their scribes. This step may have taken place when Q first took literary form. At any rate we may assume that the identification was present in the archetype of Q^{Mt} and Q^{Lk}.

What this means for our study is that the application to the scribes and Pharisees of this seventh woe implies no intensified anti-Pharisaism on Matthew's part. Such anti-Pharisaism is an inherited part of Matthew's religious outlook. Its roots may very well lie in controversies between Jesus and Pharisaic scribes.[2] We must assume that the memory of these disputes was cherished and transmitted by the Palestinian church, which, during the pre-war period, discovered that Pharisaism was the most vigorous opponent of its messianic mission. In the light of this opposition it is not at all surprising that the Palestinian tradition should increasingly regard the Pharisees as the typical opponents of Jesus.

At first surprising, however, is the fact that this kind of anti-Pharisaism, which had its *Sitz im Leben* in the mission of the Palestinian church, remained very much alive when the Palestinian tradition was transmitted to the Gentile church and translated into Greek. Indeed, all our evidence for this tendency of identifying unspecified opponents as Pharisees is drawn from our canonical gospels, all of which are products of the Greek-speaking Gentile church. The fact that Luke, a Gentile writing for Gentiles, manifests the same tendency must

[1] Bultmann, *Hist. Syn. Trad.* pp. 52 f.

[2] Bultmann, *ibid.* p. 53, after discussing passages in which the reference to scribes and Pharisees is secondary, concedes that the reference may be original in some controversy dialogues.

not be construed as evidence that controversy with the Pharisees was a living reality for Luke's Gentile church. In the absence of more positive evidence, we must assume that this kind of anti-Pharisaism had become a literary convention by the time Luke composed his gospel.

Crucial for the present study is the question whether the intensified anti-Pharisaism of Matthew can similarly be explained as due to literary convention. If this were true, Matthew's intensification of inherited anti-Pharisaism would be of little relevance for an understanding of the historical context of the First Gospel. Before we can attempt to answer this question we must examine minutely the evidence of intensification.

Not only does Matthew prefix the seventh woe with the pejorative 'Hypocrites!'; he also appends to it two sentences not found in Luke which tend to disturb the connection between the woe and the Wisdom-saying (vv. 32 f.).[1] The consensus of modern scholarship is that Luke preserves the original character of the Wisdom-saying in ascribing it to the Wisdom of God.[2] By coupling the Wisdom-saying with the preceding woe, the Q-tradition ascribed to Jesus the application of this quotation to the situation described in the woe.[3] The connective διὰ τοῦτο

[1] Cf. Haenchen, pp. 39, 52, who regards these verses as editorial insertions added by the author in order to provide a smooth transition from the last woe to the announcement of the persecution of the Christians and of the judgment upon the persecutors. Whether or not this adequately describes the author's intention, it is our contention that Matthew has obscured the original connection by these additions.

[2] Cf. Bultmann, *Hist. Syn. Trad.* p. 114, and the literature there cited. The quotation is apparently from an apocryphal work no longer extant.

[3] While it is understandable that Matthew (or perhaps Q^{Mt}) should ascribe the saying to Jesus, feeling it inappropriate that Jesus should cite a non-canonical scripture, it is not at all probable that the reverse should occur. Nor is it possible to argue that ἡ σοφία τοῦ θεοῦ is understood by Luke and/or his *Vorlage* as a self-designation of Jesus, since the accompanying verb is in the third person and in the past tense. If the title were here understood Christologically (as in 1 Cor. 1: 24), the reference would have to be to the pre-incarnate Logos. Since Luke, however, introduces his reference to the speaker with καί, 'also', he clearly regards the Wisdom-saying as coming from a speaker other than Jesus, the speaker of the preceding saying. While Luke attributes to the Wisdom of God the sending of prophets and apostles (terms used of Christian leaders in the Gentile churches), in Matthew the messengers are 'prophets, wise men and scribes'. It is probable (a) that Matthew here retains the original terms for the

86

in Luke 11: 49 makes the relationship explicit: 'It is in view of this situation, viz. that you, like your fathers, are at heart prophet-murderers, that the Wisdom of God once declared, "I will send etc.".' While Matthew retains διὰ τοῦτο as the connective, its reference has been drastically altered; it serves to explain not a *statement* made in the past by the Wisdom of God but an *act* performed in the present by Jesus of Nazareth: 'Because of this situation just described, I, Jesus, am sending to you etc.'[1] Not only has the force of the διὰ τοῦτο been materially altered by the change effected in the saying which follows, but its antecedent has been rendered ambiguous by the insertion of two verses between it and the woe. Since verse 32 is in the imperative and verse 33 in the interrogative, it would seem probable that the διὰ τοῦτο should refer back to the indicative statements of verses 29–31; this connection has been obscured by the intervening sentences, which for this reason must be suspected of being interpolations.

Whether verse 32 had been added to the Q tradition before the latter was employed by Matthew cannot be determined with certainty, since it cannot be demonstrated that the diction of this verse is particularly characteristic of the First Evangelist. With the following verse, however, the case is different. It may be regarded as characteristic of Matthew that the pejorative γεννήματα ἐχιδνῶν, directed against the crowds in Luke's account of the preaching of John the Baptist (Luke 3: 7), is applied in Matthew's version to 'many of the Pharisees and Sadducees' (Matt. 3: 7). The same pejorative is applied to the Pharisees in Matthew 12: 34 in a sentence not found in the Lucan parallel. Since no evidence forces us to postulate that this phrase was applied to the Pharisees in Q^{Mt}, we may accept it as probable that it was the author of the First Gospel who was responsible for this usage. Also characteristic of Matthew is the use of a question introduced by πῶς addressed to the Pharisaic opponents (cf. 12: 34). It seems likely, therefore, that verse 33 is an editorial addition.[2]

messengers, and (*b*) that Jesus (to whom Matthew attributes the saying) did not promise to send wise men and scribes into the world. If this is true, Matthew, by retaining the original terms, betrays the inaccuracy of his identification of the speaker.   [1] Note the emphatic ἐγώ.

[2] Cf. Bultmann, *Hist. Syn. Trad.* pp. 130, 326; Haenchen, p. 52.

Whether or not we regard verse 32 likewise as an editorial creation depends in part upon how we understand its function in the passage. It can be argued that while verse 32 would be superfluous in the parallel Lucan passage, the change introduced by Matthew's ascription of the Wisdom-saying to Jesus requires some clarification of the relationship between Jesus' act of sending prophets and the situation described in the woe. In the Lucan version the statement concerning the sending of prophets is referred to the past and therefore the sending itself may be thought of as taking place in the past as well as in the present and future; thus the prophets whose slaughter is mentioned in the woe are included among those sent out by the Wisdom of God. In the Matthean version, on the other hand, the sending of the prophets is made by Jesus in the present *with a view to* making manifest the guilt of his contemporaries, *in order that* (ὅπως) the accumulated wrath aroused by the murder of God's prophets in former generations may be visited upon this last generation. This subtle change from the Lucan version is thus reinforced by the imperative of verse 32: 'And as for you, fill up the measure of your fathers!' Judgment cannot fall until the iniquity of apostate Israel has reached full measure (cf. Gen. 15: 16). Assuming that it is the final editor who has attributed the Wisdom-saying to Jesus, it follows that the function served by verse 32 marks it as the product of the same hand.[1]

Of greater importance for the present study is the material in verse 34 not found in the Lucan parallel. In Luke 11: 49 Wisdom prophesies: 'I will send them prophets and apostles, some of whom they will kill and persecute (καὶ ἐξ αὐτῶν ἀποκτενοῦσιν καὶ διώξουσιν).' In the Matthean version these two hostile activities are expanded to four:

Therefore I send you prophets and wise men and scribes, some of whom you will kill and *crucify* (σταυρώσετε), *and some you will scourge* (μαστιγώσετε) *in your synagogues* and persecute from town to town...

The two clauses in italics have been declared to be a later interpolation by Solomon Zeitlin on the basis that they are

[1] Haenchen, p. 52, regards verse 32 as editorial, but provides no detailed argument in support of his view.

omitted from certain manuscripts.[1] The textual evidence itself, however, is not sufficient to substantiate Zeitlin's conjecture. Only two minuscules omit both σταυρώσετε and μαστιγώσετε.[2] The evidence for the omission of the second clause alone is only slightly stronger.[3] No manuscript cited by Legg's apparatus omits only σταυρώσετε. If Zeitlin's conjecture is to be supported, it must be on the basis of internal rather than external evidence.

The present writer finds it extremely difficult to believe that Matthew wrote the words καὶ σταυρώσετε in his manuscript at this point. There is not a shred of evidence that the Jews employed crucifixion as a legal form of capital punishment.[4] It is incredible that one as well acquainted with Judaism as the author of the First Gospel should have attributed to Jesus a prophecy that the Pharisees would crucify Christians. One possible explanation, of course, is that the verb σταυρόω is here used causatively, i.e. 'cause to be crucified'. This is the way the verb must be understood in Acts 2: 36; 4: 10, where the Jews are accused of crucifying Jesus. Can the presence of σταυρώσετε in the original text of Matthew 23: 34 be justified as due to the expectation that Jews would persuade the Romans to crucify Christians?

Our answer here depends in part upon how we understand the two cross-sayings of the synoptic tradition. The Marcan saying is repeated exactly by Matthew and with only slight alterations by Luke: 'If any man would come after me, let him deny himself and take up his cross and follow me' (Mark 8: 34; cf. Matt. 16: 24; Luke 9: 23). The presence in this saying of ἀπαρνησάσθω ἑαυτόν, an expression foreign to Semitic usage, makes it probable that the Marcan saying is simply a variant of the Q saying: 'Whoever does not bear his cross and come after me, cannot be my disciple' (Luke 14: 27; cf. Matt. 10: 38).[5]

[1] S. Zeitlin, Who Crucified Jesus? (1947), p. 176.

[2] Minuscules 4, 273. The textual evidence here adduced is derived from S. C. E. Legg, Novum Testamentum Graece: Evangelium secundum Matthaeum (1940).

[3] D, a, d, Lucifer Calaritanus (fourth century), and, partially, the original hand of E.

[4] Contra E. Stauffer, Jerusalem und Rom im Zeitalter Jesu Christi (1957), pp. 123–7. Cf. Paul Winter's careful examination of the evidence, pp. 62–6.

[5] Cf. Bultmann, Hist. Syn. Trad. pp. 160 f. and notes, and additional note on p. 410.

If this saying can be attributed to the public ministry of Jesus, what meaning did it convey to his hearers? Did they under-stand it to be an exhortation to be prepared to be crucified by the Romans at the instigation of fellow Jews? Although cruci-fixion at the hands of the Romans was a lively expectation for followers of Zealot leaders, it was hardly to be expected by the followers of an anti-Zealot leader who urged pacifism and the abandonment of political hatred.[1] It must be remembered that crucifixion under Roman law was a form of capital punishment strictly limited to slaves and insurgents.[2] It is unlikely, therefore, that Jesus' reference to cross-bearing anticipates Roman cruci-fixion for his followers. Far more probable is Schlatter's sug-gestion that the expression, first used by the Zealots for whom crucifixion was a real possibility, became on the lips of Jesus simply a vivid figure for self-denial.[3] On this view the saying is not very different from the saying which precedes it in Luke: 'If any one comes to me and does not hate his own father and mother and wife and children and brothers and sisters, yes, and even his own life, he cannot be my disciple' (Luke 14: 26). 'Bearing one's cross' and 'hating one's own life' are roughly equivalent expressions. Neither necessarily involves martyrdom but only a readiness to subordinate all personal desires to the demands of the Kingdom of God.

It is unwarranted, therefore, to argue on the basis of the cross-sayings that Jesus expected his disciples to be crucified by the Romans at the instigation of Jews. Nor have we dis-covered even the slightest evidence that this did in fact take place.[4] It remains possible, of course, that the author of the First Gospel expected that Christians would be crucified at Jewish instigation even though no instance of this, apart from

[1] Matt. 5: 39, 41, 44. These sayings make it clear that Jesus was a pacifist in the sense that he was firmly opposed to the use of violence as a solution to Israel's political problem. Cf. V. G. Simkhovitch, *Toward the Under-standing of Jesus* (1947), pp. 47 f.

[2] Cf. W. C. Van Unnik, 'Corpus Hellenisticum Novi Testamenti', *J.B.L.* LXXXIII (1964), 25, who cites E. Benz, 'Der gekreuzigte Gerechte bei Plato, im N.T., und in der alten Kirche', *Akademie der Wissenschaft und der Literatur in Mainz, geistes- und sozialwissenschaftliche Kl.*, no. 12 (1950), pp. 1048 ff.

[3] A. Schlatter, *Der Evangelist Matthäus* (1963), p. 350; cited by Bultmann, *Hist. Syn. Trad.* p. 161 n. 1.

[4] See above, pp. 66–77.

Jesus' own death, had occurred. While this possibility cannot be ruled out absolutely, it seems far more likely that, had this been his meaning, Matthew would have expressed the idea less ambiguously by the use of παραδιδόναι τοῖς ἔθνεσιν (cf. 20: 19) or a similar expression.[1]

It must further be pointed out that σταυρώσετε is not only ambiguous (its causative meaning is by no means self-evident) but also rather redundant after ἀποκτενεῖτε, the more general term. The redundancy cannot be explained as due to Semitic parallelism such as we find in the Jerusalem-saying (v. 37, ἀποκτείνουσα... λιθοβολοῦσα). The reference to crucifying, moreover, seems out of place in the anticlimactic series ἀποκτε-νεῖτε... μαστιγώσετε... διώξετε. These various considerations taken together incline the present writer to accept the conjecture that σταυρώσετε was neither omitted from Q by Luke nor added to Q by Matthew (or Q^{Mt}) but clumsily added to the completed gospel by an early glossator.[2]

There is little justification, however, for attributing the following clause, as Zeitlin does, to a glossator.[3] It is a clear echo of 10: 17, agreeing far more closely with the latter than with the closest Marcan parallel.[4] It is unlikely that the original form of

[1] Haenchen, p. 54, wonders whether σταυρώσετε may not refer to Peter's death in Rome. The weight of probability is against such a suggestion, in view of two considerations: (1) there is no evidence that Peter was crucified at Jewish instigation, and (2) there is no evidence that early Christians postulated Jewish instigation in this instance. Eusebius, Eccl. Hist. II. 25, finds no motive other than Nero's depravity necessary to account for Peter's death.

[2] Still another possibility might be considered. If it was Matthew (rather than Q^{Mt}) who altered the Wisdom-saying so as to attribute it to Jesus, it is possible that Q^{Mt}, attributing the saying to the Wisdom of God, added σταυρώσετε so as to include a reference to Jesus' own martyrdom. When the saying was attributed to Jesus by Matthew, this reference was rendered inappropriate but carelessly preserved by the editor (or added by a glossator while Q^{Mt} was still extant). For the purposes of the present study this conjecture does not affect the conclusion reached above, viz. that the author of the First Gospel did not add σταυρώσετε with reference to past or anticipated Jewish persecution of Christians.

[3] See above, pp. 88 f.

[4] Whereas Mark 13: 9 employs δέρω, Matt. 10: 17 and 23: 34 use μαστιγόω. Whereas συναγωγαί is used without a modifier in Mark, both Matthean verses add a pronoun to indicate that the synagogues are alien to Christians (αὐτῶν, ὑμῶν). Matthew's μαστιγόω, used technically for

the Wisdom-saying contained the reference to scourging. The function of the logion is to predict the rejection of Wisdom's messengers by an apostate Israel. The verbs employed are consequently non-specific in character; ἀποκτενοῦσιν includes all kinds of unnatural death, and διώξουσιν is similarly vague, including probably attempted murder and the desire to murder. A specific reference to scourging is thus out of place. Nor is it likely that Luke would have omitted the reference to scourging had he found it in his source. It is probable, therefore, that this clause was added to Q either by Q^Mt or by Matthew himself. If we are correct in assuming that it was Matthew who altered the Wisdom-saying so as to attribute it to Jesus, it is probable that he was also responsible for adding the reference to scourging, since it is only when the prediction is attributed to Jesus that so explicit a detail becomes appropriate.

The same reasoning can be applied to the Matthean addition to Q following διώξετε; whereas this verb is intentionally vague and general in the original Wisdom-saying as preserved in Luke 11: 49, the addition ἀπὸ πόλεως εἰς πόλιν in Matthew 23: 34 serves to make the verb far more specific ('pursue', 'harry' or 'harass'). This alteration can best be understood as having taken place after rather than before the change in attribution of the logion. For the source of the addition we need look no further than 10: 23. Since there is no indication that Matthew took 10: 23 from Q^Mt, we may assume that it is Matthew rather than Q^Mt who borrows from 10: 23 in making the addition in 23: 34.[1]

Summing up the results of our examination of verse 34, then, we accept as probable that: (1) Matthew made Jesus the author of the Wisdom-saying, attributed in Q to the Wisdom of God, and (2) Matthew added details tending to make more explicit the predicted persecution of Jesus' messengers, viz. the scourging in 'your synagogues' and the 'harrying from town to town'. Each of these changes represents an intensification of the anti-Pharisaism already present in Q.

Further evidence of intensification may be found in verse 35. In the Lucan version the purpose clause (expressing both the purpose and the result of Wisdom's prediction) employs the

judicial flogging, provides a clearer reference to synagogal *makkoth* than the more colloquial δέρω; see above, pp. 43–6, below, p. 104.

[1] For a discussion of the origin of 10: 23, see below, pp. 110 f.

Semitic idiom 'require the blood of someone from someone' (Luke 11: 50; cf. 2 Sam. 4: 11). In this instance it is 'this generation' from whom the blood of all slain prophets will be required.[1] The Matthean version substitutes an equivalent Semitic idiom, 'the blood of someone is upon someone' (cf. Lev. 20: 9; Jer. 26: 15; Jon. 1: 14). Matthew's preference for the alternative idiom is indicated perhaps by its occurrence in 27: 25. Since Luke knows and uses the second idiom in Acts 5: 28 and 18: 6, it may be assumed that he is retaining the original in Luke 11: 50 and that it is the Matthean version which substitutes. One effect of the substitution is that it permits a more emphatic judgment. The Matthean ἐφ' ὑμᾶς, coming near the beginning of the purpose clause, lays heavy stress upon the recipients of the divine judgment: 'in order that upon *you* etc.' The substitution of 'you' for the more impersonal 'this genera-tion' (which is retained in verse 36) associates the judgment even more closely with the opponents of Jesus.

Still another indication of intensified anti-Pharisaism in verse 35 is the relative clause ὃν ἐφονεύσατε, 'whom you murdered', which Matthew substitutes for Luke's impersonal middle par-ticiple, τοῦ ἀπολομένου.[2] The distinction between prophet-murderers and descendants of prophet-murderers of verses 29–

---

[1] The use of ταύτης in a prediction concerning the future is problematical. Two conclusions are possible: (1) the ἵνα-clause is not part of the original Wisdom-saying but an application of it attributed to Jesus, or (2) the ἵνα-clause is part of Wisdom's prediction, carelessly altered by the substitution of ταύτης in order to make the application more explicit. The former alternative is the simpler, and has been accepted by many recent interpreters (cf. the punctuation of the R.S.V., N.E.B. and Moffatt translations); it involves the difficulty, however, that so short a quotation is really pointless. The original Wisdom-saying must have included some promise of judgment similar to what is now found in the succeeding verse. The present writer is inclined, therefore, to believe that the apocryphal quotation continued down to οἴκου in the earliest form of the Q tradition, where it was followed by Jesus' affirmation of its validity in the statement, ναὶ λέγω κτλ. Haenchen, p. 54, argues that Luke 11: 51 a is superfluous inasmuch as a temporal determination has already been provided by ἀπὸ καταβολῆς κόσμου. He regards 51 a, with its inappropriate references to non-prophets, as an early gloss added to the Q tradition. This is entirely possible, especially in view of the embarrassment over Abel and Zechariah, which constrains Matthew to substitute πᾶν αἷμα δίκαιον for Luke's prophetic blood.

[2] That this is due to the final editor and not to Q^{Mt} is indicated by the fact that it is dependent upon the attribution of the Wisdom-saying to Jesus.

32 is here forgotten; the sons are charged with the fathers' crime. Apostate Israel is here seen as a corporate personality whose individual members in the present (i.e. those who reject Jesus and his messengers) must bear full responsibility for the murderous rejection of God's messengers in the past. Matthew's ἐφονεύσατε gives expression to his conviction that the scribes and Pharisees, the proponents of that form of Judaism which became normative in Jewry, were incarnations of the spirit of apostate Israel.[1]

The Jerusalem-saying, verses 37–9, provides no evidence of intensified anti-Pharisaism except for the fact that it is placed here in the context of an anti-Pharisaic discourse, a context quite different from the one in which it is found in Luke (13: 34 f.). There are scholars who maintain that it is Matthew who has preserved the original context of the pericope as it was found in Q.[2] Underlying this view is the assumption that the Jerusalem-saying is from the same apocryphal source as the Wisdom-saying and uttered by the same speaker, viz. the divine Wisdom.[3] Against this view Haenchen argues that the point of view of the Jerusalem-saying is essentially different from that of the Wisdom-saying; while the latter looks forward to the sending of the prophets, the former looks backward to the failure of their mission.[4] Even if we accept the hypothesis that the Jerusalem-saying was originally attributed to Wisdom, the connection between the two was not immediate.[5] To Haenchen's criticism we might add the observation that the judgment contemplated in the Wisdom-saying is different in kind from that announced in the Jerusalem-saying; in the former it is a case of active revenge, in the latter, of passive abandonment. While these two kinds of judgment are by no means mutually exclusive, the contrast in expression suggests, as does the contrast in verb tense, that the two logia were originally found in separate contexts.[6]

---

[1] See below, p. 151.

[2] Cf. Bultmann, *Hist. Syn. Trad.* p. 115, and authors there cited.

[3] Cf. Bultmann, *ibid.* pp. 114 f.

[4] Haenchen, p. 56.   [5] Haenchen, *ibid.*

[6] It is entirely possible that the Jerusalem-saying is based upon a genuine word of Jesus, whose mission was to the lost sheep of the house of Israel (Matt. 15: 24). It is by no means necessary that the speaker here be a 'supra-historical entity' as Bultmann insists, *Hist. Syn. Trad.* p. 114. The

It is probable, as J. P. Brown has suggested, that the original Q-context of the Jerusalem-saying may be discovered in Luke when we omit the three editorial verses which Luke has supplied as an introduction (13: 31–3); the Jerusalem-saying continues the thought of Luke 13: 24–30, whose theme is the rejection of Israel.[1] It must be remembered in this connection that as far as we know Q was not a gospel, that is, it did not present its materials within a carefully worked out chronological frame-work. This is implied in the present instance by the fact that Luke can take the logion as a reference to Jesus' forthcoming triumphal entry, while Matthew understands it as referring to the parousia.[2] It is unlikely that Luke would have attempted so radical a reinterpretation had his source clearly indicated that the logion was uttered by Jesus as his valedictory to the Jewish people, as Matthew suggests.[3]

For these various reasons, then, we conclude that Matthew found the Jerusalem-saying in a Q-context other than the Q discourse against the scribes and Pharisees. By appending the Jerusalem-saying to his attack on the scribes and Pharisees, Matthew effects two subtle changes in the force of the logion: (1) in the new context, the saying suggests that it is the scribes and Pharisees who are primarily responsible for the nation's

observation that the O.T. image of a bird signifies God (Bultmann, *ibid.*) is irrelevant; it ignores the fact that what we have here is not metaphor but simile. The emphasis is not upon the simile but upon the verb ἐπισυναγαγεῖν; Jesus' mission had been governed by the continuing desire (ποσάκις ἐθέλησα) to gather the lost sheep of the house (οἶκος) of Israel into a people prepared for the Kingdom of God. Support for the view that 'house' here refers to the nation, not the Temple, is provided by Billerbeck, *S.–B.* I, 943 f. Haenchen, p. 55, takes a contrary view. Bultmann's argument that the reference to οἶκος confirms the view that the saying derives from a Wisdom myth is beside the point (*op. cit.* p. 115).

[1] J. P. Brown, *N.T.S.* VIII, 35 n. 1. In favour of Brown's view that verses 31–3 are editorial, it may be observed that verse 33 contradicts the fact well known to Jesus that prophets had perished outside Jerusalem; indeed, four out of the six martyr-prophets remembered by name met their fate else-where; cf. Jeremias, *Heiligengräber*, p. 66.

[2] While it is strange that Luke would so interpret the logion in view of the judgment of Luke 13: 35 *a*, this interpretation seems to be confirmed by the context in which he places it. Matthew's interpretation is indicated both by the context and by the addition of ἀπ' ἄρτι. Cf. also W. L. Knox, *The Sources of the Synoptic Gospels*, vol. II, *St Luke and St Matthew* (1957), p. 82.

[3] Cf. Haenchen, p. 57.

contemporary rejection of divine messengers; (2) in the light of verse 34, the reference to 'the prophets' and 'those who are sent' now includes the missionaries of the Christian church.

Let us recapitulate. In our examination of the redactional probabilities of 23: 29–39 we have found the following indications of intensified anti-Pharisaism: (1) the addition of pejorative epithets; (2) two verses have been supplied by the editor to bring the Pharisaic persecution of Christian missionaries into closer relationship with the persecution of the prophets by former generations (vv. 32f.); (3) additions to verse 34 have made more specific the nature of the contemporary persecution (flogging in the synagogues, pursuit from town to town); (4) in verse 35 the substitution of 'upon you' for 'this generation' and of 'whom you murdered' for 'who perished' relates both the guilt and the judgment mentioned in the Wisdom-saying unambiguously to the Pharisees; (5) the location of the Jerusalem-saying as the capstone of the discourse against the Pharisees gives it an anti-Pharisaic force which it did not originally possess.

The kind of anti-Pharisaism here evidenced is far too intense to be a matter of literary convention as in Luke. Some kind of unhappy contact with Pharisaism is required to explain the hostility of the author. The question of the nature of this contact must be delayed until all the relevant material has been examined.

Matthew 10: 16–33

In contrast to 23: 34, chapter 10 contains no references to persecution which can be attributed to the author. The allusions to trials and floggings in 10: 17 f. are taken directly from Mark 13. The reference to flight from persecution in 10: 23 is non-Marcan, but, as we shall see, is probably taken from some other source and not the creation of the author. The way these allusions are employed by the author, however, suggests their significance to him.

Before we examine these and other allusions in detail, we must make some observations about the wider context.

In his treatment of Mark 1–6, Matthew has taken considerable liberties with the Marcan order, replacing the Marcan scheme with one of his own, in which a summary of Jesus' activity as teacher and healer (4: 23–5) is followed and illustrated by the Sermon on the Mount (chs. 5–7) and ten miracle stories (chs. 8–9). At 9: 35 the author repeats almost verbatim the summary of 4: 23, and then prepares for a chapter on discipleship by borrowing from Mark 6: 34 the saying about shepherdless sheep (9: 36), to which he attaches the Q saying about praying for harvesters (9: 37 f.; cf. Luke 10: 2). It seems probable that Matthew's decision to insert the Marcan material concerning the Mission of the Twelve at this point, well in advance of its position in the Marcan story, is inspired by Q.[1]

Having decided, therefore, to pursue the discipleship theme at this point, Matthew conflates material from Q with Marcan material from two different chapters in the earlier gospel (Mark 3: 13–19, the Call of the Twelve, and Mark 6: 7–11, the Sending Out of the Twelve).[2] To this conflation are added pertinent sayings from another source, possibly already present in Q^{Mt} (10: 15 f.).[3]

The mission itself is unimportant to Matthew, who not only fails to report the mission and the return (Mark 6: 12, 30; cf. Luke 9: 6, 10) but also explicitly states that when Jesus had completed these instructions to his disciples it was *he* who went on from there to teach and preach in their cities (11: 1). It is clear from this that Matthew is interested solely in the instructions Jesus gives relating to mission. That is to say, Matthew is interested in the missionary instructions of Jesus not as an

---

[1] Although little can be established concerning the original content and structure of the hypothetical Q, it is to be observed that in both Matthew and Luke the Q material of the Sermon on the Mount/Sermon on the Plain is followed by a narrative concerning the centurion (Matt. 8: 5–13; Luke 7: 1–10), sayings about following Jesus (Matt. 8: 19–22; Luke 9: 57–60), the saying about praying for harvesters (Matt. 9: 37 f.; Luke 10: 2), and instructions to a group of missionaries (Matt. 10 *passim*; Luke 10: 1–12). The presence within the above series of other Q material—the Baptist's question and Jesus' response, Luke 7: 18–35, which is found after the discipleship material in Matthew (11: 2–19)—does not detract from the coincidence of order within the series.

[2] Cf. W. L. Knox, *Sources*, ii, 48.

[3] The clumsiness with which this conflation is effected is indicated by the abruptness with which the Twelve are introduced at 10: 1 without a word of explanation. Such an explanation is not needed in Mark 6: 7–11, because it has been given previously in 3: 13–19. (The Q passage in all probability identified the missionaries simply as 'disciples'.) Matthew partially overcomes the deficiency by supplying a modifier at each occurrence of οἱ δώδεκα, 10: 1 f., 5; 11: 1), a phrase used absolutely by Mark (Mark 6: 7; cf. 3: 16).

appendage to a historical event occurring during Jesus' life but rather as instructions relevant to the Church's mission in the period after the Resurrection.

In the light of this it is important to note how large a proportion of the material in the chapter is concerned with the non-acceptance of the gospel and the hostility with which the missionaries are treated. There is no instruction regarding what is to be done with converts in a successful mission! Nor is there any suggestion concerning how long missionaries are to stay in an accepting community. Indeed, the closing verse of the chapter suggests that acceptance is unusual—even a cup of cold water, a token of minimal acceptance, will receive its due reward.

The contrast between Matthew 10 and the two primary sources which inspire the chapter is startling. Neither the Marcan nor the Q account of the sending out of the disciples betrays any evidence of violent resistance to the proclamation of the gospel. The most that the Marcan narrative anticipates is non-acceptance of the gospel, against which the missionaries are to bear witness by shaking the dust off their shoes.[1] The Marcan account of the mission and return likewise reports no active resistance (Mark 6: 12 f., 30). The Q version perhaps hints at the possibility of violence in its use of the saying about sheep in the midst of wolves (Matt. 10: 16a; Luke 10: 3b), but beyond this contemplates only the problem of non-acceptance (Luke 10: 10–12).[2]

[1] W. L. Knox, *Sources*, II, 48 f., argues convincingly that Q's prohibition of sandals (Matt. 10: 10; Luke 10: 4) is not original in view of the difficulties in conceiving a dramatic gesture for shaking dust off bare feet. Mark's clumsy addition, ἀλλὰ ὑποδεδεμένους σανδάλια (Mark 6: 9), represents the author's attack on the ascetic practice of travelling barefoot supported by Q.

[2] Bultmann, *Hist. Syn. Trad.* pp. 158, 163, justifiably regards this 'I'-saying as a product of the Palestinian church in its mission to Israel. There is no evidence anywhere in the New Testament that the disciples met with active hostility from fellow Jews during Jesus' ministry; even the Fourth Gospel, which reports attempts on Jesus' life during the ministry (John 5: 18; 7: 1, 25; 8: 59; 10: 31), gives no evidence that the disciples were included as objects of violent hatred. Whether or not the Q tradition intended this saying to be taken as an allusion to violence cannot be determined. The Q account probably concluded with the woes on the Galilean cities, Luke 10: 13–15 (placed by Matthew after the Q material concerning Jesus' testimony to the Baptist, Matt. 11: 20–4). In these woes Chorazin, Bethsaida

Matthew has altered the tone of his material drastically by intruding into this context material taken from Mark's apocalyptic section (Mark 13) and from later Q sections concerning fearless confession, household divisions and the conditions of discipleship (Luke 12: 2–9, 51–3; 14: 26 f.; 17: 33). This intrusion is possible only because Matthew is concerned not with the Galilean mission of the Twelve during Jesus' ministry but with the Church's mission at a later date.

The transfer of Mark 13: 9–13 from its position in an apocalyptic discourse to a missionary discourse not only changes the tone of the latter but also alters the significance of the transferred material. That is to say, Matthew's use of this passage provides it with a meaning different from that intended by Mark.

Willi Marxsen has pointed out that in his apocalyptic discourse Mark has brought together disparate materials whose only unity is the use the author makes of them.[1] Thus in verse 9 the reference to governors and kings seems to require a Diaspora setting, while verse 14 apparently refers primarily to Jerusalemites and verses 15 f. have rural people (Judeans?) in mind.[2] Regardless of the original intent of the separate sayings, the complex created by Mark is intended to depict the eschatological situation of the Church. The persecution portrayed in verses 9–13 is not temporally insignificant but is clearly a necessary prelude to the final apocalyptic events. If, as is generally conceded, Mark is here reflecting actual experiences of the early Church in Palestine and the Diaspora, the way in which he reports the experiences indicates that he regards the End as at hand. Thus the period contemporary with the evangelist is described as the ἀρχή of the messianic woes which precede the End.[3]

As Marxsen points out, Matthew has de-eschatologized the Marcan passage by removing it from its eschatological context;

and Capernaum are upbraided, not for treating Jesus' emissaries as wolves treat sheep, but simply for non-acceptance. In later passages in Q, however, the possibility of active persecution is clearly in mind, not only in Luke 11: 47–51 but also in subsequent passages (Luke 12: 4, 8 f., 11 f.).

[1] Willi Marxsen, *Der Evangelist Markus: Studien zur Redaktionsgeschichte des Evangeliums* (1959), pp. 108–12.

[2] *Ibid.*

[3] Mark 13: 8, ἀρχὴ ὠδίνων ταῦτα; cf. Marxsen, p. 121.

that which is described by Mark as pertaining to the period immediately preceding the Parousia has become for Matthew characteristic of a continuing situation.[1] While according to Mark the persecution suffered by Christians belongs to the period of messianic woes, for Matthew this persecution is a normal concomitant of the Church's mission.

By placing the persecution material found in Mark 13: 9–13 in the context of missionary instructions to the disciples, Matthew further suggests that persecution arises *precisely on account of the Church's mission*.[2] In the Marcan context no motivation is provided for the phenomenon of persecution; like the other messianic woes, persecution requires no explanation other than that it is foreordained. For Mark persecution provides an *occasion* for witnessing rather than being the *result* of witnessing.[3]

Matthew thus takes from the missionary instructions of Mark and Q the theme of non-acceptance, and extends it in the direction of increasing hostility by bringing into the context of the mission the persecution-predictions of Mark 13: 9–13 and several Q passages implying persecution (concerning fearless confession, household divisions and conditions of discipleship) which seem not to have belonged to a missionary context in Q.[4]

[1] Marxsen, p. 138.

[2] Marxsen, p. 138, observes briefly that in Matt. 10: 18 the occasion for witnessing against the Jews (αὐτοῖς) and the governors and kings (τοῖς ἔθνεσιν) results from the missionary proclamation.

[3] Mark 13: 9. According to H. Strathmann, 'μάρτυς', *T.W.N.T.* IV, 508 f., μαρτύριον in Mark 13: 9 does not refer to missionary proclamation; the purpose of this testimony is rather to render the opponents guilty. Marxsen, pp. 118 f., maintains that while Strathmann's interpretation holds for the verse itself, it is not reflected in the use made of the verse by Mark; by attaching to it verse 10, Mark indicates that he understands the μαρτύριον of verse 9 to be a preaching of the gospel to the Gentiles. According to Marxsen, p. 138, the Matthean version (Matt. 10: 18) reverts to the original meaning of the verse, taking μαρτύριον as testimony which renders opponents guilty. For a contrary view, see below, pp. 106 f.

[4] If Luke preserves the original order of Q at this point, then the passage concerning fearless confession was probably preceded in Q by the discourse against the Pharisees and lawyers, whose penultimate logion is the Wisdom prediction concerning the persecution of prophets, wise men and scribes ('apostles' is undoubtedly a Lucan substitution). Persecution is thus associated with divine messengers in the Q context, but not explicitly identified as the result of missionary activity.

A comparison with the Lucan parallel suggests that Matthew 10: 26f. has been altered for purposes of adaptation to a missionary context; for Luke's future indicative κηρυχθήσεται (Luke 12: 3) Matthew substitutes an imperative, κηρύξατε (Matt. 10: 27b). Similarly Luke's prediction, 'Whatever you have said in the dark shall be heard in the light', becomes 'What I tell you in the dark, utter in the light!' (10: 27a). The saying about confessing and denying Jesus before men (10: 32 f.) becomes in the present context an exhortation to Christian missionaries to remain steadfast in their loyalty to Jesus when undergoing trial in the synagogues or civil courts. By itself the saying implies persecution of Christians because of their religious allegiance; missionary activity is not implied.[1] The catena of discipleship-sayings concerning bearing one's cross and losing one's life (10: 38 f.) is given a more specific application by being placed in a missionary context; imperatives which in Q (Luke 14: 27; 17: 33) and Mark (8: 34 f.) are associated with *followers* of Jesus are here directed to *missionaries*. It is the heralds of the gospel, rather than Christian believers as such, who must risk death.[2]

With the Matthean context in mind, let us turn now to a more careful examination of the allusions to persecution. παραδώ-σουσιν γὰρ ὑμᾶς εἰς συνέδρια (v. 17). The only alteration from the Marcan text is the addition of γάρ. There is little indication in the Marcan passage that the 'councils' here referred to are Jewish, or that those who 'deliver' Christians to the courts are

---

[1] *Contra* Bultmann, *Hist. Syn. Trad.* p. 128, it must be asserted that the Q logion in its Lucan form (Luke 12: 8 f.) concerns not simply the judgment of a man on the basis of 'his attitude to the teaching of Jesus' but rather the matter of steadfast loyalty to Jesus in the face of public pressure. Bultmann's interpretation seems to be derived primarily from the Marcan parallel, Mark 8: 38 (Luke 9: 26); cf. *op. cit.* p. 151. Whatever the original form of the logion, its meaning for the Q tradition is indicated by the negative member, ὁ δὲ ἀρνησάμενός με ἐνώπιον τῶν ἀνθρώπων κτλ. The question is not one of private apostasy but of apostasy due to external pressure. The warning would therefore more appropriately be addressed to ordinary Christians than to outspoken evangelists who would be less likely to yield to such pressure.

[2] Whether or not the parallel expressions λαμβάνειν τὸν σταυρόν and ἀπολέσαι τὴν ψυχήν were originally understood literally as references to martyrdom (see above, pp. 89 f.), in the present context they clearly imply the risk of martyrdom; cf. 10: 21, 28.

Jews.[1] The fact that this prediction is followed by a reference to floggings in the synagogues has inclined scholars to identify 'councils' as Jewish, but it is by no means impossible that the author intended both the συνέδρια and the παραδώσουσιν to be understood in a neutral sense, having reference to both Jewish and Gentile persecution. The reference is far less ambiguous in Matthew, who has altered the context of the persecution by the addition of αὐτῶν after συναγωγαῖς. This addition requires that we understand the subject of *both* verbs ('deliver' as well as 'flog') to be members of the synagogues, i.e. Jews.

The reference to συνέδρια, however, remains ambiguous. In Palestinian communities there were local councils or sanhedrins distinct from the synagogal ruling body (Mish. Sanh. 1 : 6), but it is probable that in the Diaspora local Jewish courts were generally closely identified with the synagogal structure.[2] In Jewish usage, however, not every kind of court was referred to as a 'sanhedrin'. In Palestine the local court which received this designation was the Court of Twenty-Three, not the smaller Court of Three.[3] The Mishnah informs us that the lesser sanhedrin was concerned primarily with capital cases (although

---

[1] Although there is little evidence in support of the use of συνέδριον as the designation of local courts of justice among non-Jewish populations, the fact that this Greek word became a loan-word in rabbinic Hebrew and Aramaic suggests the possibility that there were hellenistic συνέδρια which functioned in much the same way as the lesser sanhedrins of the Jewish legal system. E. Lohse, 'συνέδριον', *T.W.N.T.* vii, 859, maintains that the word had not become a technical term in hellenistic political law, but he provides three instances in which the word refers to a court of justice. It is possible, therefore, that civic institutions such as the one referred to in Acts 17 : 6 by the collective term οἱ πολιτάρχαι may have been referred to at times as a συνέδριον, although, on the basis of available evidence, we cannot say that this was common usage. The use of an uncommon term here by Mark (or by the tradition before him) could be explained as due to familiarity with the term in Jewish circles (just as the United States Congress is occasionally referred to as a 'parliament' by those more familiar with the British tradition).

[2] Tos. Sanh. 3: 10: 'Within the land of Israel they make them [sanhedrins] in every city; but outside the land, they make them in every province.' This suggests an organization independent of the synagogal structure. Lohse, in the article cited in the preceding note, maintains that there were Jewish sanhedrins in Syria and Asia Minor, but does not cite his evidence. Quotations from Tos. Sanh. are taken from H. Danby, *Tractate Sanhedrin: Mishnah and Tosefta* (1919).

[3] Mish. Sanh. 1: 6; Tos. Sanh. 3: 7.

certain capital crimes were reserved for the Great Sanhedrin, Mish. Sanh. 1: 5). This is supported by the statement of Tos. Sanh. 6: 3 that 'non-capital cases are tried by three judges'. Since there is no evidence that either the profession or the propagation of the Christian faith was identified as a capital crime by Jewish legal authorities, there is no reason to believe that Christians were brought before the lesser sanhedrins, whether in Palestine or the Diaspora.[1] If we are correct in the conclusion that the charge most commonly preferred against Christian missionaries was breach of the peace, there was little cause to bring such defendants before a session of the lesser sanhedrin. Any court of three judges was competent to try such cases.[2]

The alternatives are clear. If συνέδρια in Mark 13: 9 and Matthew 10: 17 refers to the lesser sanhedrins described by our rabbinic sources, *either* we have been misinformed by the Mishnah concerning the function of the lesser sanhedrin in the latter half of the first century, *or* the synoptic tradition and/or its editors preserve here an unfulfilled prediction which anticipated that the profession or propagation of the Christian faith would be identified as a capital crime and prosecuted as such.[3] To the present writer it seems far more likely that the reference is not to the lesser sanhedrins but to other councils, both Gentile and Jewish. Just as the πολιτάρχαι of Acts 17: 6 constituted a συνέδριον when in session, whether or not the term was commonly used, the same would be true of a session of the elders of a synagogue.[4] Since these συνέδρια, both civic and synagogal, were charged with the responsibility of preserving the peace,

[1] See above, pp. 25–30, 42 f.
[2] See above, pp. 43–6. In the Diaspora responsibility for maintaining peace in the synagogue community probably rested with the council of elders.
[3] Billerbeck, *S.–B.* I, 575, identifies the συνέδρια of Matt. 10: 17 with the lesser sanhedrins of Tractate Sanhedrin, assuming, apparently, that Christians were liable to capital prosecution. Frend, *Martyrdom*, p. 154, equates συνέδρια with 'Sanhedrins', but does not consider the legal implications of this identification.
[4] E. Schürer, Div. II, vol. II, p. 151, suggests that the elders of Luke 7: 3 belong to a local sanhedrin; by this term he apparently means any local court, not specifically the Court of Twenty-Three. C. E. B. Cranfield, *The Gospel According to St Mark* (1963), p. 397, interprets συνέδρια in Mark 13: 9 as 'councils of synagogues'.

it is probable that Christian missionaries were frequently prose-cuted before such bodies.

Whether or not the clause παραδώσουσιν γὰρ ὑμᾶς εἰς συνέδρια represents a genuine dominical prediction, it is clear that it reflects the actual experience of the Christian church. It cannot be said that Matthew has exaggerated the role of Jewish persecutors by limiting the subject of παραδώσουσιν to members of the synagogue; this limitation simply indicates that *it is with Jewish persecution, not persecution as such, that Matthew is primarily concerned.* Gentile participation is implied by 10: 18, where the ἡγεμόνες (if not also the βασιλεῖς) refers to Gentile rulers, but the role of Gentiles is minimized.[1]

καὶ ἐν ταῖς συναγωγαῖς αὐτῶν μαστιγώσουσιν ὑμᾶς. Matthew substitutes μαστιγώσουσιν for Mark's δαρήσεσθε. The latter is the more general term, 'beat', which can be used more appropriately of non-judicial beating (cf. Mark 12: 3, 5); μαστιγόω is the verb preferred for judicial flogging, whether the reference is to the Jewish or the Gentile form of the punish-ment.[2] Matthew's substitution makes it clear that the reference here is to the legal punishment, not mob violence.

The addition of αὐτῶν by Matthew serves not only to identify clearly the authors of the persecution as Jews but also to provide a clear distinction between Jews and Christians, between syna-gogue and Church. This contrast is missing from Mark's ver-sion of the prediction. Those addressed are all Jews, and it is predicted that it will be in their own synagogues that they will be beaten by their own people. The Matthean version suggests that the Jewish disciples no longer 'belong' in the synagogue; it is an alien institution belonging to an alien people. This view is consistently maintained in the First Gospel. In each of nine references to synagogues Matthew adds αὐτῶν (Matt. 4: 23; 9: 35; 10: 17; 12: 9; 13: 54) whenever the context fails to indi-cate that the synagogue is an institution belonging to 'the hypo-crites' (Matt. 6: 2, 5; 23: 6, 34).[3] The addition of αὐτῶν after

---

[1] See below, p. 108.   [2] Cf. Bauer, p. 496.

[3] Cf. Kilpatrick, *Origins*, pp. 110 f.; Reinhart Hummel, *Die Auseinander-setzung zwischen Kirche und Judentum im Matthäusevangelium* (1963), p. 29. Hummel, p. 17, notes the use of the same pronoun to describe the scribes in Matt. 7: 29, where the Marcan *Vorlage* does not have it (Mark 1: 22). W. Trilling, *Das wahre Israel: Studien zur Theologie des Matthäusevangeliums* (1959), p. 61, observes that the pronoun is used with 'cities' in 11: 1.

συναγωγή is also found in Mark (1: 23, 39), but in the earlier gospel there is no attempt at consistency. In three instances Matthew adds the modifier where his Marcan *Vorlage* does not have it (with Mark 3: 1; 6: 2 and 13: 9 cf. Matt. 12: 9; 13: 54 and 10: 17). The Third Gospel, written, it is generally believed, by a Gentile, contains συναγωγή fifteen times, and only once is αὐτῶν found as a modifier (4: 15, where we are perhaps to see the influence of Mark 1: 39). Twice Luke omits the αὐτῶν supplied by his source (with Mark 1: 23, 39, cf. Luke 4: 33, 44). This phenomenon suggests that while for Luke the synagogue has always been a foreign institution, for Matthew it has *become* a foreign institution in which Christians of Jewish blood no longer belong.

For Matthew, therefore, the reference to floggings in the synagogues is a prediction already fulfilled in the past rather than a contemporary experience. We have seen in the preceding chapter that there is little evidence that the profession of Christianity *per se* was treated by the synagogues of Jewry as a crime punishable by flogging.[1] In all probability the charge for which Christians received this punishment was breach of the peace.[2] This charge could only be made while Jewish Christians were still clearly identified with the synagogue community and propagating their faith in that community. When Christians, ostracized from the synagogue, withdrew into the Gentile community for both fellowship and missionary activity, they were no longer liable to the disciplinary action of the synagogue, nor could any legal charge be raised against them except before the civil courts.[3]

Again it must be observed that it is the missionaries of the

---

[1] See above, pp. 43–6.   [2] See above, p. 45.

[3] Tiberius Alexander, the nephew of Philo who served briefly as Judean procurator, was an apostate from Judaism (Josephus, *Ant.* xx. 5.2 [100]). In the light of this political appointment it must be regarded as certain that the Jewish legal system no longer had jurisdiction over one who had apostasized. Although the case with the Christians is different, yet surely by analogy we may say that those Jews who became assimilated into a Gentile community were thereby removed from Jewish jurisdiction, which in the Diaspora was primarily synagogal. Christians who no longer attended services in the synagogue but who persisted in living in the Jewish quarter would still be considered Jews by the civil authorities as well as by the Jewish authorities. The present writer is of the opinion that Matthew and his friends have left both the synagogue and the Jewish quarter.

gospel who are flogged in the synagogues. That this was Matthew's understanding is indicated by the parallel in 23: 34, where it is the prophets, wise men and scribes sent by Jesus who are to be flogged in the synagogues. If we are correct in our conclusion that the author is looking back upon an experience of the past, we may find here confirmation of the view presented in the preceding chapter that it was primarily missionaries, not rank-and-file Christians, who were persecuted in this way.[1]

καὶ ἐπὶ ἡγεμόνας δὲ καὶ βασιλεῖς ἀχθήσεσθε ἕνεκεν ἐμοῦ, εἰς μαρτύριον αὐτοῖς καὶ τοῖς ἔθνεσιν. The only significant alteration from the Marcan form of this prediction is the addition of καὶ τοῖς ἔθνεσιν. This addition is clearly inspired by the verse immediately following in the Marcan source: καὶ εἰς πάντα τὰ ἔθνη πρῶτον δεῖ κηρυχθῆναι τὸ εὐαγγέλιον (Mark 13: 10). The idea of the Gentile mission is inappropriate in the context of the Galilean mission, and consequently Matthew can retain here only this brief allusion.[2] A fuller parallel to Mark 13: 10 is reserved by Matthew for his eschatological discourse, 24: 14.

For the purposes of the present study, the significant question concerning this verse involves the reference of αὐτοῖς: Does the verse refer to Gentile persecution through Jewish agency or is purely Gentile persecution meant? The tradition received from Mark may intend βασιλεῖς to include the two Jewish kings of the period, viz. Herod Agrippa I and Herod Agrippa II, but it cannot be maintained that the term is used with these two kings primarily in mind. In the Marcan context the immediately following reference to the Gentile mission indicates that for Mark both the ἡγεμόνες and βασιλεῖς refer to Gentiles.[3] The context also indicates that Mark understood the phrase εἰς μαρτύριον αὐτοῖς as meaning 'for the purpose of witnessing to them, the judges, concerning Christ'.[4] Did Matthew in taking

[1] See above, p. 46.
[2] Cf. W. C. Allen, *A Critical and Exegetical Commentary on the Gospel according to St Matthew* (1912), ad loc.
[3] *Contra* Frend, who assumes that the 'governors and kings' are 'local Jewish officials and rulers' (*Martyrdom*, p. 154).
[4] The view that αὐτοῖς in Mark 13: 10 includes both the Gentile judges and the Jewish accusers who brought charges against the Christians in Gentile courts (so Cranfield, p. 398) rests entirely upon the assumption that Mark had Jewish persecutors in mind when writing this clause. There

over the phrase from Mark understand it in the same way? Marxsen maintains that while Mark reinterpreted the phrase as a reference to missionary proclamation, Matthew reverted to the original meaning, 'for testimony against them'.[1] Since Marxsen believes that it was Mark's insertion of verse 10 into the context of verses 9, 11 f. which altered the meaning of the phrase, he can argue that Matthew's omission of verse 10 indicates that Matthew explicitly rejected Mark's interpretation.[2] We have seen, however, that another, equally satisfactory, explanation for the omission can be supplied: in the context of the Galilean mission the reference to preaching the gospel to all nations is inappropriate and is therefore reserved by Matthew for the apocalyptic context provided by Mark (Matt. 24: 14). There is therefore no justifiable reason for believing that Matthew understood the phrase otherwise than Mark. The meaning of μαρτύριον here and in Matthew 24: 14 is basically the same: the gospel must be proclaimed to the Gentiles, with the expectation of both positive and negative response (28: 19 f.; 10: 22; 24: 9). Only with respect to those who refuse to accept the gospel does μαρτύριον become 'testimony which renders the opponents guilty'.[3] This being the case, there is no reason to regard αὐτοῖς as referring to persons other than those indicated by the nearest antecedents, viz. ἡγεμόνας and βασιλεῖς. That is to say, if the *primary* meaning of μαρτύριον here as in Mark 13: 9 is missionary proclamation, it is inappropriate that Jewish persecutors, who have already heard and rejected the gospel, should be included in the αὐτοῖς.[4]

is little evidence in the Marcan text itself to justify the assumption. Indeed, if one agrees with Cranfield that μαρτύριον refers in the first place to witnessing to the truth of the gospel (*op. cit.* p. 397), then it is more natural to understand αὐτοῖς as referring primarily to Gentile judges who had not previously had the opportunity of hearing the gospel; the postulated Jewish accusers would presumably have haled the Christians before Gentile courts precisely because they had heard the gospel.

[1] P. 138. [2] Pp. 137 f.

[3] G. R. Beasley-Murray, *A Commentary on Mark Thirteen* (1957), p. 40 and note, likewise rejects Strathmann's view (cited above, p. 100 n. 3).

[4] Those who understand the Matthean μαρτύριον as condemnatory testimony are inclined to interpret αὐτοῖς as a reference to Jews and τοῖς ἔθνεσιν as a reference to the governors and kings; so Marxsen, pp. 137 f. Strathmann, p. 509, takes the αὐτοῖς in Mark 13: 9 as a reference to Jews; similarly C. H. Turner, 'The Gospel according to St Mark', *A New Com-*

The view that the addition of καὶ τοῖς ἔθνεσιν requires that we understand αὐτοῖς as referring to Jews alone rests upon the assumption that the author would not refer to Gentile judges and then to Gentiles generally without qualifying the second reference—καὶ τοῖς λοιποῖς ἔθνεσιν (cf. Rom. 1: 13). Such care is not always observed in the New Testament, however. In Acts 2: 37 λοιπούς is employed to distinguish Peter from 'the rest of the apostles', but in 5: 29 the author feels no need of this qualifier. A parallel example of overlapping terms is found in Acts 9: 15, '... Before the Gentiles and kings and the sons of Israel', where the second category includes members belonging to the first and third (cf. also Mark 16: 7). Matthew's addition simply extends the effects of the testimony to Gentiles beyond those directly involved in the trial of Christians.[1]

It must be concluded, therefore, that while Matthew has made it clear in the preceding verse that Christians will be delivered up to councils by Jews, it cannot be said that he has introduced the Jews as agents of persecution in verse 18. As it stands, this verse refers primarily to Gentile persecution.[2] Had Matthew wished to implicate Jews as the instigators of this Gentile persecution, he could easily have carried through the parallelism of the preceding clauses by substituting an active verb with ὑμᾶς as object as he has done in verse 17.[3] The fact that he chooses to substitute yet supplies a passive rather than an active form is surely sufficient evidence that Matthew had no intention of implicating the Jews in this reference to Gentile persecution.

ὅταν δὲ παραδῶσιν ὑμᾶς... (verse 19). The changes made here by Matthew are matters of style only. As in Mark 13: 11,

mentary on Holy Scripture (1928), part III, p. 103. H. A. W. Meyer, *A Critical and Exegetical Commentary on the New Testament*, part I, *The Gospel according to St Matthew* (1880–1), I, 297 f., argues strongly against the interpretation of μαρτύριον as 'testimony against', but nevertheless supports the view that αὐτοῖς in Matt. 10: 18 refers to the Jews while τοῖς ἔθνεσιν denotes the procurators and kings and their Gentile environment.

[1] Cf. Phil. 1: 12 f.

[2] While the two Agrippas are included, they are primarily secular rulers, deriving their authority from the emperor in the same way as the procurators.

[3] Why not ἄξουσιν ὑμᾶς as in Mark 13: 11 (ὅταν ἄγωσιν ὑμᾶς)? In verse 17, where it is clearly his purpose to cite the Jews as persecutors, he substitutes the active μαστιγώσουσιν ὑμᾶς for Mark's passive δαρήσεσθε.

the subject of the verb is ambiguous. In the light of the preceding reference to Gentile persecution, it could be inferred that the subject of the verb is 'Gentiles'. Because, however, of the close parallel with παραδώσουσιν in verse 17 and παραδώσει in verse 21, where the context indicates Jewish subjects, it is probable that the reference here is primarily to Jewish opponents. Because the reference is left ambiguous, however, it cannot be maintained that Matthew intended verse 19 to be taken as further comment on verse 18 in such a way that Jews are regarded as the instigators of the Gentile persecution there mentioned. Had Matthew regarded the Jews as primarily responsible for Gentile persecution, these two verses supplied by Mark afforded him an excellent opportunity to give expression to the conviction. The fact that this first-century author fails to take advantage of the opportunity should teach us caution in dealing with the wholesale charges levelled against the Jews by later writers.[1]

παραδώσει δὲ ἀδελφὸς ἀδελφὸν εἰς θάνατον (v. 21). The use of θάνατος and θανατόω in this verse must not be taken as evidence that many Christians had experienced martyrdom for their faith at the time this gospel was written. It may, of course, have been a fact that a considerable number of Christians had perished as martyrs during the chaotic period of the war with Rome.[2] This verse, however, is merely a piece of apocalyptic prophecy, borrowed verbatim from Mark 13: 12.[3] The prediction seems to have been inspired by traditional apocalyptic expectations (cf. Mic. 7: 6; Ezek. 38: 21).[4] Mark's use of the logion is to be explained not on the basis of actual experience but on the basis of the theological motif which conditioned Christians to expect suffering in the last days.[5] Matthew's employment of the logion in a non-apocalyptic context does not alter its significance; he gives us no hint that he regards the prediction as having already been fulfilled. The same must be

---

[1] See above, pp. 66–77.

[2] See above, pp. 37 f.

[3] The only change is the substitution of δέ for καί.

[4] For parallels, cf. Billerbeck, S.-B. IV, 978 f.

[5] Beasley-Murray, p. 50, is quite mistaken in proposing the alternative: either a genuine saying of Jesus or a *vaticinium ex eventu* ('a piece of purely Jewish apocalyptic, taken over here in view of the experience of these sufferings within the primitive Christian community'). See below, p. 124.

said concerning the prediction of universal hatred preserved in the following verse (v. 22).

ὅταν δὲ διώκωσιν ὑμᾶς ἐν τῇ πόλει ταύτῃ, φεύγετε εἰς τὴν ἑτέραν (v. 23). This non-Marcan verse is probably not derived from Q^{Mt}, since there is no discernible reason for its association with the Q material which follows. It is more probably an independent logion which Matthew found in circulation in the Diaspora church. Regarded as missionary instruction, the logion stands in sharp contrast to the missionary material from Mark and Q used by Matthew in the earlier part of the chapter, in which the persecution of missionaries is not envisaged. From Matthew 10: 14 we infer that the decision of the missionary to move from one location to another was due to the non-acceptance of the gospel, not to persecution.

If we are justified in ascribing greater historical credibility to the picture of the Palestinian mission provided by Mark and Q, we must conclude that in its present form verse 23 is not a *vaticinium ex eventu* created by the Palestinian church on the basis of its own experience.[1] It is possible that the logion in its original form was a genuine prediction based upon the motif of eschatological flight.[2] Its present form, however, lends support to a different explanation of its origin. It has been suggested by a number of scholars that 23 a and 23 b are of separate origin.[3] On this hypothesis we may understand 23 b as having to do only with the mission and its urgency, with no reference to persecution implied; the change of location from town to town is due to the briefness of the time, not to persecution. It must be assumed that in the earliest form of the logion the words 'cities of Israel' referred exclusively to Palestinian cities.[4] Later, however, the phrase may have been exegeted by

---

[1] See above, pp. 62–4, 98. Bultmann, *Hist. Syn. Trad.* p. 122, describes 10: 23 as a *vaticinium* 'deriving from the missionary activity of the Church', but does not specify the geographical location of the experience which gave rise to the logion. Herbert Braun, *Spätjüdisch-häretischer und frühchristlicher Radikalismus* (1957), II, 102 n. 4, simply echoes Bultmann's opinion.

[2] Braun, *ibid.*, discusses the occurrence of the motif in the Qumran literature.

[3] Cf. C. G. Montefiore, *The Synoptic Gospels* (1927), II, 149–51, and authors there cited.

[4] The term 'Israel' must here be taken as a geographical rather than as an ethnic term, since 'cities' is primarily geographical and only secondarily sociological in connotation.

those evangelists who transferred their attention to the Diaspora as having reference also to the Diaspora Jewish communities. The words themselves would not suggest such an understanding.[1]

The eschatological prediction of 23a, when employed, as here, apart from a strictly eschatological setting, probably reflects the experience of Diaspora missionaries such as Paul, who were chased by Jewish hostility from one community to another.[2] It is possible that 23a did not first circulate separately but was created precisely as an introduction to 23b, providing for the latter an interpretative context which reveals the understanding of 23b which prevailed in the Diaspora. On the other hand, it may have originated as a prophetic 'word from the Lord' in a situation such as that described in Acts 17: 10, where the brethren take the initiative in removing missionaries from threatened persecution.

Whether or not 23a and 23b had separate origins, we can be fairly certain that the author of the First Gospel received them as a unit. In view of Matthew's method of constructing discourses, we may infer that it would not have occurred to him to introduce 23b at this point had he found it as an independent logion. The first half of the double logion suits Matthew's purpose admirably; the immediate context is concerned primarily with the fate of the missionaries and only secondarily with the mission itself. The context thus ignores 23b, which is concerned with the geographical and temporal limits of the mission. Since no further allusion is made to the mission, we may assume that Matthew employs the double logion only in order to report the prediction that Jewish persecution will harry missionaries from

[1] J. Munck, *Paul and the Salvation of Mankind* (1959), p. 256 n. 1, suggests that 'it was thought later that the towns of Israel included the Jewish Diaspora in the East', but does not cite his evidence. Cf. also Kilpatrick, *Origins*, p. 119. The application of this phrase to the Diaspora may indicate a very early attempt to deal with the problem of the delay of the parousia. We must assume that the Palestinian mission was completed (in the preliminary way which seems to be implied here and in Rom. 15: 19, 23) at an early date. The non-occurrence of the parousia at the conclusion of this mission would give impetus to the Diaspora mission, which, although in existence from the earliest period (cf. Acts 9: 10), had apparently not been treated seriously by the apostles. The reinterpretation of 23b may have coincided with the departure of Peter (and possibly other apostles) to the Diaspora.

[2] Cf. B. H. Streeter, *The Four Gospels* (1924), p. 255 n. 1.

town to town. The recurrence of this motif in 23: 34 as an editorial addition argues strongly in favour of the view that for Matthew this is a fulfilled prediction.[1]

Those who are anxious to preserve a Palestinian locale for the fulfilment of the prediction suggest that for Matthew the logion reflects the experience of Christians during the war of A.D. 66–70.[2] This is improbable. The initial mission to Palestine had long before been completed, with little success. It is unlikely that a missionary campaign of this kind was again conducted during the chaotic period of the war. Taken in isolation, 23a might suggest the flight of ordinary Christians (not missionaries) during the war, but in combination with 23b it is clearly a reference to the persecution of missionaries.[3] Matthew's location of the double logion leaves no doubt that this is how he understood it. To the extent, therefore, that this is a fulfilled prediction for Matthew, we may regard it as probable that the historical reference is to the Jewish persecution of Jewish Christian missionaries in the Diaspora. Such a conclusion supports the hypothesis suggested earlier in this study that Jewish hostility to Christianity was more intense in the Diaspora than in Palestine because of the Gentile problem.[4]

With reference to the Q passage concerning fearless confession (10: 26–33; cf. Luke 12: 2–9) we have already suggested that Matthew has altered the passage to make it more relevant to the missionary context in which he places it.[5] If we are

[1] See above, p. 92.

[2] Hummel, p. 30; J. A. T. Robinson, *Jesus and His Coming* (1957), p. 76, regards 10: 23 as the Pella oracle mentioned by Eusebius. S. S. Smalley, 'The Delay of the Parousia', *J.B.L.* LXXXIII, 46, maintains that the logion is a genuine saying of Jesus which 'foreshadows' Pella.

[3] W. G. Kümmel, *Promise and Fulfilment* (1961), pp. 61 f.

[4] See above, pp. 62–4. *Contra* Munck, pp. 123, 200–9, we would argue that 'mixed' congregations were as common in the Diaspora as they were uncommon in Palestine. The churches at Antioch and Corinth contained Jews (Gal. 2: 13; 1 Cor. 1: 14; cf. Acts 18: 8). Paul greets no less than five Jews belonging to the church addressed in Rom. 16 (probably Ephesus). There is no reason to doubt the report of Acts that the nucleus of many of the Pauline churches was drawn from the synagogue and included both Jews and 'God-fearers' (e.g. Acts 17: 11 f.). Munck is undoubtedly correct, however, in insisting that the membership of the Pauline churches was overwhelmingly Gentile. [5] See above, pp. 100 f.

correct in assuming that Luke here preserves the original order of Q, we can infer that the sayings in this little collection already implied Jewish opponents in their Q context.[1] The new context provided by Matthew likewise implies that the antagonists are Jews.[2] The geographical *Sitz im Leben* of the Q sayings is not clear.[3] For our purposes it is sufficient to note that the vagueness of the reference to 'those who kill the body' renders it unlikely that this saying was preserved primarily because it was associated with the Church's experience of martyrdom. Similarly, the allusion to denying Jesus is too general for us to draw any conclusions about the kind of social or legal pressure which was expected to have this result. While Matthew alters the material in order to adapt it to the missionary context, none of his changes reflect the historical situation out of which he wrote. The passage thus provides no additional evidence of Jewish persecution of Christians. Matthew's use of the material here serves to illustrate again that for him it is the missionaries of the gospel who are most liable to persecution from the Jews.

Before leaving chapter 10, let us review our findings. By inserting persecution material into his missionary discourse, Matthew suggests that persecution has been brought about by the Church's mission and that it is missionaries rather than rank-and-file Christians who are the primary object of persecution. By the addition of a personal pronoun ('*their* synagogues'), he indicates: (1) that he is concerned primarily with Jewish persecution, not persecution in general; (2) that the synagogue has become for him an alien institution; (3) that the era of persecution in the synagogues is largely past. The kinds of persecution mentioned are not different from those alluded to

---

[1] See above, p. 100 n. 4. The verses under consideration are followed in Luke (with one verse intervening, also from Q) by the logion which promises the help of the Holy Spirit to those brought before the synagogues etc. (Luke 12: 11). Comparison with the Matthean version (10: 19) indicates that this logion also belonged to the Q persecution collection.

[2] The introduction provided by the editor in 26a refers to the subject of the preceding sentence, i.e. those who call the master of the house Beelzebul. Matthew surely intends this as an allusion to the Pharisaic opponents of Mark 3: 22 (cf. Matt. 12: 24).

[3] The reference to Gehenna in Matt. 10: 28/Luke 12: 5 suggests a Palestinian origin.

in chapter 23; besides the vague references to death (*vv.* 21, 28) there are specific references to floggings in the synagogues and pursuit from town to town. In both cases the Diaspora situation seems to be implied.

Matthew 5: 10–12

With respect to the Beatitudes, the history of the tradition is unclear. It may be presumed that the form of Q anterior to Q^{Mt} and Q^{Lk} contained the outline of a dominical 'sermon' which began with beatitudes, among which was a beatitude for the persecuted.

Of Matthew's two versions, the first (5: 10) has been suspected of being the creation of the author, who allegedly combined the theme of 5: 11 f. with the form of the earlier beatitudes (5: 3–9).[1] Whether or not the suspicion is justified, this brief version of the beatitude for the persecuted is of little help to us in assessing the sociological situation.[2]

If we isolate the common elements of the two Q versions, we can reconstruct the Q archetype as follows:

Blessed are you when they revile you and slander you because
    of me;[3]
Rejoice and exult, because your reward is great in heaven,
For so they did to the prophets.

The absence of the verb διώκω from the Lucan version argues strongly against its presence in the archetype; it is more probable

---

[1] Cf. Bultmann, *Hist. Syn. Trad.* p. 110; Braun, II, 103 n. 1; J. Dupont, *Les Béatitudes* (1954), p. 85.

[2] We shall examine this verse later in connection with the author's understanding of the causes of persecution. See below, pp. 130–32.

[3] Luke's 'on account of the Son of man' appears more primitive, in view of the fact that 'Son of man' is a Semitic title which failed to achieve popular acceptance in the Gentile church. Its employment in our gospels, however, is not always primitive. Matthew adds it to his source at 16: 13. Luke has been suspected of creating the 'Son of Man' saying of Luke 18: 8b (cf. Bultmann, *Hist. Syn. Trad.* p. 175 and supplement). The title is probably editorial in most instances in the Fourth Gospel. A. Harnack, *The Sayings of Jesus* (1908), pp. 52 f., regards both ἕνεκεν ἐμοῦ and ἕνεκα τοῦ υἱοῦ τοῦ ἀνθρώπου as secondary; similarly Bultmann, p. 151, who argues that references to the person of Jesus are generally secondary in such sayings. Even if Harnack and Bultmann are correct in regarding ἕνεκεν ἐμοῦ as secondary, the idea is none the less implied by the ἐστε; i.e. it is those related to Jesus who are addressed by the logion, and it is precisely because of their relationship to him that they will suffer persecution.

that Matthew added than that Luke omitted.[1] The use of μισέω and ἀφορίζω in the Lucan version may have been inspired by the Hebrew text of Isaiah 66: 5, as Hunzinger suggests.[2] The hypothesis of a Semitic archetype has been employed to explain the equivalence of Matthew's εἴπωσιν πᾶν πονηρὸν καθ' ὑμῶν with Luke's ἐκβάλωσιν τὸ ὄνομα ὑμῶν ὡς πονηρόν. Matthew Black has conjectured that the Lucan ἐκβάλωσιν represents a fairly literal rendering of the Hebrew verb יצא used idiomatically in the Hiphil to mean 'publish abroad'.[3] He apparently assumes that the Matthean version represents a much freer translation of the same Semitic idiom. Harnack, on the other hand, maintains that ἐκβάλλειν in the metaphorical sense 'to defame' is good Greek and that on the contrary the Matthean phrase εἰπεῖν πᾶν πονηρόν is not; he concludes that the Matthean version is anterior to the Lucan.[4] Neither scholar, it must be pointed out, has succeeded in explaining the unusual Greek of *either* version on the hypothesis of a literal rendering of a Semitic *Vorlage*. Nor can it be maintained that either version represents an idiomatic Greek translation of a Semitic expression rendered more literally by the other. Although we are unable to explain the variants, however, the underlying idea is the same; both versions speak of defamation of character by slander.[5]

[1] Harnack, *Sayings*, pp. 50 f., argues that ὀνειδίσωσιν, διώξωσιν and εἴπωσιν were omitted by Luke in favour of three other verbs which exhibited a more logical sequence; Luke then substituted ἐποίουν for ἐδίωξαν in the conclusion, 'because in the preceding clauses not only persecutions but also other trials are mentioned'. *Contra* Harnack it must be maintained that διώκω is sufficiently general in its application to serve here just as well as ποιέω; consequently there is no need to postulate an editorial substitution. Later Harnack admits difficulty in explaining Luke's avoidance of διώκω in this passage: 'Why, I know not' (*Sayings*, p. 61).

[2] Claus-Hunno Hunzinger, *Die jüdische Bannpraxis im neutestamentlichen Zeitalter* (1954), as reported in *T.L.* LXXX (1955), col. 114.

[3] M. Black, *An Aramaic Approach to the Gospels and Acts* (1954), pp. 97 f. Black properly credits Wellhausen with pointing out the correspondence with Hebrew idiom, but Wellhausen does not introduce the Hebrew term into the discussion in the context cited, *Evangelium Lucae* (1904), *in loc.*

[4] *Sayings*, p. 52; similarly Dupont, p. 97. Bauer, p. 236, cites parallels to Luke's use of ἐκβάλλω from Plato and Sophocles.

[5] This failure to explain variants in Q on the basis of a common Semitic archetype should caution us against assuming that Q existed as an Aramaic document. It is clear that the bifurcation of the Q-tradition into Q^{Mt} and Q^{Lk}

A Semitic *Vorlage* has likewise been postulated in order to explain the wide variation between the Matthean τοὺς πρὸ ὑμῶν and the Lucan οἱ πατέρες αὐτῶν. Wellhausen suggested that Luke's source contained the Aramaic expression דקדמיהון (literally, 'which [were] before them'), which was read in Matthew's source as דקדמיכון ('which [were] before you').[1] Because of the difficulty of deriving the Greek variants from the suggested Aramaic original, the present writer is inclined to the opinion that τοὺς πρὸ ὑμῶν and οἱ πατέρες αὐτῶν do not represent a common Aramaic archetype.[2] The absence of the reference to οἱ πατέρες αὐτῶν from Matthew can more easily be explained by the hypothesis that this is an interpretative addition made by Luke.[3] It is equally probable that Matthew's τοὺς πρὸ ὑμῶν is an addition made either by Matthew himself or by his source, Q^Mt.[4] At any rate it is improbable that τοὺς πρὸ ὑμῶν can be derived from *ipsissima verba Jesu*. As it stands the phrase clearly implies that those addressed stand directly in the prophetic tradition. Yet nowhere else in the synoptic tradition does Jesus draw so close a parallel between his followers and the prophets.[5] It must be assumed that it was not until after the appearance of pneumatic phenomena that followers of Jesus were referred to as prophets. We can go even further and argue that the concluding clause, with its reference

took place at the Greek stage and not the Aramaic, in view of the large number of Q passages which are unmistakably dependent upon a common Greek archetype. Cf. Black, pp. 270–4.

[1] J. Wellhausen, *Einleitung in die drei ersten Evangelien* (1st edn, 1905), p. 36 (omitted from 2nd edn); cf. also his *Evangelium Lucae*, p. 24.

[2] See Appendix III for a fuller discussion of this matter.

[3] As a denominative for the ancestors of contemporary Jews, οἱ πατέρες is found five times in Luke and twenty-one times in Acts; it occurs twice only in Matthew, four times in John, and is absent from Mark. In the Pauline epistles the expression is used three times to designate the patriarchs, and once in the more general sense in which it is used here (1 Cor. 10: 1). Harnack, *Sayings*, p. 51, argues that the expression is editorial here, derived from the Q woe against the lawyers (Luke 11: 47 f.).

[4] Harnack, *ibid.*, maintains that Matthew's version represents the original text of Q.

[5] Matt. 10: 41 is too ambiguous to be adduced as evidence that Jesus regarded his followers as prophets. Matt. 23: 34 cannot be regarded as evidence, since it is a secondary formulation (see above, pp. 86 f.); in the Lucan version (Luke 11: 49) the parallel between Jesus' disciples and the prophets is not evident.

to the persecution of the prophets, is a post-resurrection addition because of the parallel it draws between disciples and prophets. The secondary character of this line is indicated perhaps by the fact that it is essentially superfluous; the beatitude is fully complete without it.[1] The point of the beatitude is not that all who are persecuted are fortunate, since this indicates that they are truly righteous like the prophets, but rather that those who are persecuted because of their relationship to Jesus are fortunate, since an eschatological reward to recompense them for their suffering is prepared in heaven.[2] The reference to the persecuted prophets is thus an afterthought, having no vital connection with the logion as long as we treat it as a genuine beatitude.

It is possible, however, that this is not a true beatitude but rather a prediction which has been given the form of a beatitude.[3] In this case the reference to the prophets explains not the blessedness but the prediction: 'They will persecute you, for so they treated the prophets.' The logic of this argument, however, requires the premise: 'You stand in the prophetic succession.' Since we have found no satisfactory evidence that Jesus accepted this premise, it will be better to treat the logion as a genuine beatitude, and regard the reference to the persecution of the prophets as an afterthought added by the Palestinian church.[4]

[1] F. C. Grant, *The Gospel of Matthew*, Harper's Annotated Bible Series, vol. I (1955), p. 31, suggests that the whole final clause, which sounds like an anticlimax, is 'perhaps an after-thought...added by the compiler of Q from other sayings of Jesus in the same vein'.

[2] The former seems to be the understanding which forms the basis of Black's reconstruction, p. 275. In support of the view here presented, cf. Dupont, p. 136; he also notes the correlation between the promise of punishment to the persecutors in 23: 29 ff. and the promise of reward to the persecuted in the present passage.

[3] Makarisms generally employ the present tense in the primary clause: 'Blessed is the man who [now, or at any time—the gnomic use of tense] is...' There are, however, other exceptions to this rule in addition to the present instance; cf. Luke 11: 27 (past); Matt. 24: 46 par., Luke 12: 37 f. and 14: 14 f. (future).

[4] Bultmann, *Hist. Syn. Trad.* pp. 110, 151, distinguishes Matt. 5: 11 f./ Luke 6: 22 f. from the older beatitudes in form and content and argues that these verses are *ex eventu*; similarly Braun, vol. II, p. 103 n. 1. Although Bultmann's argument from form is far from convincing (cf. the makarisms in Matt. 11: 6/Luke 7: 23; Matt. 13: 16; Luke 10: 23), analysis of the

The force of the original beatitude is indicated by the parallel woe in Luke 6: 26: 'Woe to you, when all men speak well to you, for so their fathers did to the false prophets.'[1] Both the malediction and the beatitude are concerned primarily with oral persecution, that is, name-calling, ridicule, public insults and the like. The key word in the beatitude is ὀνειδίζω. This verb is translated by 'revile' in the Revised Standard Version, and, like the English verb, it implies the presence of the object of reproach; that is, this verb is not ordinarily employed to denote the use of abusive language directed at a person who is absent.[2] The reference is not to the use of insulting language when describing Christians to a third party but rather to face-to-face insults. Face-to-face encounter seems also to be implied by Matthew's use of κατά in the clause καὶ εἴπωσιν πᾶν πονηρὸν καθ᾽ ὑμῶν ψευδόμενοι ἕνεκεν ἐμοῦ. If the reference were to rumour-mongering, one would expect a different preposition—περί or ἐπί.[3] While ὀνειδίσωσιν implies the use of insulting language with or without any specific charges being made (cf. Matt. 27: 44; Mark 15: 32), εἴπωσιν πᾶν πονηρὸν κατά refers to specific charges involving various kinds of disapproved behaviour. The following ψευδόμενοι makes it clear that the reference is to public accusation, in this case false accusation. The context

content reveals that many of the details are secondary. If we take ὀνειδίζω, the one descriptive verb common to the two versions, as the kernel of the underlying dominical logion, there is no need to treat the logion as *ex eventu*; the Beelzebul controversy suggests a possible *Sitz im Leben Jesu*. We cannot agree with Lohmeyer, *Das Evangelium des Matthäus* (1958), p. 95, who suggests that both variants derive from Jesus himself. Taking both versions as references to persecution in the courts, Lohmeyer fails to provide any historical justification for the view that Jesus expected his followers to be so persecuted. The gospels provide no evidence that Jesus himself was ever haled into court prior to the Passion; what would encourage Jesus to believe that his disciples would be legally persecuted?

[1] In support of the translation 'to you', cf. Blass–Debrunner–Funk, p. 84 (151.1). Even if this verse is a Lucan formulation (so Bultmann, p. 111; Dupont, pp. 104 ff.), it serves to indicate how Luke understood the beatitude (cf. Dupont, p. 110).

[2] ὀνειδίζω can also mean 'reproach justifiably' (cf. Matt. 11: 20), but in the present context so neutral a meaning can hardly be intended; cf. Bauer, p. 573.

[3] This suggestion is made by Lohmeyer, p. 95. He insists that the clause must refer to adverse testimony in court, since otherwise it is tautologous after 'revile'. This is not true.

may be the court, as Lohmeyer suggests, but it is by no means necessary to define the context so narrowly.[1] The words can just as well describe the use of lies by hecklers to discredit Christian missionaries as they proclaim their message.[2]

If we have correctly understood the meaning of ὀνειδίσωσιν and εἴπωσιν πᾶν πονηρὸν καθ' ὑμῶν, what is the significance of Matthew's διώξωσιν? We have already suggested that its omission from the Lucan parallel indicates that it is secondary.[3] Lohmeyer, who believes that διώξωσιν was part of the original logion, argues that the verb is here used as a *terminus technicus* of the court, meaning 'to bring legal charges against someone'.[4] The argument requires that εἴπωσιν πᾶν πονηρόν κτλ refer to judicial testimony. There is nothing, however, in the context to suggest that judicial action was in the mind of either Jesus or Matthew. Presumably διώκω is used in the same way in verse 11 and in verse 12, yet there is no evidence of a tradition that the prophets were persecuted judicially in the courts of law. From the editorial modification of 23: 34 we have discovered that Matthew interprets διώκω as signifying those hostile activities which drive Christian missionaries out of a community.[5] Such activities may very well include legal action, but can by no means be limited to the latter. We suggested 'harry' as a translation of the verb in 23: 34.[6] Another possible English equivalent is 'hound', which can be defined as 'pursue relentlessly'. Perhaps the meaning here is 'violently oppose'. Included under this general term are perhaps blows (including slaps on the cheek, cf. Matt. 5: 39), the throwing of refuse and stones (intended not to kill but to intimidate) and the use of threats of violence.

If διώξωσιν is secondary, its position in the sequence of verbs is unusual. One would expect the added verb, since its meaning is less specific than that of the other two, to be placed either at the beginning or at the end of the series. With this sequence, however, we may compare 23: 34, where the editorial inser-

---

[1] *Ibid.*

[2] The Lucan formulation, ἐκβάλωσιν τὸ ὄνομα ὑμῶν ὡς πονηρόν, seems to refer to rumour-mongering rather than to direct accusation (see above, p. 115). In view of the Lucan woe, we are inclined to take the Matthean version as more nearly representing the archetype at this point.

[3] Above, pp. 114 f.   [4] P. 95.

[5] Above, p. 92.   [6] Above, *ibid.*

tion is likewise placed in the middle of a sequence. Although the logic of the sequence is more appropriate in the latter case, the addition itself ('And some you will scourge in your synagogues') is logically inappropriate since the passage is concerned with the murder of the prophets. Consequently we ought not to expect the editor to be scrupulously concerned for logic in his adaptation of source material.[1]

Although διώξωσιν is vague in its application, it probably does not here include murderous violence. From the use of the verb in 10: 23 and 23: 34 we gather that for Matthew the activities subsumed under διώκω fall short of mortal persecution (whether murder or legal execution). Although the logic of the sequence of verbs in verse 11 is not clear, it is highly improbable that the author would be so insensitive to logical sequence as to insert a reference to mortal persecution between two allusions to oral persecution. It is probable, therefore, that 'persecute' in verse 12 is likewise to be construed in a general sense, having reference to those forms of persecution which do not seek the death of the victim.[2]

Although the persecutors are not specified by the logion or by the context in which the two evangelists have placed it, it is clearly implied that the persecutors are Jews.[3] Even if we regard the final line as secondary, it is clear that the reference to the persecution of the prophets belonged to the archetype of Q^{Mt} and Q^{Lk} and is therefore probably of Jewish Christian origin. Although we regard οἱ πατέρες αὐτῶν as a Lucan addition, it is probable that this represents not an anti-Judaic bias on the part of a Gentile but rather a faithful interpretation of the current Jewish tradition that the prophets of Israel have always been persecuted by unfaithful Israel.[4] That is to say, Luke merely makes explicit what is implicit in the logion in

[1] Cf. also the odd sequence in 21: 35—'beat...kill...stone'. The order of the verbs added by Matthew ('kill', 'stone') may be inspired by the Jerusalem-saying (23: 37).

[2] This seems to be the way Paul uses διώκω when referring to his own role as a persecutor of the Church (1 Cor. 15: 9; Gal. 1: 13; Phil. 3: 6); see above, pp. 35 f.

[3] Cf. W. D. Davies, Setting, pp. 289 f. Davies argues convincingly that the contrast between the synagogue and the Christian community is further amplified in 5: 13-16, for which 5: 11 f. forms an introduction.

[4] Cf. S.-B. I, 943; Josephus, Ant. ix. 13. 2 (264 f.). See below, pp. 137-41.

the pre-Lucan form; the reference to the prophets indicates that the logion was understood as referring to Jewish persecution. Matthew's τοὺς πρὸ ὑμῶν may have been part of the original Q-addition.[1] Regardless of its origin, however, this phrase does not alter the force of the tradition with respect to the source of persecution; it simply emphasizes the view (already implicit in the Q-addition) that the followers of Jesus who are being persecuted stand in the prophetic tradition and must therefore expect to be persecuted by unfaithful Israel.

The Matthean version thus suggests that for Matthew this beatitude applied primarily to Christian prophets in their mission to unbelieving Israel. This, of course, was to be expected on *a priori* grounds; historical probability indicates that it was the active propagators of the Christian faith who were most frequently the object of public insults and false accusations. Matthew's insertion of διώξωσιν, a verb reserved by him for the treatment accorded missionaries by unbelieving Jews, indicates that the hostile activities mentioned in this beatitude are for him not speculative possibilities but matters of historical experience drawn from the mission to Israel.

Matthew 22: 6

In this verse a note of violence is introduced into Matthew's Parable of the King's Marriage Feast which is entirely absent from the closest parallel, Luke's Parable of the Great Supper (Luke 14: 16–24). We are told that some of those invited made light of it, 'while the rest seized his servants, treated them shamefully, and killed them'.

The theme of the allegory is clearly the rejection of God's messengers by Israel and the consequent rejection of Israel by God.[2] The problem is to determine whether the two sets of servants mentioned in verses 3 and 4 represent the prophets of the old and new dispensations respectively or signify only pre-Christian messengers.[3] The former alternative is probably to be

---

[1] Cf. Harnack, *Sayings*, p. 51; see above, pp. 116 f.

[2] See below, pp. 139, 154.

[3] The possibility that only one group is intended is suggested by the two sets of servants in the Parable of the Wicked Tenants (21: 34, 36), both of which precede the Son. Harnack, *Sayings*, p. 120, was convinced that only pre-Christian prophets were intended in 22: 3 f.; similarly Schniewind, *Das Evangelium nach Matthäus* (1962), p. 221.

preferred.[1] Matthew's meaning here is probably indicated by his treatment of the Wisdom-saying in 23: 34 f., where Christian missionaries are clearly included among the divine messengers whose sufferings bring about the doom of Jerusalem.[2]

Although the allegory designates the unbelieving Jews as murderers (v. 7), the number of martyrs implied must not be exaggerated. Despite the generalization of verse 6, it is clear that many servants remain for the subsequent mission to the Gentiles (vv. 8–10).

Ambiguous References to Persecution
(5: 44; 7: 6; 13: 21; 24: 9; 25: 43 f.)

Matthew 5: 44 ('But I say to you, Love your enemies and pray for those who persecute you') is surely one of the least contested dominical sayings.[3] The original context of the saying, however, is not clear.[4] The enemies may have been Roman soldiers (cf. 5: 41), money-lenders and legal suitors (cf. 5: 40), personal enemies or religious opponents (cf. 5: 39). The reference to τῶν διωκόντων ὑμᾶς in no way serves to indicate which enemies were primarily in mind in the original use of the saying, for although διώκω with a personal object is used in the New Testament primarily of religious persecution, it is not impossible that the obligations imposed by the Roman occupational forces were regarded subjectively as a form of religious persecution.[5]

It is possible, however, that τῶν διωκόντων is secondary and that Luke's τῶν ἐπηρεαζόντων (Luke 6: 28) represents the original rendering of the Q saying. Harnack argues that since ἐπηρεάζειν does not belong to the vocabulary of common speech it is probably secondary in Luke.[6] This fact, however, can be

---

[1] Cf. J. Jeremias, *The Parables of Jesus* (revised edn, 1963), p. 68; Dupont, p. 132 n. 1.

[2] See above, p. 88.

[3] Cf. Bultmann, *Hist. Syn. Trad.* p. 105.

[4] W. D. Davies, *Setting*, pp. 245–8, suggests that 5: 43–8 is directed specifically against the sectarians of the Dead Sea Scrolls. V. G. Simkhovitch, *Toward the Understanding of Jesus* (1947), pp. 47 f., believed that these verses were directed against the Zealots' hatred for the Romans.

[5] Cf. the tendency in the Psalms of interpreting all kinds of enmity in religious terms, e.g. Pss. 140–3. The same tendency is seen in Paul's allegorical treatment of Ishmael and Isaac (Gal. 4: 29).

[6] *Sayings*, p. 61.

used with equal effectiveness to demonstrate that Luke's reading is to be preferred as the more difficult. If we are correct in regarding διώκω as secondary in Matthew 5: 11 f., it is possible that the same is true in this case.[1] The argument must not be pressed, however. The injunction of Romans 12: 14, 'Bless those who persecute you', suggests that from an early period a reference to persecutors belonged to the instructions concerning love for enemies. Regardless of the origin of the phrase, however, it is highly probable that Matthew, who elsewhere in his gospel is concerned primarily with Jewish persecution, understood the injunction as applying primarily to the conflict between the Church and the synagogue.

Matthew 7: 6 ('Do not give dogs what is holy...') is an enigmatic saying which has persistently eluded the ingenuity of exegetes.[2] The only justification for suspecting an allusion to persecution here is, of course, the reference to violence in the concluding line ('...and turn to attack you'). This line is superfluous if the meaning is simply 'Do not share sacred mysteries with the unworthy'. If we give the concluding words their full weight, the preceding imperatives may be taken as designating a course of action intended to avoid violence.

It is probable that 'dogs' and 'swine' refer to Gentile opponents rather than to Jewish.[3] The allusion is far too vague, however, to be taken as evidence that Gentile persecution of Christians was a matter of serious concern to the author of this gospel.

Matthew 13: 21 '...And when tribulation or persecution arises on account of the word, immediately he falls away'. These words are taken from Mark 4: 17, with only minor changes.[4] The source of persecution is unspecified in Mark, and Matthew adds nothing to indicate his understanding of the reference. The verse is therefore of little value for our study.

[1] See above, pp. 114 f.

[2] Cf. M. Dibelius, *From Tradition to Gospel* (1934), p. 250 n. 2.

[3] Cf. S.–B. I, 449 f. W. D. Davies, *Christian Origins and Judaism* (1962), p. 123, believes that the reference is to outsiders of any kind.

[4] The words θλῖψις and διωγμός, which are lacking in the Lucan parallel (Luke 8: 13), are regarded by C. H. Dodd, *Parables of the Kingdom* (revised edn, 1961), p. 3, as belonging to the vocabulary of the apostolic period rather than to the primitive tradition of the words of Jesus; cf. Jeremias, *Parables*, pp. 77 f.

Matthew 24: 9 'Then they will deliver you up to tribulation, and put you to death; and you will be hated by all nations for my name's sake'. This verse is clearly an editorial résumé, inserted here to take the place of Mark 13: 9–13, which Matthew has already employed in 10: 17–22. We can therefore infer that θλῖψις here refers to the judicial persecution of Mark 13: 9, 11. Similarly we infer that ἀποκτενοῦσιν ὑμᾶς echoes the prediction of Mark 13: 12, 'And brother will deliver brother to death...'. As we saw in the case of the earlier use in Matthew 10: 21, there is no need to regard this as a *vaticinium ex eventu*; it may just as well be taken as a genuine prediction, an expression of apocalyptic expectation.[1] The verse remains ambiguous with respect to the agents of persecution. Although our author is elsewhere concerned primarily with Jewish persecutors, we cannot infer that it is so here; this is a genuinely eschatological section, in which the author is concerned with events, still in the future, which belong to the category of 'messianic woes'.[2] In view of the immediately following reference to universal hatred, it is probable that Gentile as well as Jewish persecutors are intended.

Matthew 25: 36. The reference to imprisonment in this and succeeding verses (*vv.* 39, 43 f.) could be an allusion to religious persecution, since imprisonment was sometimes employed against Christians.[3] The possibility that this was the intention requires that we take 'the least of these, my brethren' of 25: 40 as referring to Christians, not the poor generally.[4] This is improbable. Although ἀδελφός is used regularly in the New Testament to denote either physical brothers or members of the same religious group, the use here is surely an exception to the general rule. The universality of the judgment requires a universal norm; not all men can be judged on the basis of the treatment accorded a small group of Christians.[5] Indeed, the view that the eternal destiny of all men will depend upon their treatment of Christians is essentially immoral! We are on safer

---

[1] See above, p. 109.   [2] Matt. 24: 8. Cf. Marxsen, p. 138.

[3] See above, pp. 47 f. With reference to this verse, Montefiore, II, p. 325, writes: 'It points to the era of persecutions.'

[4] So Allen, p. 265; H. F. von Soden, art. 'ἀδελφός', *T.D.N.T.* I, 145; Trilling, pp. 130, 189; Davies, *Setting*, pp. 98, 249, but the possibility of the broader interpretation is acknowledged on p. 329.

[5] Cf. Jeremias, *Parables*, p. 207; Schniewind, p. 254.

ground exegetically when we interpret the narrative in the light of its probable Jewish antecedents, taking as an inspired Christian addition the identification of the Judge with the world's needy.[1] In this view there is no allusion to religious persecution in verse 36. Imprisonment probably represents the helplessness of the debtor who has no one to rescue him from the impatience of a hard-hearted creditor.

SUMMARY AND EVALUATION

In Matthew 23 we have found evidence of an intensified anti-Pharisaism reflecting the unhappy contact between Christians and Pharisees. In his redaction of 23: 29–39 Matthew indicates that his hostility toward the Pharisees is related to their treatment of Christian missionaries. That it is missionaries who are the primary target of Jewish persecution is clearly and consistently presented by the First Gospel. Nowhere does this gospel intimate that rank-and-file Christians are liable to Jewish persecution.

Of the various forms of persecution studied in the preceding chapter, only two (imprisonment and economic reprisals) are completely ignored by Matthew. There is no evidence of formal exclusion from the synagogues, but Matthew's description of the synagogue as an alien institution indicates that, whatever the cause, Christians are no longer members. Nothing in Matthew militates against the conclusion reached in chapter II that social ostracism and mutual hostility constituted the primary cause of this exclusion.[2] There are a number of references to violent death (10: 21, 28; 22: 6; 23: 34, 37), but the references are sufficiently vague that a large number of martyrs need not

---

[1] Cf. Bultmann, *Hist. Syn. Trad.* pp. 123 f., 402; Braun, II, 94 n. 2.

[2] See above, pp. 55 f. Hummel, p. 29, points out that, in view of the fact that there is no mention of the *Birkath ha-Minim* in the persecution logia of Matthew, there is no justification for Kilpatrick's assumption (*Origins*, p. 11) that the separation from the synagogue to which Matthew witnesses was due to the *Birkath ha-Minim*. Hummel, p. 31, maintains that Matt. 23: 2 f. argues against a date after the effective application of this liturgical change. Although we may disagree with Hummel's interpretation of the meaning of these verses to Matthew, he is quite correct in regarding it as incredible that they could have been retained after the rabbinic decree concerning the *Birkath ha-Minim* became well known.

be implied. The only exaggeration which may be suspected here is the claim that the Pharisees are primarily responsible. Of the three known martyrdoms examined in chapter II, two are clearly attributed to non-Pharisees and in the third case (the martyrdom of Stephen) our source does not permit us to say that Pharisees were primarily responsible. If martyrdoms occurred during the war, fanatical nationalists were probably the instigators, not the Pharisees, who were generally less enthusiastic in the nationalist cause. In any event, Matthew nowhere suggests that Pharisees brought capital charges against Christians and had them executed. The conclusion reached in chapter II is unaffected by our examination of the Matthean data.

Matthew adds nothing to Mark's testimony concerning floggings in the synagogues, except to make it certain that the reference is to judicial flogging (by substituting μαστιγόω) and to indicate that the Pharisees are responsible (23: 34). On the basis of the conclusion reached in chapter II that floggings were administered to Christians by Jewish authorities primarily for breach of the peace, it is not at all improbable that Pharisees were occasionally involved in the employment of this sanction against missionaries whose work had a disruptive effect upon Jewish communities.

Under the general category of social reprisals we could include Matthew's use of διώκω in 5: 11 f.; 10: 23 and 23: 34. This would include various kinds of ill-treatment, including blows, insults and threats, all of which would be designed to drive a missionary out of the community. The reviling and slander referred to in 5: 11 f. would contribute to the same end. There is no reason to suspect exaggeration here. Matthew's portrayal is corroborated by Acts' description of Paul's mission.

In the redaction of his source at 10: 18 Matthew seems to imply that Jews have on occasion delivered Christians over to Gentile courts, but this implication is by no means certain, and the idea is not given any emphasis anywhere in the gospel. Gentile persecution, with or without Jewish instigation, is of little concern to Matthew.

The chronology of the persecution described by Matthew is difficult to establish. Although it is probable that the role of the Pharisees and their rabbis in this conflict increased after A.D. 70, it cannot be insisted that they played an insignificant role before that time.[1] The argument of 23: 29–39 requires that the persecution there alluded to took place in the pre-war period, since the destruction of Jerusalem and the Jewish nation is regarded as a divine punishment brought about in part by the sufferings inflicted on Christian missionaries. On the other hand, it is probable that persecution persisted after the war and did not cease until the mission to Israel waned with the withdrawal of Christians from the synagogues. The insertion of the *Birkath ha-Minim* into the Eighteen Benedictions in the latter part of the first century provides evidence that this separation was still in process at that time. Although it is unlikely that the First Gospel was written after this action was taken by the rabbinic leaders, it surely belongs to the period immediately preceding, when in some areas at least the separation had already been completed.[2] We may assume, therefore, that Matthew, written a decade or more after the war, looks back at the era of persecution, surveying both its pre-war and post-war phases from a vantage point outside the synagogue community. Floggings in the synagogues belong to the past. Henceforward the mission is to the Gentiles!

The geographical reference is even more difficult to establish with any certainty. Violent deaths may have occurred in the Diaspora as well as in Palestine, but we have no specific evidence. Matthew's allusions may be based entirely on a handful of martyrdoms in Palestine before and during the war. The floggings in the synagogues to which he refers took place more probably in the Diaspora than in the Jewish towns of Palestine, if we are correct in assuming that local civil government in Palestine resided with secular officials who employed the sanctions entrusted to them in public places other than synagogues.[3] The harrying of missionaries from town to town probably did not take place in Palestine during the early pre-war period; our earliest sources suggest that non-acceptance, not violent opposi-

---

[1] D. W. Riddle, *Jesus and the Pharisees* (1928), p. 64, notes that Acts does not picture the Pharisees as the implacable opponents of the Christian movement but gives this role rather to the Sadducees. It must be remembered, however, that Paul, erstwhile persecutor of the Church, had been a Pharisee.   [2] See above, pp. 55 f., 105 n. 3.

[3] Cf. Jos. *Bell.* ii. 14. 1 (273): τῆς παρ' ἑκάστοις βουλῆς.

tion, was the common response. On the other hand, Diaspora missionaries such as Paul were liable to this kind of treatment in the early period. In the years immediately preceding the war the Palestinian situation was aggravated by intense nationalism, and Christian missionaries undoubtedly found their work impossible in many communities. After the war the Christian mission to Israel was probably reactivated as Christians took advantage of the despondency of a defeated people.[1] During the same period, however, the rabbis were successfully gaining control of the Jewish religion and its institutions.[2] As synagogues which had formerly been independent of Pharisaic control came under the domination of Jamnia, Christian missionaries found that toleration of their work sharply decreased. It is probable that in post-war Palestine Pharisaic hostility drove Christian missionaries out of many communities. In view, however, of the fact that Minim persisted in Palestine into the second century and later, it cannot be maintained that Pharisaic antipathy attempted to banish Christians from the land; the intention of the rabbis was rather to bring Christian influence in the synagogues to an end.[3] In the Diaspora, where Jews constituted a self-conscious minority living together in the Jewish quarter of a hellenistic city, controversial missionaries were probably driven not only from the synagogue but from the residential community as well. This left the missionaries with two alternatives: they could remain in the same city, living and proclaiming their faith among the Gentiles and enjoying the fellowship of the Gentile church, or they could move to the Jewish quarter of another city and begin a new mission. As the years passed the second alternative became less and less viable, as opposition to the Christian movement was gradually consolidated with the help of Pharisaic leadership.[4] The First Gospel, in which ambivalence toward the Jews and concern for the Gentile mission probably reflect the failure of the mission to Israel, is to be seen as representing the reluctant abandonment of the second alternative in favour of the first.

[1] Cf. Jacob Jocz, *The Jewish People and Jesus Christ* (1949), pp. 42 f.
[2] See the excellent study of the influence of Jamnia in W. D. Davies, *Setting*, pp. 256–315.
[3] Cf. Israel Abrahams, *Studies in Pharisaism and the Gospels* (Second Series, 1924), p. 59.   [4] See above, p. 65.

Since the abandonment of the Jewish mission by those who believed themselves 'entrusted with the gospel to the circumcised' (Gal. 2: 7) could occur only after the failure of the Diaspora mission, not after the earlier Palestinian failure, we may regard the Matthean allusions to the pursuit from town to town as referring in their present context to the Diaspora situation.[1]

We have found no reason for believing that Matthew's portrayal of the conflict between synagogue and Church is greatly distorted. Although Matthew's treatment of the Pharisees manifests the kind of stereotyping and exaggeration which is normal in the heat of religious controversy, it cannot be said that he exaggerates with respect to the kinds of persecution Christians suffered in this conflict. Nor is Matthew open to the charge of having exaggerated the number of Christians who were molested or judicially flogged; his careful limitation of this suffering to missionaries of the gospel indicates that the number was relatively small. If the persecution to which this gospel witnesses has been exaggerated, it has not been by the evangelist himself but rather by careless or biased readers.

[1] See above, p. 111 and note.

CHAPTER IV

MATTHEW'S UNDERSTANDING OF THE CAUSES OF PERSECUTION

In our examination of the relevant Matthean passages we discovered that for Matthew Jewish persecution is directed primarily against missionaries of the Gospel. This indicates the occasion of persecution but not the cause. In chapter 1 a sociological explanation was offered: persecution occurred when Christians challenged the symbols of ethnic solidarity so sharply that they placed themselves beyond the tolerance-limits of the Jewish community. Almost every point of friction mentioned in that chapter can be documented from the Gospel according to St Matthew.[1] Our concern here is not to identify the historical causes of the conflict as they are reflected in this gospel but rather to discover which elements are perceived by Matthew as the primary causes of persecution.

ἕνεκεν δικαιοσύνης (5: 10)

The significance of δικαιοσύνη ('righteousness') in Matthew has been greatly debated. The fact that Deutero-Isaiah has elsewhere influenced Matthew has inclined some scholars to regard δικαιοσύνη as a reference to God's saving righteousness. Thus Lohmeyer argues that in 5: 10 δικαιοσύνη refers not to a human condition of righteousness but to the reality (*Wirklichkeit*) of God in which the disciples live.[2] Lohmeyer's view has not been widely accepted. Schlatter, noticing the absence of the definite article, insists that ἕνεκεν δικαιοσύνης must be taken as a reference to human conduct (*Verhalten*).[3] The present

---

[1] There is nowhere in the First Gospel any explicit depreciation of circumcision, but this is surely implicit in Matthew's treatment of the Gentile question; for Matthew circumcision is no longer a problem. Cf. R. Hummel, p. 26.

[2] Lohmeyer, p. 94.

[3] A. Schlatter, *Der Evangelist Matthäus*, p. 140. Schlatter is here followed by Georg Strecker, *Der Weg der Gerechtigkeit* (1962), p. 145, who, however, tries to mediate between the two positions by arguing that it is wrong to ask 'God's righteousness or man's?' since the righteousness de-

writer is convinced that in every instance Matthew intends δικαιοσύνη to denote the God-demanded behaviour which is characteristic of those who are to enter the Kingdom of heaven.[1]

What then does it mean to be persecuted 'on account of righteous behaviour'? The meaning of ἕνεκεν is not clear. The phrase may be descriptive rather than interpretative; that is to say, ἕνεκεν δικαιοσύνης may serve simply to identify the persecuted ('Blessed are the persecuted righteous') rather than to indicate the cause of persecution ('Righteous behaviour excites violent antagonism'). Although Matthew does not maintain that only those who believe in Jesus manifest righteousness, it is sufficiently identified with those who are to enter the Kingdom that the beatitude could be paraphrased, 'Blessed are those who are persecuted as Christians'.[2] If this is the meaning, the phrase indicates not the cause of persecution but only the occasion.[3] If, on the other hand, we take ἕνεκεν δικαιοσύνης as a reference to the cause (sufficient condition) of persecution, the beatitude may be regarded as an expression of the view that the righteous are perennially persecuted by the wicked because their righteous behaviour incites hatred.[4] This sentiment is not

manded of man is the righteousness of God. This confusion of God's saving righteousness with God's demand of righteous behaviour from man is not helpful.

[1] Note the close relationship between δικαιοσύνη and ἡ βασιλεία in 5: 10; 5: 20; 6: 33; although less obvious, the relationship is also present in the wider context of 21: 32 (cf. 21: 31, 43). For Matthew δικαιοσύνη is the abstract noun which corresponds to the phrase ποιεῖν τὸ θέλημα τοῦ πατρός; thus 5: 20 is to be understood by reference to 7: 21. Again, a close relationship may be observed between τὸ θέλημα τοῦ πατρός and ἡ βασιλεία in 6: 10; 7: 21 and 21: 31. That this δικαιοσύνη is not simply a matter of human achievement is suggested by the petition of 6: 10, γενηθήτω τὸ θέλημά σου. Nevertheless, voluntarism is predominant in Matthew; cf. W. Trilling, p. 165.

[2] The possibility of non-Christian righteousness is acknowledged in 5: 20 and 21: 32.

[3] This appears to be the meaning of ὡς Χριστιανός in 1 Peter 4: 16.

[4] Cf. 1 Peter 3: 16; 4: 4. The same idea may be implicit in 1 Peter 3: 14, a verse which seems to reflect the beatitude. The view that the righteous are continually persecuted by the wicked is very pervasive in the Psalms, but it is not stated that righteousness is the cause of persecution. Instead it is frequently stated that the wicked persecute (or hate) *without a cause*, חִנָּם (LXX: δωρεάν, μάτην); cf. Ps. 35: 7; 69: 4; 109: 3; 119: 161.

specifically Christian and is not otherwise reflected in Matthew's treatment of the theme of persecution.[1] Of these two possibilities, the former seems the more probable.

A third possibility may be considered. Because of the proximity and parallelism of verses 10 and 11, ἕνεκεν δικαιοσύνης may be regarded as synonymous with ἕνεκεν ἐμοῦ; that is to say, those who are persecuted because of their righteous behaviour are in reality being persecuted because of their relationship to Jesus, who is the source and cause of their distinctive way of life.[2] In this view 5: 10 is simply an anticipation of 5: 11 and provides no additional understanding of the causes of persecution.[3]

A fourth possibility must be mentioned in order to be excluded. It is improbable that δικαιοσύνη in 5: 10 has reference to Torah-obedience, thus making the beatitude an allusion to the conflict between the synagogue and the Church concerning the correct interpretation of Torah. In 5: 19 f. it is suggested that righteousness involves 'doing' the commandments of Torah, but Matthew's δικαιοσύνη can by no means be limited to legal righteousness (cf. 3: 15). Although the First Gospel reflects the dispute over Torah, it is unjustifiable to find in this verse a reference to that dispute.

ἕνεκεν ἐμοῦ (5: 11)

We have already argued that ἕνεκεν ἐμοῦ has at least as good a claim to a place in the Q archetype of the concluding beatitude as Luke's ἕνεκα τοῦ υἱοῦ τοῦ ἀνθρώπου.[4] Whether or not

[1] J. Schniewind, p. 49, associates 5: 10 with the general expectation that the righteous must suffer (citing Ps. 34): those who trust in God are continually persecuted precisely because they are righteous. Although this generalized view of suffering as the lot of the righteous is found in the New Testament, it is almost everywhere transformed by the fact of Christ's sufferings. That is to say, while the Old Testament idea underlies New Testament thinking about suffering, the New Testament view involves in addition the idea that the suffering of Christians is a participation in the suffering of Christ (cf. 1 Peter 2: 21; 4: 13). Even if Schniewind were correct in his understanding of 5: 10, it would remain true that such a view of persecution is not found elsewhere in Matthew. It is not the suffering of Christians generally which concerns Matthew but the persecution of Jesus' messengers by an unbelieving Israel.

[2] G. Bornkamm, 'End-Expectation and Church in Matthew', in G. Bornkamm, G. Barth and H. J. Held, *Tradition and Interpretation in Matthew* (1963), p. 30, notes this parallelism.

[3] Cf. J. Dupont, pp. 85 f.   [4] Above, p. 114 n. 3.

the phrase was created by Matthew, the idea is surely implicit in the Q archetype, in view of the fact that it is addressed to those who stand in the prophetic tradition.[1] The Q beatitude speaks of the persecution of Jesus' messengers; the phrase ἕνεκεν ἐμοῦ makes it clear that it is precisely on account of their relationship to Jesus that the Christian messengers are being persecuted.[2]

Beyond this, however, the meaning of the phrase is not immediately apparent. As we saw with respect to ἕνεκεν δικαιοσύνης, the ἕνεκεν-phrase may specify only the occasion of persecution, providing no clue as to the cause. That is to say, while the phrase indicates that the Christians are slandered because they are Christians, it does not state unambiguously that the primary issue in the dispute is Jesus himself. Since the verb in this instance is active (not passive as in 5: 10), it is at least possible that the ἕνεκεν ἐμοῦ is intended to indicate the central point of the conflict.[3]

On a priori grounds we should expect Matthew's 'high' Christology to arouse hostility in his fellow Jews.[4] For Matthew the meaning of Jesus' person is conveyed primarily by the title 'the Son of God'.[5] This title articulates the highest faith of

---

[1] See above, pp. 120 f.

[2] W. D. Davies, Setting, p. 99, suggests that the phrase be rendered 'on account of your relationship to me', but cautions that this meaning cannot be pressed.

[3] This is the only instance in Matthew in which ἕνεκεν ἐμοῦ or its equivalent διὰ τὸ ὄνομά μου is used with an active verb, the subject of which denotes the opponents of Christians. In those instances in which the causal phrase is used with a passive verb (5: 10; 10: 18, 22; 24: 9) it is best to take the causal phrase as indicating the motivation for Christian involvement in the activity of being persecuted or hated, not the motivation of the persecutors or haters. This is more clearly the case, of course, where the phrase is used in a clause in which the verb is active and the subject denotes Christians, as in 16: 25, 'Whoever loses his life on account of me' (cf. 10: 39; 19: 29), where the causal phrase clearly refers to the subjective cause of Christian involvement. Because of its frequent use in the gospel as an indicator of the subjective cause of the involvement of Christians in persecution, it is not certain that the phrase may be taken as referring to the motivation of the opponents in 5: 11. The N.E.B. supports the possibility that the phrase refers to the internal or subjective cause by altering the voice of the verb from active to paraphrastic passive.   [4] See above, p. 5 and note.

[5] The use of the title ὁ υἱὸς τοῦ θεοῦ in Matthew reflects a liturgical use which has fixed the title so that τοῦ θεοῦ is used despite Matthew's preference for a circumlocution in the case of the phrase 'the Kingdom of God'.

the disciples (14: 33; 16: 16). It is claimed by Jesus for himself (26: 63 f.; cf. 11: 27; 24: 36), and it is this claim which is the direct cause of his rejection by the leaders of Israel and his condemnation to death. Although, apart from the uncertain reference of 5: 11, Matthew nowhere clearly suggests that the persecution of Christians by Jews is the result of the Christological claims they make for Jesus, it is most probable that wherever he speaks of the Jewish rejection of Jesus he implies that this is the central point at issue in the conflict between the Church and Judaism.

Let us examine briefly the material pertinent to this theme. The rejection motif appears first in 9: 3.[1] Here the scribes accuse Jesus of blasphemy because he declares a paralytic's sins forgiven. Matthew omits the statement which Mark attributes to the critics ('Who can forgive sins except God alone?', Mark 2: 7), yet his use of the story suggests that the matter of remitting sins was still an issue in the dispute between the Church and the synagogue. In 16: 19 and 18: 18 Matthew claims this authority for the Church, and derives it directly from Jesus who possesses all authority (28: 18). It is for this reason that he can modify Mark's conclusion to the pericope by adding that the authority which the Son of man has upon earth to forgive

Thus in the trial scene, where Mark has the circumlocution ὁ υἱὸς τοῦ εὐλογητοῦ, Matthew substitutes ὁ υἱὸς τοῦ θεοῦ. The argument that this title could be used to express a 'high' Christology only in hellenistic Christianity, since the corresponding Semitic appellative could be used of any human being, is indefensible. The Semitic title 'the Son of man' was capable of the same ambiguity yet was used meaningfully by the Palestinian church. It is furthermore exceedingly improbable that the title ὁ υἱὸς τοῦ θεοῦ, an inherited part of Paul's Christianity, should have been created *de novo* in the hellenistic church within five years or so of the crucifixion, that is, by the time of Paul's conversion. Whether or not the messianic title 'Son of God' was used of Jesus in a 'low' Christology prior to his death, its use as part of a 'high' Christology was almost inevitable as soon as the Resurrection-faith gave birth to the doctrine of the exaltation of Jesus to the right hand of God (cf. Acts 2: 33). Although at this point the title may not yet have implied the developed incarnational doctrine of Paul and John, it clearly implied belief in a divine being whose rank exceeded that of the archangels and was second only to that of God himself. The incarnationalism of Matthew is found in his programmatic statements concerning the coming of Christ (ἦλθον, 5: 17; 9: 13; 10: 34 f.; cf. ἦλθεν, 20: 28); these statements clearly imply the pre-existence of Christ.

[1] The rejection in 8: 34 is non-theological.

sins has been given to *men* (plural, 9: 8). What is the meaning of
the charge of blasphemy? It would not have been considered
blasphemy for Jesus, as a prophet, to have announced God's
forgiveness.[1] The charge seems rather to be related to the
Christian claim that Jesus possessed this authority in a unique
way because of his status as heavenly Son of man. That is to
say, the reference to blasphemy reflects the response which
Christians met when they proclaimed Jesus' unique relation to
God in terms of the authority to remit sins.

The rejection motif appears again at the conclusion of
Matthew's miracles-collection. The Pharisees respond to the
healing of a dumb demoniac with the charge: 'He casts out
demons by the prince of demons' (9: 34). This, of course, is an
anticipation of the Beelzebul controversy which Matthew places
at a later point (12: 22–32). The accusation is reflected also in
10: 25 *b*, 'If they have called the master of the house Beelzebul,
how much more will they malign those of his household?' This
allusion indicates that the argument which attempted to prove
the divine status of Jesus on the basis of his miracles frequently
faced the counter-argument that Jesus was simply a magician,
a charge encountered often in the talmudic references to
Jesus.[2] Those who presented the claim on behalf of Jesus were
liable to be called the agents of the devil.

The Sabbath controversy of 12: 1–14 contains the daring
claim that Jesus, as the Son of man, is Lord of the Sabbath,
and that consequently his disciples can profane the Sabbath
because a higher obligation takes precedence over the Sabbath:
'Something greater than the Temple is here' (12: 6). It is at
the conclusion of this controversy that Matthew, following
Mark, first notes the intention of the Pharisees to destroy Jesus.
This can be regarded as an indication that intense hostility was
aroused by the Christian declaration that Jesus was Lord of
the Sabbath and able therefore to free his followers from the
Pharisaic Sabbath. The claim that Jesus' divine authority
exceeded even the authority of Torah was bound to have this

---

[1] C. G. Montefiore, I, 47, notes the instance of Nathan and David,
2 Sam. 12: 13, cited by Windisch, *De tegenwoordige stand van het Christus-
probleem* (2nd edn, 1924), pp. 24, 70 f.

[2] Cf. H. L. Strack, *Jesus, die Häretiker und die Christen nach den ältesten
jüdischen Angaben* (1910).

response. The same claim and the same response are present, less clearly, in the controversy over the traditions of the elders (15: 1–20) and the discussion concerning divorce (19: 3–9).

In his account of the Passion, Matthew supplies no motivation for the intention to destroy Jesus on the part of the high priests and elders.[1] Matthew apparently assumes that his readers are familiar with the tradition that it was the claim to divine authority made by Jesus which stirred up the jealousy (φθόνος, 27: 18) of Israel's religious leaders. In the trial before Caiaphas this claim is articulated in terms of the titles 'Christ' and 'Son of God' (26: 63). On the basis of his acceptance of these titles and the application to himself of the Danielic prediction of the Son of man, Jesus is condemned to death on the charge of blasphemy. We have seen that it is exceedingly improbable that the formal charge of blasphemy was sustained against Jesus by the highest court of Jewry.[2] The appearance of this motif in the narrative is therefore to be understood as a reflection of the Jewish rejection of the claims made on behalf of Jesus by his followers in their mission to the Jews. Later in the Passion narrative the claim that Jesus is the Son of God is the object of ridicule (27: 40–3). Contrasted with the rejection of the claim by Jesus' own people is the believing response of the centurion and his soldiers: 'Truly this was the Son of God.'[3] The Jewish leaders, incapable of faith, call Jesus a deceiver (πλάνος, 27: 63).[4] Even when presented with evidence of the Resurrection by their soldiers they are concerned only for the suppression of the evidence by means of a lie (28: 11–15). Matthew adds that this lie still circulates among Jews in his own day.

All these references to the rejection of Jesus can be seen as reflections of the experience of Christian missionaries in their mission to the Jews. Their declaration that Jesus was the Son of God was ridiculed: How could one cursed by execution be

---

[1] Contrast John 11: 47–53.   [2] See above, pp. 25–30.

[3] Matt. 27: 54. The omission of the English article by the R.S.V. was unjustified; the same phrase is translated with the article at 14: 33. Cf. E. C. Colwell, 'A Definite Rule for the Use of the Article in the Greek New Testament', *J.B.L.* LII (1933), 12–21. A recent edition of the R.S.V. has corrected this mistake.

[4] For the talmudic tradition that Jesus was a deceiver of the people, see above, p. 17 n. 3, and Strack, *Jesus*.

the Son of God? (cf. Gal. 3: 13). The claim that Jesus had been vindicated by his Resurrection was dismissed as a forgery. Their insistence that his teaching and healing were evidence of his authority brought the response: 'A servant of Beelzebul and a deceiver of the people!'

Matthew indicates that the rejection of Jesus and the rejection of the missionaries belonged together ('...How much more those of his household', 10: 25). It is probable therefore that ἕνεκεν ἐμοῦ in 5: 11 is intended to mean that the reviling and persecution which Christian missionaries suffer at Jewish hands is intimately related to the Jewish rejection of Jesus and of the high claims made for him by the Christians.

It must be noted again, however, that apart from 5: 11, Matthew nowhere explicitly derives the persecution from the Christian proclamation of the divine status of Jesus. Although there is good reason for believing that this was in fact a major factor in the complex situation which produced the persecution, it cannot be said that Matthew lays great stress upon it.

οὕτως γὰρ ἐδίωξαν τοὺς προφήτας (5: 12)

Christians inherited from Judaism the view that Israel had persistently persecuted her own prophets. Historical research indicates that the number of prophetic martyrdoms was greatly exaggerated in popular tradition. Of the three major and twelve minor prophets of the canon, none died a violent death.[1] The Old Testament does, however, report the death of two non-literary prophets who are remembered by name (Zechariah, son of Jehoiada, 2 Chr. 24: 20 f., and Uriah, son of Shemaiah, Jer. 26: 20–3) as well as a slaughter of unnamed prophets in Elijah's day (1 Kings 19: 10, 14). It is noteworthy that although 1 Kings 18: 4 suggests that it was Jezebel who cut off the prophets of Yahweh, Elijah's complaint in 19: 10, 14 is that the people of Israel have slain the prophets. Here we see the beginnings of the belief that Israel as a whole is responsible for the death of her prophets and must bear the guilt corporately. This is the meaning of the indictment of Jeremiah 2: 30: 'Your own sword devoured your prophets.' With this we may compare the generalization found in 2 Chronicles 36: 15 f., where the reference is not to violence but to ridicule:

[1] Cf. H. J. Schoeps, *Die jüdischen Prophetenmorde* (1943), p. 4.

The Lord, the God of their fathers, sent persistently to them by his messengers, because he had compassion on his people and on his dwelling place; but they kept mocking the messengers of God, despising his words, and scoffing at his prophets, till the wrath of the Lord rose against his people, till there was no remedy.

The Chronicler's generalization is easily understood as an explanation of the destruction of the nation by the Babylonians in the sixth century. It is not as easy to see why this kind of generalization was intensified in the post-exilic era. It may be that the development of a prophetic martyrology was due to the anti-Judaism of sectarianism.[1] Whatever the origins of the martyr-traditions associated with various prophets, these traditions were apparently widely accepted in the first century A.D.[2] Josephus gives ample evidence of the currency of the view that suffering was the prophetic lot.[3] The popularity of the tradition is further indicated by the fact that in the time of Jesus shrines were erected on the supposed sites of prophetic martyrdoms. Jeremias suggests that these memorials, intended as expiations for the blood of the murdered prophets, were popular centres for healing.[4]

It is not surprising, therefore, that the motif of Israel's rejec-

---

[1] The Martyrdom of Isaiah is thought by some scholars to derive from sectarianism of the Qumran type; K. Schubert, 'The Sermon on the Mount and the Qumran Texts', in *The Scrolls and the New Testament*, ed. K. Stendahl (1957), p. 123, concurs with this opinion, which he derives from D. Flusser.

[2] Schoeps, *Die jüd. Prophetenmorde*, p. 10, notes that in the *Vitae Prophetarum* six prophets are associated with unnatural death: Amos, Micah, Isaiah, Jeremiah, Ezekiel and Zechariah ben Jehoiada. Persistence of this theme in rabbinic circles is evidenced by a passage in a ninth-century midrash, Pesiqta Rabbathi 26 (129 a), cited by S.–B. I, 943: 'Jeremiah spoke to God: I cannot prophesy against them [the Israelites]; what prophet has arisen among them whom they have not tried to kill?'

[3] In *Ant.* ix. 13. 2 (264 f.) Josephus, reproducing the story of the sending of messengers to the Northern Kingdom by Hezekiah (2 Chr. 30: 1 ff.), adds to the biblical narrative the following: '...And when their prophets exhorted them in like manner, and foretold what they would suffer if they did not alter their course to one of piety toward God, they poured scorn [literally, spat] upon them and finally seized them and killed them.' In *Ant.* x. 3. 1 (38) he speaks of Manasseh's daily slaughter of prophets; although it is the king and not the people who is here responsible, the exaggeration nevertheless indicates the role played by the theme in the popular mind, as Schoeps, *Die jüd. Prophetenmorde*, p. 7 n. 7, suggests.

[4] J. Jeremias, *Heiligengräber*, pp. 126 ff. See above, pp. 83 f.

tion and persecution of the prophets plays a significant role in the literature of Christianity. Indeed, the surprise is that it does not occur more frequently.[1] In Christian polemic the charge is generalized to its fullest extent: 'Which of the prophets did not your fathers persecute?' (Acts 7: 52). A new idea is added to the charge to adapt it to Christian use: 'And they killed those who announced beforehand the coming of the Righteous One, whom you have now murdered and betrayed' (Acts 7: 52). Schoeps is probably correct in seeing in this verse a causal relationship between the prophetic proclamation of the Messiah and the persecution of the prophets,[2] but this cannot be regarded as certain in view of the fact that none of the other allusions to the theme in the New Testament make this connection.[3]

A further step is taken when Christians interpret the persecution of their missionaries as the contemporary manifestation of the 'law of history' that Israel continually persecutes the messengers sent by God.[4] This employment of the tradition probably derives from the early Palestinian mission.[5] It is reflected in Matthew in the final beatitude (5: 12), the allegory of the Wedding Feast (22: 6), and the conclusion of the discourse against the Pharisees (23: 29–39).[6] Insight into Matthew's understanding of the tradition is provided primarily by the last of these passages. Here we learn that the 'law of history' applies not only to prophets in the narrower sense of the term (i.e. men moved directly by the Holy Spirit) but to various kinds of divine messengers, including wise men and scribes. The Wisdom-saying, taken by Matthew from Q, contained in its pre-Matthean form a confusion between two kinds of guilt: guilt for the murder of God's messengers, and guilt for the

---

[1] The motif is explicitly alluded to in Matt. 5: 12 (Luke 6: 23); 23: 29–31, 34–6, 37 (Luke 11: 47–51; 13: 34); Luke 13: 33; Acts 7: 52; 1 Thess. 2: 15; and is implicit in Mark 12: 5 par. The allusion in Jas. 5: 10 is uncertain; cf. Bauer, p. 398, art. 'κακοπάθεια'. In the Apostolic Fathers it is found in Ignatius Magn. 8: 2 and Barn. 5: 11. Justin makes frequent allusions to the theme: *Dial.* 16, 73, 95 (cf. 93), 112, 120.

[2] *Die jüd. Prophetenmorde*, p. 11.

[3] Matthew is less explicit than Acts 7: 52 and 1 Peter 1: 10–12 in identifying Christological prediction as the primary function of the prophets of the old dispensation, yet this idea is surely the basis for his use of the prophets as a quarry for Christological proof-texts.

[4] The term 'law of history' is suggested by Trilling, p. 61.

[5] See above, pp. 116 f.   [6] See above, pp. 120 f., 121, and 88, respectively.

murder of the righteous. Matthew does not remove this confusion, but his additions show awareness of the problem created
by the inclusion of Abel in the Q text.[1] By placing the Jerusalem-
saying immediately after the Wisdom-saying, Matthew indicates that of the two types of guilt mentioned in this passage
he is concerned primarily with the first: the persecution of the
prophets. It is not the suffering of ordinary Christians nor the
suffering of missionaries as δίκαιοι but rather the suffering of
missionaries *as divine messengers* which is the burden of the
passage.[2] The only distinction between the divine messengers
of the two dispensations is that the Christian messengers are
sent by Jesus.[3]

Although the parallel between the former and latter-day
prophets is not as explicit in the beatitude, it seems probable
that Matthew intended his concluding phrase, τοὺς πρὸ ὑμῶν,
to indicate this parallelism.[4] Matthew's concern is with the
persecution of Christian missionaries, and he locates the cause
of this persecution in the age-old rejection of God's messengers
by Israel. The cause, as Matthew perceived it, is not ordinary
wickedness such as is common to Jews and Gentiles but rather
that specific kind of wickedness which is peculiar to God's
Chosen People. Israel alone has received God's special favour,
but she has persistently responded to God's good with evil,
and has rejected his fatherly correction, persecuting and killing
his messengers. Yet in the midst of her murderous rebellion
against God, Israel maintains that she is faithfully performing
God's will ('You tithe mint and dill and cummin', 23: 23) and
claims her privileged position as a right ('We have Abraham
as our father', 3: 9).

[1] Cf. E. Haenchen, 'Matthäus 23', *Z.T.K.* XLVIII (1951), 54.

[2] This confusion persists in many modern treatments of the New Testament doctrine of suffering. See Appendix IV.

[3] The daring Christological claim implicit in 23: 34 ought not to be over-
looked. The absence of distinction between the messengers of the two dispensations is to be noted in the allegory of the Wedding Feast, 22: 1 ff., in
which the function of the two sets of messengers is identical. See above, pp. 121 f.

[4] It is difficult to understand why Trilling, p. 63, maintains that this
logion presents the disciples neither as prophets nor as belonging to the prophetic succession. His paraphrase of the concluding line ignores the force
of the crucial phrase, and fails to take account of the fact that the parallel
depends not on the righteousness of the prophets but on their function.
See above, pp. 117, 121.

The obduracy of Israel is a mystery to Matthew as to Paul and the pre-exilic prophets. In the light of this obduracy, however, the persecution of God's latter-day prophets is to be expected. There is nothing in the conclusion of Stephen's speech which Matthew himself could not have written: 'You stiff-necked people, uncircumcised in heart and ears, you always resist the Holy Spirit. As your fathers did, so do you' (Acts 7: 51). The adoption of so pessimistic an article of faith was not, however, inevitable. It may well be that the appropriation of this theological viewpoint represents the reaction of Jewish Christian theology to the intolerance shown to its messengers. This question will be examined in the next chapter.

THE DISPUTE OVER THE INTERPRETATION OF TORAH

In the passages alluding to the persecution of Christian missionaries there is no suggestion that the persecution is due to the fact that the Christians proclaim the abrogation of the Torah and/or fail to observe the Torah themselves. The relationship of Christians to the Torah is not presented by Matthew as a cause of persecution. We can go further and point out that in those controversy narratives in which the dispute over the correct interpretation of Torah is presented by means of criticism of the behaviour of the disciples, there is not the slightest suggestion that the antagonists intended to take legal action against the followers of Jesus or to persecute them in any other way (Matt. 12: 1–8; 15: 1–20). This should serve to remind us again that there was greater tolerance for halakic nonconformity than has sometimes been supposed. Such nonconformity persisted for years even within Pharisaic circles, and was not easily overcome in the non-Pharisaic population.[1] It

[1] The persistent nonconformity of the 'amme ha'areṣ continued to be a problem for rabbinic Judaism in the second and third centuries when the rabbinic control of the synagogues was undisputed. Cf. A. Büchler, *The Political and Social Leaders of the Jewish Community of Sepphoris in the Second and Third Centuries*. It should be observed in this connection that Matt. 5: 19, one of the most conservative logia in the gospel, manifests a surprising tolerance toward nonconformity: those Christians who annul even one commandment will be called least in the Kingdom of heaven, but will not

must be assumed, furthermore, that Christians involved in the mission to the Jews were much concerned not to cause offence in this area. The pericope concerning the Temple tax illustrates well the point of view of those who, as sons of the Kingdom, are free yet nevertheless observe the old requirements in order not to give offence.[1] Thus Peter, the apostle to the circumcision, withdrew from table fellowship with the Gentiles at Antioch, not because of his loyalty to the *halakoth* involved but because of loyalty to the principle enunciated in Matthew 17: 27, ἵνα μὴ σκανδαλίσωμεν αὐτούς.[2]

There can be little doubt, however, that the kind of Jewish Christianity reflected in the First Gospel evinced an attitude toward Torah which was bound to bring Christian missionaries into conflict with the Pharisees and their teachers. While the validity of Torah is maintained, the rabbinic exegesis is treated ambivalently. Although Matthew retains a logion which seems to give blanket approval to the scribal interpretation of Torah (23: 2), there are many other passages in which the authority of the Pharisaic scribes as interpreters is seriously challenged. Matthew retains the Marcan charge that the scribal tradition nullifies the word of God (15: 6; cf. Mark 7: 13). It is Jesus who teaches with authority (an authority which is from God, 21: 23–7), not the scribes (7: 29). The Pharisaic scribes are blind guides (15: 14; 23: 16, 24; cf. 23: 17, 19, 26) whose teaching must be treated with great caution (16: 12). Christian exegetes have replaced the Pharisaic scribes as the authoritative interpreters of Scripture within the Church (13: 52; 23: 34; cf. 23:

forfeit membership in the Kingdom on that account! Cf. H. A. W. Meyer, *Critical and Exegetical Commentary on the N.T. Part 1, The Gospel according to St Matt.*(1880–1), I, *ad loc.*; A. B. Bruce, 'The Synoptic Gospels', *E.G.T.* I, *ad loc.*

[1] Matt. 17: 24–7; cf. 1 Cor. 9: 20. In the period in which the gospel was written the tax was paid not to Jerusalem but to Rome. As it stands, therefore, the pericope exhorts against giving offence to the representatives of Roman government; cf. W. D. Davies, *Setting*, p. 391, and H. Montefiore, 'Jesus and the Temple Tax', *N.T.S.* xi (1964–5), 64 f. It is probable, however, that *v.* 27 originated in the pre-war period and had reference in that situation to the matter of offending Jews through the exercise of Christian freedom. Cf. R. Bultmann, *Hist. Syn. Trad.* pp. 34 f.

[2] Gal. 2: 12. Paul's use of 'fear' with respect to Peter is probably polemical; it is far more probable that Peter's action was taken as a matter of expediency in order not to further alienate unconverted Jews. Cf. Dom Gregory Dix, *Jew and Greek*, pp. 43 f.

7 f., 10). Their authority is divine, since it is derived directly from Jesus, to whom God has entrusted all authority (28: 18), and who has communicated authority to the leaders of his Church (16: 19; 18: 18).

We have already suggested that hostility was aroused in Jewish hearers by the Christian proclamation of Jesus as Lord of the Sabbath, since such a claim attributed to Jesus an authority above that of Torah itself.[1] It is probable that the Torah-dispute was focused not so much on the attitude of Christians toward individual *halakoth* as on the question of the exegetical authority of Jesus and his Church *vis-à-vis* the authority of the rabbis. It is to be expected that this dispute at times reached such intensity that it resulted in the ill-treatment of Christian missionaries. It must be noted again, however, that Matthew does not allude to the Torah-dispute in connection with the persecution.

THE ESCHATOLOGICAL CAUSE

A common feature of Jewish eschatological thought is the motif of the messianic woes which will come upon the righteous immediately prior to the coming of the Messiah. Although it has always been the lot of the righteous to suffer at the hands of the wicked, this suffering will reach unprecedented intensity in the last days.[2] That Christians early appropriated this motif is indicated by its employment in the so-called Little Apocalypse of Mark 13.[3] How prevalent this expectation was among Christians of the earliest period cannot now be determined, because of the scantiness of our records. The motif is almost completely absent from Paul's letters. Inevitably the doctrine was of greatest interest when the outlook was blackest; believers faced with the prospect of severe distress could find hope in the belief that their ordeal would be brief and that eschatological salvation was at hand.

In the Marcan apocalypse the persecution of Christian

[1] See above, p. 135.

[2] For a review of the pertinent Jewish sources, see Billerbeck's excursus, 'Vorzeichen und Berechnung der Tage des Messias', *S.–B.* IV, part 2, pp. 977 ff.

[3] Mark 13: 8, ἀρχὴ ὠδίνων ταῦτα. Cf. Bultmann, *Hist. Syn. Trad.* pp. 122, 400 f., and authors there cited.

missionaries is included among the woes of the last days.[1] We have seen how Matthew de-eschatologizes this passage by removing it from the Marcan context and placing it in the missionary discourse of Matthew 10.[2] Thus the eschatological cause of persecution is essentially irrelevant in Matthew's treatment of the theme. Matthew retains the traditional view of eschatological persecution in his abbreviated summary of the same passage in 24: 9, but there is good reason for believing that Matthew regards the events alluded to in 24: 9 ff. as genuinely future, not contemporary.[3] The contemporary persecution of the missionaries to Israel, the only persecution which is of real concern to Matthew, is not attributed to eschatological necessity but rather to historical necessity: Israel always persecutes her prophets. The proximity of the end does not alter this law of history.[4]

The eschatological cause ought not to be dismissed entirely, however. Although for Matthew the sufferings borne by the messengers to Israel do not belong among the messianic woes, they are nevertheless eschatologically conditioned. The eschatological judgment of Israel requires that the full measure of her sins be filled up; not until this measure has been completed can the End come. Thus it is that the scribes and Pharisees, who symbolize for Matthew the rebelliousness of Israel, are urged to fill up the measure of their fathers (23: 32). Jesus sends messengers to Israel *in order that* the guilt of Israel may be made manifest and be punished according to its deserts (23: 34–6).[5]

SUMMARY

Scant attention is paid by Matthew to the causes of persecution. Since his concern is primarily for the persecution of Jesus' messengers to Israel, the historical law that the righteous are

---

[1] Mark 13: 9–11; these verses follow immediately the reference to the messianic woes in verse 8.   [2] See above, pp. 99 f.

[3] Cf. W. Marxsen, pp. 138 f. For a fuller treatment of this theme, see below, pp. 163 f., 177–9.

[4] Trilling, pp. 29 f., notes that the delay of the parousia is no problem for Matthew. This may be partly due to the fact that Matthew is able to de-eschatologize the persecution and accept the Gentile mission as the precondition without which the End cannot come (24: 14).

[5] See above, p. 88.

always persecuted by the wicked and the eschatological law that the sufferings of the righteous will be intensified in the last days are accorded only a passing glance. The hostile rejection of Jesus' messengers is interpreted in the light of Israel's rejection of the Son of God and her rejection of God's prophets in former days.[1] The dispute over Torah, while clearly perceived by Matthew as a point of friction between the Church and the synagogue, is not treated by him as a cause of the persecution. This is in keeping with his avoidance of sociological explanations. Only the theological cause, the obduracy of Israel, is of interest to the author. Nor is the mystery of Israel's sin probed, whether in terms of dualistic categories or in terms of predestinarianism.[2] Israel's sin is a fact of history which requires no explanation. It is the sufficient cause of the persecution. For Matthew no other explanation is necessary.

[1] These two strains of interpretation are parallel but not identical, and must not be confused.   [2] See below, pp. 149 f.

CHAPTER V

THE CHRISTIAN RESPONSE TO
PERSECUTION BY THE JEWS AS
EVIDENCED BY MATTHEW

IT is to be expected that the conflict situation which we have
examined would have provoked a response from the Church.
The hostility experienced by Jesus' messengers in the mission
to Israel was bound to affect both the Church's theological
understanding of the place of Israel in God's plan and the
Church's missionary strategy. It was bound also to affect the
way Christians interpreted the destruction of Jerusalem. It
stimulated reflection concerning the attitude to be shown toward Jewish opponents: should it be eschatological hatred or
patient love? Were the sufferings of the missionaries to be
treated as a sign that the End was at hand, or were they simply
a part of the Church's on-going life in the world? We shall
examine Matthew's answers to these questions.

PESSIMISM CONCERNING THE POSSIBILITY OF
THE CONVERSION OF ISRAEL

It must be assumed that the post-Resurrection mission to Israel
was initiated in the expectation that many of the descendants
of Abraham would respond favourably and receive a place in
the Kingdom. Despite early resistance to the Gospel, missionaries persisted in their work in the belief that they were destined
as the instruments of salvation for the lost sheep of the house
of Israel.[1] When the mission to Palestine proved unfruitful, the
missionaries turned to the Diaspora, expecting to rescue lost
sheep there.[2] This persistent optimism concerning the mission

---

[1] Trilling, pp. 83 f., argues that Matthew understands the limitation of
Jesus' mission in 15: 24 as necessary for the establishment of Israel's guilt.
While this may accurately reflect Matthew's view, it must be maintained that
the concern for the lost sheep is ultimately derived from Jesus' own mission,
in which salvation, not condemnation, was the goal; this is reflected in the
earlier form of the Q Parable of the Lost Sheep, Luke 15: 3–7.

[2] See above, pp. 110 f.

to Israel seems to be reflected in Paul's account of his conference with the apostles in Jerusalem.[1]

As the years passed, and resistance to the Gospel became increasingly prevalent in the Diaspora as well as in Palestine, the initial optimism inevitably gave way to a growing pessimism. This pessimism was intensified by the experience of persecution. Matthew's missionary discourse in chapter 10 reflects the pessimism of missionaries who expect non-acceptance and persecution to be the *normal* response to their message.[2] It would appear that this response did not at first prevent the missionaries from persisting in their work. When work in one community was no longer possible, attention was transferred to another. It may be assumed that this process continued until virtually all the synagogues of Jewry were closed to Christian evangelism.

At what point on this time-line is the Gospel according to St Matthew to be located? Does the First Gospel regard the mission to Israel as essentially a thing of the past, or as a continuing project despite discouraging results?

A. Schlatter expressed the view that the abandonment of the mission to Israel was unthinkable for Matthew, who saw it as his Church's mission to suffer and die on behalf of the Chosen People.[3] Although perhaps few scholars would go as far as Schlatter in this direction, many feel that the conflict between the Church and the synagogue is still for Matthew a conflict *intra muros*, that is, 'a dialogue within Judaism' rather than 'an appeal or apologetic to the synagogue from a church that was already outside it'.[4] The view of the present writer is that the First Gospel, addressed not to Israel but to the Church, assumes

---

[1] Gal. 2: 9. Romans, written probably no more than two years after the conference, reflects the failure of the mission to Israel (Rom. 10: 18; 11: 7). Although Rom. 11: 14 anticipates future conversions, the outlook on the whole is dark apart from the eschatological event referred to in 11: 25–32.

[2] See above, p. 98.

[3] A. Schlatter, *Die Kirche des Matthäus* (1929), pp. 13, 17–19.

[4] W. D. Davies, *Setting*, p. 290. Cf. G. Bornkamm, 'End-Expectation and Church in Matthew', in *Tradition and Interpretation in Matthew*, p. 39 and p. 22 n. 2. G. D. Kilpatrick, *Origins*, p. 122, writes 'Despite these harsh measures the opposition between Christian and Pharisee is for the evangelist an opposition within Judaism', yet he maintains, p. 111, that the First Gospel reflects the exclusion of Christian Jews from rabbinical synagogues. In what sense can the dispute or opposition be said to be *intra muros* when one party has been successfully excluded by the other? R. Hummel,

the abandonment of the mission to Israel. The synagogues of Jewry, the primary *locus* of the mission, have become hostile institutions.[1] The floggings in the synagogues are an experience of the past.[2] The invitation to the messianic banquet, offered so persistently and as persistently refused, will be offered no more (22:8f.). In the future converts from Israel will not be refused, but their conversion will not be sought. Henceforward the mission is not to Israel and the Gentiles but only to the Gentiles! The dual mission of Galatians 2: 7–9 is replaced by the single mission of Matthew 28: 19 f.: 'Go, make disciples of all the Gentiles...'[3] These words form the climax of the gospel and express the considered opinion of its author.[4]

The pessimism of Matthew is not limited in a temporal way, as is the pessimism of Hosea, Jeremiah and Paul. There is no suggestion that after the full number of the Gentiles have been

pp. 28–33, maintains that Matthew's Jewish Christians no longer participate in the synagogue services but nevertheless belong to the synagogue community (*Synagogenverband*). Perhaps Kilpatrick and Hummel mean that the Jewish Christians are continuing to live in the Jewish quarter, despite the fact that they have been ostracized by the Jewish community and are thus restricted in their personal relationships to fellowship with other Christians, including Gentiles. It is far more probable that, under these circumstances, the Jewish Christians left the Jewish quarter, and lived ἐθνικῶς with their Gentile friends, as did Peter at Antioch (Gal. 2: 14).

[1] Above, p. 105.   [2] Above, *ibid.*

[3] The following phrase, βαπτίζοντες αὐτούς, indicates that we must take τὰ ἔθνη as 'Gentiles', not 'nations'. For a contrary view, cf. Trilling, pp. 12–14, and literature there noted. Trilling, who argues that πάντα τὰ ἔθνη here includes Israel, fails to note that ἔθνη in this instance must refer to individuals, not nations, and can therefore refer only to non-Jews. Nor can we agree with him that the same expression in 25: 32; 24: 9, 14 would be for Matthew an inclusive term, implying no *Spannungsverhältnis* between Jews and Gentiles (*op. cit.* p. 13). Kenneth W. Clark, 'The Gentile Bias in Matthew', *J.B.L.* LXVI (1947), 166, translates: 'Go and make disciples of all the Gentile peoples', correctly understanding the reference as being to non-Jews, but failing to note that it is Gentile individuals who are meant.

[4] Evidence of a continuing mission to Israel has been found by some in Matthew's use of the pericope concerning the tax: so Schlatter, *Die Kirche des Matthäus*, p. 13. In a similar vein Bornkamm, *Trad. and Interpr.* pp. 19 f., argues that this pericope shows that Matthew's church was still attached to Judaism; likewise Hummel, pp. 32, 159. Although circumcised Christians may have been expected by Rome to pay the *fiscus iudaicus*, it by no means follows that these Christians were still a part of the Jewish community. See above, p. 105 n. 3.

admitted to the Kingdom the resistance of Israel will be supernaturally overcome, as in Romans 11: 25 f. For Israel the future holds only Judgment.[1]

ISRAEL'S REJECTION OF THE GOSPEL FOREORDAINED

The failure of the mission to Israel posed a theological problem to Jewish Christians. Paul gives expression to the inevitable response in Romans 9: 6, 'But it is not as though the word of God had failed'. Christian faith, instinctively trusting the sovereignty of God, could not but infer that the resistance of Israel to the Gospel was predestined.

This view is given expression by Matthew in the passage in which the purpose of teaching in parables is explained (13: 10–17). The Matthean departures from the Marcan *Vorlage* are here most instructive.[2] To the Marcan statement ὑμῖν δέδοται Matthew adds the antithesis ἐκείνοις δὲ οὐ δέδοται (13: 11). This contrast is then clarified by means of a verse taken from a later Marcan passage (Mark 4: 25): 'For to him who has will more be given, and he will have abundance; but from him who has not, even what he has will be taken away' (13: 12). The reference of the ὅστις δὲ οὐκ ἔχει is indicated by the following verses. In verse 13 Matthew substitutes ὅτι for Mark's ἵνα. Whereas Mark's ἵνα suggests that Jesus spoke in parables *in order that* the people might hear and yet not understand, Matthew indicates that this inability to understand was a condition already existing in an obdurate people. This point is then further established by means of a citation from the Septuagint of Isaiah 6: 9 f., in which the imperative of the masoretic text has been abandoned in favour of an aorist indicative; in this way Israel's resistance to repentance is presented not as the result of Jesus' ministry but as its precondition. The scriptural citation serves another purpose for Matthew; its reference to 'this people' (τοῦ λαοῦ τούτου) serves to make the meaning of ἐκείνοις in verse 11 and ὅστις δὲ οὐκ ἔχει in verse 12 unambiguous: Israel as a whole is cited for obduracy. To Israel

---

[1] See below, pp. 154–6.
[2] In what follows I am much indebted to Trilling's analysis of the passage, *Das wahre Israel*, pp. 59 f.

it has not been given to know the secrets of the Kingdom. Although the mystery of foreordained obduracy is not pursued, we are probably justified in seeing in the Matthean passive, οὐ δέδοται, a view similar to that expressed less ambiguously by Paul in Romans 11 : 7 f. (alluding to Isa. 29 : 10) : 'God gave them a spirit of stupor...'

The possibility of a dualistic answer to the problem is suggested by the reference to the devil in the interpretation of the Parable of the Tares: an alien will is here made responsible for the existence of 'the sons of the evil one' within the Church (13 : 38 f.).[1] It is to be noted, however, that Matthew refused to exploit this possibility. His avoidance of a dualistic explanation is probably due not only to his belief that God's will is sovereign but also to the conviction that Israel must be made responsible for her own guilt. It is for this reason, we may believe, that the allusion to foreordained obduracy is not more clearly made: there must be no weakening of Israel's responsibility.[2]

It is instructive to contrast Matthew's interest in the guilt of Israel with Paul's lack of interest. Whereas Matthew makes the whole people accept voluntarily the guilt of Jesus' death (27 : 25), Paul, in his discussion of the destiny of Israel in Romans 9–11, makes no mention of this guilt, and elsewhere attributes the death of Jesus to 'the rulers of this age'.[3] Whereas Matthew makes a dogma of the view that Israel has always persecuted the messengers sent her by God, Paul, himself the object of Jewish persecution, makes no mention of this guilt in Romans 9–11. For Matthew the guilt of Israel is her rejection of God, concretely manifested in the murder of Messiah, prophets and apostles and in the rejection of the Gospel.[4] Israel's doom issues

---

[1] Cf. C. W. F. Smith, 'The Mixed State of the Church in Matthew's Gospel', *J.B.L.* LXXXII (1963), 149 ff.

[2] This is a reflection of Matthew's voluntarism; by an act of will one may enter the Kingdom (19 : 17), and by an act of will one may refuse (23 : 37). Cf. the discussion of Matthew's voluntarism in Trilling, p. 165.

[3] 1 Cor. 2: 8. Only in 1 Thess. 2: 14–16 are the Jews cited as responsible for Jesus' death. This passage is suspected of being an interpolation; see above, p. 63.

[4] Although this is not as explicitly stated in Matthew as in the Fourth Gospel (e.g. 15: 20–4), it is surely implicit in Matt. 10: 40; just as acceptance of the disciple is equivalent to acceptance of Jesus and the one who sent him, so also is the rejection of the Gospel offered by the disciple ultimately equivalent to the rejection of God.

from this guilt. For Paul, on the other hand, the obduracy of Israel is seen as having a God-ordained function in *Heilsgeschichte*. As a result of Jewish hardness of heart, salvation has come to the Gentiles (Rom. 11: 11). The rejection (temporary) of Israel has resulted in the reconciliation of the whole world (Rom. 11: 15). After the full number of the Gentiles have been admitted, all Israel will be saved (Rom. 11: 25 f.). Nothing of this positive understanding of Israel's obduracy can be seen in Matthew. Israel's guilt is heavily underlined in order to justify her doom.

Matthew sees both Jesus' mission and the mission of his messengers as having the purpose of exhibiting and bringing to completion the already existing guilt of Israel. Although this is not clearly articulated with respect to Jesus' own mission, it is implied in the allegory of the Wicked Tenants, in which the sending of the Son serves only to demonstrate conclusively the guilt which had characterized the Tenants from the beginning. While the Marcan version of the allegory, taking the vineyard as representing Israel (cf. Isa. 5: 7), serves to indict only the religious leadership of Israel, Matthew's version indicts the whole people; 21: 43 indicates that for Matthew the vineyard represents not Israel but the Kingdom of God, which has been Israel's special prerogative up to this point but which has now been taken from Israel and given to another people.[1] Thus the purpose of Jesus' mission to Israel is to accomplish the transfer of the Kingdom. Likewise the purpose of the mission of Jesus' messengers is to bring to completion the full measure of Israel's guilt, so that her judgment may be consummated.[2] Although Matthew, even more than Mark, censures the religious leadership of Israel, the censured leaders do not constitute a separate group whose destiny is distinguishable from that of Israel. Although the Pharisaic opponents are made primarily responsible for Israel's rejection of Jesus and his messengers,[3] they simply incarnate the spirit of apostasy which has characterized Israel throughout her history.[4] Thus the condemnation of the Pharisees in the seventh woe shades almost

---

[1] See below, pp. 153 f.
[2] Matt. 23: 34–6; see above, p. 88.
[3] See above, pp. 95 f.
[4] See above, p. 94.

imperceptibly into a condemnation of the people as a whole, symbolized by 'this generation' (23: 36) and Jerusalem (23: 37).[1]

GOD HAS REJECTED ISRAEL

In the prophetic tradition pessimism with respect to the response of Israel to God goes hand in hand with the doctrine of the rejection of Israel by God. Because Israel rejects God, God rejects Israel.[2] With the possible exception of Amos, however, the pessimism of the prophets is never absolute; it is always tempered by the hope that, after punishment has been executed upon the faithless nation, Israel will be restored to her former privileges. This restoration may be understood in terms of a miraculous salvation from sin (Jer. 31: 31–4) or in terms of a chosen remnant (Isa. 1: 9; 10: 20–2). Paul, who clearly belongs within this prophetic tradition, employs both ideas: at present, despite Israel's obduracy, there is a chosen remnant (Rom. 11: 5); after the full number of the Gentiles have been admitted, all Israel will be saved, when God miraculously removes the faithlessness of his people (11: 25–7). Paul's confidence is based on his conviction that the election of Israel is irrevocable (11: 28 f.). He finds it unthinkable that God has rejected his people in a permanent way.[3]

It has been claimed that Matthew's denunciation of Israel is to be interpreted in the light of this prophetic tradition. Gregory Baum writes:

Matthew and his version of the message of Jesus fit perfectly into the tradition of Hebrew prophecy. In the eyes of the true prophet the sins of God's people, of the people with which he, the prophet, identifies himself, are infinitely worse than the vices of foreigners. Thus it was not dislike of his own nation, but on the contrary his love for the people called by God, which prompted Matthew to be so severe with the Jewish people.[4]

[1] Trilling, p. 73, points out that Mark's tripartite scheme (leaders, people, disciples, all of whom fail to understand Jesus) is altered to a bipartite scheme (unbelieving Israel and true Israel, distinguished by ability to understand).

[2] Cf. Jer. 6: 19, 30; Isa. 5: 24 f.; Amos 9: 7, 8a; Hos. 13: 4–16.

[3] Rom. 11: 1 f. Trilling, p. 115, notes that the final conversion of Israel in Paul's thought issues not simply from Paul's affection for his own people but from the theological problem of the *Verheissungstreue Gottes*.

[4] G. Baum, *The Jews and the Gospel* (1961), p. 44.

While we may agree with Baum that Matthew's anti-Judaism is not simply a matter of dislike, it must be maintained that Matthew's pessimism concerning Israel is unrelieved. There is no doctrine of the remnant. There is no prophecy of a future restoration. In Matthew's gospel the rejection of Israel is permanent and complete.

Let us examine the relevant passages: 21 : 43; 22 : 7 f.; and 23 : 37–9.

The first of these, 21 : 43, is an addition to the Marcan allegory of the Wicked Tenants, and must be regarded as the creation of the author.[1] The vineyard of the allegory is interpreted as symbolizing the Kingdom of God. Since Matthew's ordinary designation for the eschatological Kingdom is ἡ βασιλεία τῶν οὐρανῶν, it is probable that the use of ἡ βασιλεία τοῦ θεοῦ in this instance indicates that the reference here is not to the eschatological Kingdom but rather to the presently existing sphere of God's rulership, which can also be described as the special relationship between God and his chosen people.[2] This possession is now to be taken away from Israel and given to another people, who will produce the fruit expected by God, as Israel has not.[3] Matthew's use of ἔθνος here must be taken with full seriousness. Its presence in verse 43 means that not only the religious leadership but the whole of Israel is cited in the ὑμῶν.[4] The Kingdom of God is not being transferred from one part of Israel to another, however these parts might be described (false Israel, true Israel; unbelieving majority, faithful remnant; old Israel, new Israel); the transfer is from Israel to *another people, non-Israel.* It is this radical discontinuity between Israel and her successor which requires that we regard the rejection of Israel in Matthew as final and complete. This does not mean, of course, the rejection of the individual members of Israel. The ἔθνος to which the Kingdom is to be given is not 'the Gentiles' (considered corporately) but the Church, and Matthew

---

[1] Cf. Allen, p. 231.   [2] Cf. Allen, p. 362; E. Lohmeyer, p. 315.

[3] Lohmeyer, *ibid.*, points out the discrepancy between this verse and the allegory to which it is attached; the allegory maintains that fruit has been produced, but because of those responsible for the vineyard it has never been delivered to the owner. Lohmeyer is incorrect, however, in suggesting that the logion derives from a Jewish Christian community which regarded itself as the true Israel. The use of ἔθνει prohibits such an understanding; see below.   [4] Cf. Trilling, p. 45.

makes it quite clear that Jews compose the nucleus of the Church (cf. 16: 16; 19: 28). What is rejected is the nation Israel; this corporate entity has no more place in God's grace or God's plan.

This distinction between the nation and its individual members must be kept in mind as we consider 22: 7 f. Here the temporal punishment of Israel is identified with the destruction of Jerusalem. The invitation which had been spurned by Israel is now offered to others. In the present context the 'others' who are now invited for the first time can only refer to the Gentiles.[1] Those who had been previously invited were unworthy and are excluded. In view of the important place held by Jewish Christians in the Church, this can only be taken as a reference to Israel considered as a corporate whole. As a nation Israel refuses the invitation, and as a nation she is judged unworthy and is excluded. Henceforward the mission is to the Gentiles.

While Matthew takes the Jerusalem-saying (23: 37–9) from Q and makes no major alteration in it, the position he gives it illuminates his doctrine of the rejection of Israel.[2] It is made the final word in Jesus' valedictory to the Jewish nation. Placed between the promise of judgment upon 'this generation' and the subsequent prediction of the destruction of the Temple (24: 1 f.), the Jerusalem-saying declares that Israel's 'house' has been abandoned. Not the Temple but the commonwealth of Israel is meant by ὁ οἶκος ὑμῶν.[3] Not the desolation of the city but the rejection of the rejecting nation is here predicted. The abandonment of Israel by God is then symbolized by the departure of the Messiah and his disciples from the Temple and the city to the Mount of Olives (24: 1, 3). The abandonment is permanent. Henceforward the Messiah will no longer show tender concern for Israel; ἀπ' ἄρτι Israel will know him only as Judge.[4]

[1] Cf. J. Jeremias, *Parables*, p. 64.

[2] With respect to Matthew's addition here of ἀπ' ἄρτι, Trilling, p. 68, notes that the phrase here as in 26: 29, 64 marks a division between major periods of time. Cf. A. H. McNeile, *The Gospel according to St Matthew* (1915), p. 402.

[3] See above, p. 94 n. 6. Cf. Trilling, p. 67: 'Mit οἶκος wird das Gemeinwesen, die Stadt mit ihrer Bewohnerschaft, gemeint sein.' For a contrary opinion, cf. W. D. Davies, *Setting*, p. 298.

[4] So Trilling, pp. 67 f., who compares 23: 39 with 26: 29, 64. The point of the verse for Matthew, says Trilling, is not the Psalmic blessing but the removal of the Messiah until his return as Judge. He argues convincingly

G. Bornkamm maintains that a comparison of Matthew 21: 43 with Mark 12: 1 ff. indicates that while for Mark the rejection of Israel has already taken place, for Matthew it is to occur in the future.[1] While it is true that the future tense is used in 21: 43, this by no means proves that the rejection was regarded as still future by the author of the gospel; it only indicates that the transfer of the Kingdom had not yet taken place at the point in history where Matthew places the logion. Bornkamm's discussion ignores the fact that the Kingdom of God is here not a future reality but one which Israel already possesses; it can hardly be taken away if it is not first possessed. Since it is the Church which replaces Israel, the transfer must in some sense coincide with the birth of the Church. Matthew shows no interest in precision at this point, however. Matthew 22: 7 f. suggests that the moment of rejection is the destruction of Jerusalem. If our analysis of the history of persecution is correct, the mission to Israel persisted with vigour beyond this point, and was not abandoned for ten or fifteen years after this date.[2] Although the abandonment of the mission could be regarded as the point of final rejection by God, it is probable that Matthew would say that the abandonment of the mission and the destruction of Jerusalem were both simply concrete signs of the divine rejection which occurred at the time of the death of Jesus and the birth of the Church. This is suggested by 23: 39 f.: Jesus' last word to the inhabitants of Jerusalem is that their 'house' is abandoned to them and that the Messiah whom they have rejected is no longer their saving Messiah but only their Judge. Since the Jewish rejection of Jesus is for Matthew consummated in the crucifixion, it is at this point that God rejects Israel.

The rejection of God is manifested in punishment. It has been suggested that for Matthew the destruction of Jerusalem was the punishment for Israel's rejection of God's messengers and Messiah. This is clearly suggested by the allegory of the

that in the light of 8: 11 f. we cannot regard the blessing of 23: 39 as an indication that Matthew expected a miraculous conversion of Israel at the last moment. Similarly Baum, p. 65.

[1] *Trad. and Interpr.* p. 43. Is it clear, as Bornkamm maintains, that Mark 12: 1–12 proclaims the rejection of *Israel*? The context as well as the content of the allegory suggests rather that it is Israel's religious leadership which is rejected, not the nation.

[2] See above, p. 128.

Wedding Feast (22: 7). Although the allusion to the destruction of the city is not as clear in 23: 34–9 as has often been supposed, it seems probable that ἥξει ταῦτα πάντα ἐπὶ τὴν γενεὰν ταύτην points in this direction. Matthew 27: 25 is also to be seen in this light; the inclusion of the following generation (καὶ ἐπὶ τὰ τέκνα ἡμῶν) in the guilt for the murder of the Messiah has its significance in the fact that it was the second generation which bore the horrors of war and defeat. It cannot be maintained, however, that for Matthew the destruction of Jerusalem was the decisive punishment of Israel's guilt. This temporal punishment was merely the visible sign of the truly severe punishment which was visited upon Israel when God deprived her of possession of the Kingdom.[1] This crucial punishment, symbolized by the destruction of the city, will be consummated at the final judgment, when the erstwhile sons of the Kingdom will be cast out into outer darkness (8: 11 f.). It is none the less a present reality. Israel is no longer the People of God.

ISRAEL REPLACED BY THE CHURCH

The New Testament writers are concerned to affirm both the continuity and the discontinuity between the old and new dispensations. What has happened is new, and yet it is the fulfilment of the old. There is only one *Heilsgeschichte*, which begins with Abraham and is fulfilled in the community of the saints which are in Christ Jesus.

The tension between continuity and discontinuity is especially evident in New Testament thinking about the Church. When Paul wishes to emphasize the continuity of *Heilsgeschichte*, he suggests that the Church *is* Israel. This is established either by relating believers to Abraham (Rom. 4: 11, 16; Gal. 3: 29) or by suggesting that Gentile believers have been grafted on to the olive tree which is Israel (Rom. 11: 17). The discontinuity between Israel and the Church in Paul's thought is evident when he insists that a special place is retained in *Heilsgeschichte* for Israel κατὰ σάρκα; God's original Chosen People continues its existence as an entity over against the Church. Paul makes little effort to be consistent at this point. Although he distinguishes between the elect and non-elect in Israel 'according

---

[1] So Trilling, p. 47.

to the flesh' (Rom. 9: 6, 8, 24; 11: 7), he cannot abandon the inherited conviction, based on the promises to the Fathers, that all Israel has a place in the Age to Come (Rom. 11: 1, 11 f., 26–9).

This tension between continuity and discontinuity is almost non-existent in Matthew's view of Israel and the Church. Here there is almost no continuity between Israel, the People of God in the old dispensation, and the Church, the new People of God.

Matthew's radical discontinuity has been obscured when scholars have attributed to him a doctrine of a New Israel or True Israel.[1] Although there have been protests against calling Matthew's church a New Israel, this term is perhaps less misleading than the other, for although it mistakenly retains a reference to Israel, it none the less suggests that a *different* Israel is denoted, thus testifying to the discontinuity.[2] The appellative True Israel, on the other hand, suggests a continuity which is not to be found in Matthew's thought. Matthew does not suggest that Gentile members of the Church are related to Abraham by faith or that they have been grafted onto the elect remnant of Israel.[3] The doctrine of the remnant is not employed. The Church is in no sense a continuation of Israel but a different ἔθνος, non-Israel, which replaces Israel in *Heilsgeschichte* (21: 43). This new People of the Kingdom is neither Jewish nor Gentile but, although Matthew does not use the term, a 'third race'.

One of the most enthusiastic supporters of the view that Matthew regards the Church as True Israel is Wolfgang Trilling. Although Trilling is emphatic in maintaining that for

---

[1] The term 'New Israel' is employed by W. D. Davies, *Setting*, p. 290, who notes, however, that no such term is used by Matthew. 'True Israel' is made by Trilling the key to Matthew's theology, *op. cit. passim*; it is the term preferred by Baum, pp. 55, 63, and E. P. Blair, *Jesus in the Gospel of Matthew*, p. 149. Bornkamm emphasizes continuity when he suggests that Matthew's church regards itself as 'the true Judaism', *Trad. and Interpr.* p. 22 n. 2. Hummel, p. 160, argues that the Church is not thought of by Matthew as the replacement of Israel, nor as true or new Israel, but as the eschatological community within Judaism.

[2] Protests are raised by Trilling, p. 76, Baum, p. 63, Hummel, p. 160.

[3] In 3: 9 it is suggested that God is able to raise up children to Abraham from stones, but this motif is not developed in relationship to Gentile believers.

Matthew Israel has been rejected and is no longer God's People, he insists that 'True Israel' is justified as a designation of the Church in Matthew's thought.[1] While admitting that Matthew uses no term corresponding to 'True Israel', he maintains that this term correctly indicates the continuity which Matthew sees between the People of God in the old dispensation and the People of God in the new; for Matthew the whole of the Old Testament *Heilsgeschichte* flows without interruption, correction or reinterpretation into the new period, and consequently the Church is not a New Israel taking the place of the old but the genuine, true Israel as God had conceived it from the beginning.[2] This continuity, he suggests, is expressed by Matthew in terms of ἡ βασιλεία τοῦ θεοῦ; consequently, 'Wem diese *Basilea* von Gott gegeben worden ist, wer sie "hat", der ist Israel'.[3] This is a misleading use of terms. There is no evidence whatsoever that Matthew regarded the Church as Israel; on the contrary, there is positive evidence that he regarded the Church as non-Israel. Where is the continuity between Israel, a nation which in Matthew's view has persistently rejected God and his messengers, and the new People of the Kingdom, which produces the fruit refused by Israel? While it may be true that Matthew sees the Church as the People of the Kingdom as God had conceived it from the beginning, there is no justification for equating this people with guilty Israel. Trilling is again using misleading terms when he opposes True and False Israel.[4] Matthew nowhere suggests that Israel is falsely claiming to be Israel; he employs 'Ἰσραήλ exclusively of Israel 'according to the flesh', which is therefore the genuine Israel.[5]

A similar error is made by Reinhart Hummel when he attempts to establish the continuity between Israel and the

[1] Cf. p. 68: 'Israel hat aufgehört, Gottes erwähltes Volk zu sein.'

[2] P. 76.

[3] P. 75. Cf. p. 47: 'So ist mit der Kontinuität des Reiches auch die Kontinuität eines Volkes Gottes gegeben.'

[4] P. 76.

[5] Exception must also be taken to Trilling's statement that both sides, that is, Church and synagogue, claimed to be the Israel of election and promise. Matthew nowhere makes this claim; nowhere does he employ these categories to describe the Church. The term οἱ ἐκλεκτοί describes individuals; it is not used in the singular to describe the elect People of God. No allusion is made to the promises to the Patriarchs.

Church on the basis of a common dependence upon Torah.[1]
He greatly exaggerates the role of the Mosaic Torah in the
Christian community.[2] In Matthew's view entrance to the
Kingdom is gained not by doing Torah but by doing τὸ θέλημα
τοῦ πατρός, which includes πίστις. Conversely, the guilt of
Israel is not neglect of Torah but the rejection of God mani-
fested in the rejection of God's messengers.

While we must agree with Trilling and Hummel that for
Matthew there is continuity between the two periods of *Heilsgeschichte*, we would insist that this is not to be located in
Matthew's idea of the Church or in his view of Torah but
rather in his Christology. Trilling approaches such a view when
he remarks that for Matthew, who takes the Old Testament
seriously, the Messiah is the *Messiah of Israel*.[3]

The Messiah, whose ministry is directed to the lost sheep of
the house of Israel (15: 24), is named Jesus because his mission
is to save his people from their sins.[4] The association of the
Messiah with Israel is so close that at one point it approaches
identity: 'Out of Egypt have I called my son.'[5] This theological
possibility is, however, repudiated at 12: 18, where Matthew
deliberately ignores the Septuagint's identification of the
Servant with Israel in Isaiah 42: 1, while resorting to the Septuagint for the last line of the quotation.[6] Nevertheless the
Jewishness of the Messiah is emphatically portrayed. His
genealogy is traced back to David and Abraham (1: 1–17), not
to Adam as in Luke (Luke 3: 38). At his birth he is recognized
by Gentiles as King of the Jews (2: 2), and it is under this title
that he dies (27: 11, 29, 37; cf. 21: 5; 27: 42). He is the son of
Abraham who fulfils all righteousness (3: 15), who comes not

---

[1] Pp. 156–60.

[2] In his treatment of Matthew's attitude toward antinomianism, pp. 67–
71, Hummel exaggerates Matthew's hostility toward those who fail to
observe the Mosaic code, ignoring the concession of 5: 19 that Christians
who teach nonconformity to Torah are none the less members of the Kingdom
(see above, p. 141 n. 1). The statement 'Ohne Tora gibt es überhaupt keine
Gerechtigkeit' (p. 69) ignores completely the implications of 8: 10 f.

[3] P. 84.

[4] Matt. 1: 21: τὸν λαὸν αὐτοῦ. In Matthew λαός is used exclusively of
Israel 'according to the flesh'.

[5] Matt. 2: 15. Here Matthew follows the Hebrew text of Hos. 11: 1,
where the LXX reads τὰ τέκνα αὐτοῦ.

[6] LXX Isa. 42: 1: 'Ιακὼβ ὁ παῖς μου...'Ισραὴλ ὁ ἐκλεκτός μου...

to destroy the Law and the Prophets but to fulfil them (5: 17), and who perfectly fulfils the will of his Father, even to the point of surrendering his life to a shameful death (26: 42). For Matthew the consummation of Old Testament *Heilsgeschichte* is in this one son of Abraham, who in his own person incarnates the obedient faithfulness that God has always demanded of Abraham's posterity. The point of continuity between the old People of God and the new is thus Jesus himself. It is the Messiah who forms the bridge uniting the two periods of *Heilsgeschichte*. This is reflected in the use made of the Old Testament by Matthew. No quotation is culled from the Scriptures to demonstrate that the Church is the fulfilment of the Old Testament hope for Israel.[1] With few exceptions the quotations are selected for the purpose of showing that *Jesus* is the fulfilment of the Old Testament hope.[2]

The new People of God is therefore to be defined primarily in terms of its relationship to the Messiah. It is the Congregation of the Messiah, ἡ ἐκκλησία τοῦ Χριστοῦ.[3] The crucified and risen Messiah is a present reality within this ἐκκλησία and the dominant force in its *heilsgeschichtlich* mission (18: 20; 28: 20). The messianic community can also be described as ἡ βασιλεία αὐτοῦ (13: 41) and its members as 'Sons of the King-

---

[1] Even the 'new covenant' motif of Jer. 31: 31–4, associated by Paul and Luke with the tradition of the Lord's Supper, is avoided by Matthew. The contrast between this gospel and the Dead Sea Scrolls is at this point quite clear. We would point out to Hummel that, unlike the Scrolls, Matthew does not cite Scripture to demonstrate that the Church is the Torah-observing community in the midst of unfaithful Israel.

[2] Exceptions such as 2: 17 f.; 27: 9 f. are related indirectly to the Messiah's story.

[3] With Matt. 16: 18, cf. Rom. 16: 16. George Johnston, *The Doctrine of the Church in the New Testament* (1943), p. 79 n. 8, points out that Rom. 16: 16 provides the only N.T. instance of ἐκκλησίαι τοῦ Χριστοῦ, and that the singular is not used, but adds that for Paul 'the Church of God is a Church in Christ...'. Whether or not the Palestinian church employed the term כְּנִישְׁתָּא דִמְשִׁיחַ, it is clear from Matt. 16: 18 that for Matthew the Church is a new entity, created by Jesus the Messiah and defined by its relationship to him. It is a mistake, therefore, to treat ἐκκλησία in Matthew as evidence of continuity between Israel and the Church, as does K. L. Schmidt, art. 'ἐκκλησία', *T.W.N.T.* III, 529 f. Although the term may have had this meaning when it was first adopted, for Matthew ἡ ἐκκλησία μου is *not* a continuation of the ἐκκλησία of the LXX but its replacement.

dom' (13: 38).[1] The new People of God comprises those who do the will of the heavenly Father (7: 21; cf. 12: 50; 21: 31; 6: 10). While for the rabbis the will of the Father is revealed in Torah, for Matthew it is Jesus who truly reveals the will of the Father, both in his exegesis of Torah (19: 3–9) and in his own pronouncements (18: 14).[2] Those who do the will of the Father (7: 21) are therefore those who hear Jesus' words and do them (7: 24). Because of this the process of becoming members of the messianic community can be called 'becoming a disciple' (μαθητευθῆναι, 13: 52; 27: 57; cf. 28: 19). Jesus' teachings are therefore of special importance to Matthew, because they reveal the will of the Father and constitute a *Lebensordnung* for the new People of God.[3] The will of the Father as presented by Jesus' teachings in this gospel is not simply a matter of ethics, although generalizations such as the Golden Rule (7: 12; cf. 22: 40) are apt to mislead us into such a view. *Faith* is the primary characteristic of those who enter the Kingdom (8: 10 f.). It too can be described as something to be *done* (23: 23). In Matthew πίστις is associated primarily with miracles and can thus be spoken of as a kind of believing which is unrelated to Jesus (17: 20; 21: 21). More frequently, however, it is faith in Jesus' ability to work miracles (8: 10; 9: 2, 22, 29; 15: 28; cf. ἀπιστία, 13: 58). The verb πιστεύω can likewise be used to describe faith in Jesus' miraculous power (8: 13; 9: 28), but in addition it is employed to describe faith in Jesus' person: those who are in the Church are those who believe in Jesus (18: 6; cf. 27: 42). Thus the faith of the Centurion of Capernaum is described as that which is lacking in Israel, and it is on account of this refusal of faith that Israel is rejected (8: 10f.; cf. 21: 31 f.). Those who believe in Jesus and do the will of his Father in accordance with his teaching constitute a spiritual brotherhood, the family of the Messiah which replaces his fleshly family (12: 46–50).

[1] Another term used of the messianic community is 'the elect', οἱ ἐκλεκτοί, but since this term is found only in the apocalyptic chapter (24: 22, 24, 31), and in each instance is taken over from Mark, it cannot be said that Matthew found it congenial to his thinking. His avoidance of the term elsewhere may be due to his voluntarism. The use of ἐκλεκτοί in 22: 14, although not here technical, indicates that Matthew's voluntarism was simply a matter of emphasis.

[2] Cf. Trilling, p. 163.

[3] Cf. Trilling, pp. 23, 162.

It is this relationship to the Messiah which marks off the new People of God as distinct from the nation which rejected him.

RENEWED EMPHASIS UPON LOVE OF ENEMIES

One would expect that Christians involved in the conflict between the synagogue and the Church would react to persecution with expressions of hostility. Such hostility is clearly manifested in the pejoratives employed by Matthew when speaking of 'the scribes and Pharisees'.[1] His attitude toward these opponents can hardly be described as one of love. There is no attempt to distinguish between good and bad Pharisees. The scribe who in Mark receives approbation is altered by Matthew into an enemy who 'tests' Jesus in an effort to gain evidence to be used against him.[2] There is no suggestion in the persecution-passages that the missionaries should suffer in love for the sake of the Jewish opponents, for whom no hope is held.[3]

The exhortation to love one's enemies (Matt. 5: 44) must nevertheless be seen in the light of this conflict and the hostility it aroused on both sides.[4] Matthew applies the dominical injunction not to enemies in general but precisely to persecutors, who in this gospel are almost exclusively Jewish persecutors. Trilling has observed that Matthew is distinguished among the evangelists for his strenuous effort to apply the traditional teachings of Jesus to his own situation.[5] In 5: 44 Matthew indicates how the dominical logion concerning love for enemies was applied in his church during the era of persecution.[6] Although this application did not prevent expressions of hostility toward the persecutors from appearing in the gospel, it can surely be taken with 5: 39 as evidence of Matthew's commitment to passive resistance. Although little positive love is extended toward the religious opponents in the First Gospel, Christians are expected to show love by praying for those who insult and abuse

[1] See above, pp. 81 f.

[2] With Mark 12: 28–34, cf. Matt. 22: 34–40, and Bauer, p. 646, art. 'πειράζω'.

[3] Matt. 23: 32 f. Contrast Rom. 9: 1–3.

[4] See above, pp. 122 f.   [5] P. 190.

[6] Trilling, p. 170, argues that the fact that Matthew has reworked this passage (5: 38–48), making the meaning even sharper and clearer, shows how very significant it was for him.

them. It must further be observed that, in contrast to the Dead Sea Scrolls, no permission to hate the enemies of God is granted by this gospel.[1]

PERSECUTION DE-ESCHATOLOGIZED

We have seen how Matthew has de-eschatologized the persecution-situation by removing Mark 13: 9–13 from its apocalyptic setting and transferring it to a missionary discourse.[2] In this way Matthew indicates that for him the persecution of missionaries is not an eschatological sign but a part of the Church's on-going life in the world. Missionaries are persecuted not because the End of all things is at hand but because throughout history Israel has persecuted the messengers sent to her by God.[3] Matthew also de-eschatologizes the destruction of Jerusalem. While the introduction to the Marcan apocalypse suggests that for Mark there was a close relationship between the destruction of Jerusalem and the consummation of all things (Mark 13: 4), Matthew's substitution distinguishes between the events of A.D. 70 and the parousia/consummation (24: 3).[4] It is probable that for Matthew the eschatological events depicted in 24: 9 ff. are still future, that is, completely unrelated to the destruction of Jerusalem; the 'desolating sacrilege' of verse 15 is not for him an allusion to the profanation of the Temple by Titus but rather a supernatural prodigy which will appear shortly before the final coming of the Son of man on the clouds of heaven (24: 29 f.).[5] In this way Matthew is able to distinguish the contemporary persecution which attends the mission to Israel from the eschatological tribulation in which all Christians (not missionaries only) will experience the hatred of all nations (24: 9). This future suffering belongs to the messianic woes (cf. 24: 8), and will serve as a sign that the End is near (24: 14).[6] At the time that Matthew writes the mission

[1] Cf. 1QS i. 7 ff. A careful examination of the relevant texts is made by W. D. Davies, *Setting*, pp. 245–8.

[2] See above, p. 99.   [3] See above, pp. 139–41.

[4] Cf. Marxsen, p. 136 and note. Hummel, pp. 90–4, treats the destruction of the Temple as an eschatological event, but concedes that it is for Matthew a matter of 'realized' eschatology.

[5] Cf. Marxsen, pp. 138 f. For a fuller discussion, see Appendix v.

[6] See above, p. 124.

to Israel is essentially a thing of the past, the mission to the Gentiles is the Church's primary responsibility (24: 14), and the End is 'neither especially near nor especially far off'.[1]

SUMMARY

Although these various theological ideas were hammered out in the heat of controversy with rabbinic Judaism, it must be remembered that they need not on that account be the direct products of that controversy. In this connection Trilling speaks of the 'immanent unfolding of faith in the bosom of the Church', accomplished by means of meditation upon the Old Testament.[2] Nevertheless, it would be difficult to explain the extreme pessimism of Matthew with respect to Israel except on the basis of historical experience. Although the Old Testament can be quarried for scriptural evidence of the obduracy of Israel, it is surely experience which stimulates the employment of such texts. The same must be said concerning Matthew's doctrine of the rejection of Israel. This is not so much an un-folding of the Church's faith as a response to a historical situation. The failure of the mission to Israel, accompanied by the mistreatment of the Church's missionaries, is understood as a sign that it has not been granted to this people to repent and believe in the Gospel. So stern a refusal of grace on God's part is regarded as certain evidence of divine rejection.

The contrast in severity between Paul's doctrine of a tem-porary rejection and Matthew's doctrine of a permanent rejec-tion of Israel has at least two explanations. Kenneth Clark has argued that this contrast is so great that it must be regarded as evidence that the First Gospel was written by a Gentile, since no Jewish Christian would have been capable of such a view of Israel.[3]

---

[1] Trilling, p. 30; cf. pp. 190 f., where he notes that although Matthew's paraenesis is sharpened by a strong emphasis upon the coming Judgment, it is not on the basis of the nearness of the End but rather on the basis of the realization that the Church is to continue to live in the world and in it must remain true to its call. Bornkamm, *Trad. and Interpr.* p. 23, points out that the Matthean Parable of the Virgins (25: 1–13), which is directed to the Church, portrays the foolishness of counting on the imminence of the parousia.   [2] P. 198.

[3] Kenneth W. Clark, 'The Gentile Bias in Matthew', *J.B.L.* LXVI (1947), 166. J. P. Brown, *N.T.S.* VIII (1961–2), 30, on the basis of his study of the sources of Matthew, maintains that the work of the final author invariably

The present writer finds Clark's thesis unacceptable, primarily because it fails to explain the intensity of Matthew's anti-Pharisaism, which, as we have found, belongs especially to the redactional elements of the gospel.[1] Whereas the Gentile Luke speaks of the synagogue with the detachment natural to one for whom it is a foreign institution, Matthew speaks as one for whom it has only recently become an alien institution.[2]

The alternative to Clark's explanation is that the contrast between Matthew and Paul is to be understood in terms of the historical situation of the two writers. Paul, writing before the war, is concerned primarily with the mission to the Gentiles. It is not as though he did not care about the salvation of his fellow Jews; it is simply a matter of fulfilling his vocation as apostle to the Gentiles. He has experienced persecution from Jews, and at the time he writes his Epistle to the Romans he fears the possibility of ill-treatment from unbelievers in Judea (Rom. 15: 31). Nevertheless, the obduracy of Israel does not prevent him from carrying out his mission, and he can still hope that all Israel will finally be saved. Matthew, on the other hand, writes after the destruction of Jerusalem, an event regarded by rabbis and Christians alike as a divine judgment on Israel's sins.[3] He writes as one who has been concerned primarily with the mission to Israel. Whereas the failure of this mission did not prevent Paul's work from going ahead, it has meant a right-about-face for Matthew and others whose vocation it has been to seek the lost sheep of the house of Israel. The persistent rejection of their message, accompanied by in-

reflects the Gentile church; none of the Jewish Christian features of the gospel need be as late as the final editor. The conservatively Jewish elements were retained by the editor only because they came to him 'in a canonical written tradition', viz. Q^{Mt}. While we may agree with Brown that the final editor is not conservatively Jewish, this does not require that he be a Gentile. The present writer is convinced that Matthew's anti-Judaism is Jewish, not Gentile.

[1] See above, pp. 81–96. [2] See above, pp. 104 f.

[3] Berakoth 3a reports that R. Jose (probably Akiba's pupil, R. Jose ben Halafta), while praying in a ruin of Jerusalem, heard a voice saying 'Woe to the children, on account of whose sins I destroyed my house and burned my Temple and exiled them among the nations of the world!' The reference to the ruin suggests a date before A.D. 132 for this tradition. Cf. also Josephus, Bell. iv. 5. 2 (323). Such an interpretation of Israel's defeat need not exclude the hope of restoration; cf. Baruch 2: 34; 4: 25.

sults, ill-treatment and threats to their lives, has gradually deepened Matthew's pessimism into one unrelieved by hope.

We may imagine that while at first the missionaries were willing to suffer and, if need be, die on behalf of Israel, expressing the kind of love for their people manifested by Paul in Romans 9: 1–3, with the passing of time this initial readiness to suffer was subject to reappraisal as suffering failed to produce the hoped-for fruit. With the consolidation of Pharisaic opposition after A.D. 70, Jewish Christians were increasingly tempted to view the obduracy of Israel as foreordained and irremediable. Gradually the pressure of opposition forced Christians to abandon the early view of the Church as the eschatological community within Israel in favour of a view which regarded the Church as the replacement of Israel. While such a view was perhaps impossible for a Jewish Christian such as Paul in the middle of the first century, it was possible for the Jewish Christian Matthew, who, writing about A.D. 85, looked back on the fruitless suffering of the mission to Israel.

CHAPTER VI

SUMMARY AND CONCLUSIONS

CONFLICT between Christians and non-Christians in the Jewish community was inevitable, in view of the disrespect shown by Christians for the cherished symbols of ethnic solidarity. Hostility toward the nonconforming minority found varied expression. In many situations the persecution suffered by Christians was simply a matter of verbal abuse and social ostracism. Indeed, there is reason to believe that this was the method most commonly employed for containing the 'Christian problem'. When hostility exceeded the bounds of moderation, Christians were liable to physical violence at the hands of a mob. In some few instances death may have resulted, as in the case of Stephen, but apart from the chaotic period of the two wars with Rome it is unlikely that many Christians suffered martyrdom at Jewish hands. Of two other early martyrs known to us by name, James son of Zebedee and James brother of Jesus, one was killed by Herod Agrippa, presumably on a political charge, and the other was executed by a Sadducaic court, apparently on a trumped-up charge. There is no evidence that Christianity was defined as a capital crime by Jewish courts and prosecuted as such.

When outspoken missionaries such as Paul strained the tolerance of the Jewish community, mob action was frequently rendered unnecessary by legal recourse to the synagogue council or, in Palestine, to the local Jewish court. Discipline was exercised by means of temporary detention (in Palestine), flogging, and exclusion, apparently on the charge of breach of the peace. On the basis of available evidence it seems unlikely that either the profession or propagation of Christianity was defined as a crime punishable by flogging. Nor is it probable that Christians generally were liable to formal exclusion from the synagogues by means of the ban. It would appear that disciplinary action was *ad hoc* and applied only in obnoxious cases.

In the pre-war period the Church in Palestine suffered little from Jewish intolerance. Our earliest sources concerning the

Palestinian mission suggest that non-acceptance, not persecution, was the normal response of the Jewish communities in
Palestine. Although evidence is lacking, we are probably safe
in assuming that the heightened nationalism of the war years
brought suffering in various forms upon Christians who remained loyal to the pacifism and anti-nationalism of Jesus.[1]
With the gradual consolidation of Pharisaic power in the post-
war years, Christians in Palestine found themselves strongly
opposed in the synagogues. It is probable that even before the
Birkath ha-Minim was introduced into the synagogue liturgy the
influence of Christians in the Palestinian synagogues had
dwindled to the vanishing point. Social ostracism was an
effective weapon, especially where Pharisaic influence was
strong. The churches of Palestine became isolated religious en-
claves, tolerated by the wider community because no longer
a threat.

In the Diaspora the tolerance-limits of the synagogue community were more frequently exceeded. We have found no
reason to doubt the testimony of Acts, supported by allusions
in Matthew, that Christian evangelists were on occasion violently expelled from the Jewish community. It is probable that
the references to floggings in the synagogues found in the New
Testament allude primarily to the Diaspora. There was probably little change in this situation in the period A.D. 50–85,
except that increasingly the synagogues of the Mediterranean
world were closed to Christian missionaries. At first this was
primarily a local response to a local problem, but there is
evidence that the Pharisaic leaders took an increasingly active
role in the anti-Christian movement after the war.

Although the influence of Pharisaism in the various regions
of the Diaspora cannot be accurately ascertained because of
inadequate evidence, it is probable that Syria was of special
concern to Jamnia.[2] We can assume, therefore, that Christians
in Antioch and other Syrian cities felt Pharisaic opposition with
special force. The intensified anti-Pharisaism of Matthew seems
to reflect such a situation. It is characteristic of Matthew that
he is concerned not with persecution in general but rather with
the Jewish persecution of Christian missionaries. His hostility
toward the Pharisees is closely associated with the ill-treatment

[1] See above, p. 90.   [2] Cf. W. D. Davies, *Setting*, pp. 295 f.

of Jesus' messengers which he attributes to them. An examination of the Matthean allusions to persecution reveals exaggeration at this point only; his charge that the Pharisees are primarily responsible for the death of Christian missionaries must be regarded as without foundation in view of the available evidence. Nor does it seem probable that these opponents were *primarily* responsible for the floggings inflicted upon missionaries in the synagogues, although it need not be doubted that the Pharisees' role in such disciplinary action was increasingly important in the later period. Matthew's suggestion that the flight of missionaries from town to town is the result of Pharisaic opposition, while perhaps not justified for the pre-war period, may be an accurate reflection of Pharisaic opposition to Christian propaganda in the decades following the war. Matthew does not, however, introduce the Pharisees into all his allusions to persecution, and there is no reason for believing that he regarded them as the only Jewish persecutors. The Matthean references to insults and slander probably have the wider Jewish community in mind as well. Although the Pharisees are singled out for special responsibility, Matthew indicts the entire community for rejection and ill-treatment of the latter-day messengers of God.

Our sources, including Matthew, indicate that the persecution was generally restricted to missionaries and confined primarily to the Jewish community. There was little inclination on the part of Jews to persecute Gentile Christians or to instigate Gentile persecution of the Church. While Christian 'agitators' were occasionally turned over to Gentile authorities for punishment, this kind of persecution is of little concern to Matthew. We may regard it as a rather exceptional procedure and one that for Matthew belongs largely to the past. There is no reason to doubt Matthew's implication that the synagogues were able to take care of the 'Christian problem' without resorting to Gentile authorities.

The causes of persecution are of little concern to Matthew. Of little interest to him is the belief that the righteous are perennially persecuted by the wicked. The eschatological expectation that this suffering will be intensified in the last days is not employed with respect to the contemporary persecution. Sociological explanations are avoided; while he shows awareness of the role played in the conflict by disputes over the Messiah and Torah, he makes little effort to explain the persecution on this basis. Of greater interest to Matthew is the 'law of history' that Israel continually persecutes the messengers sent to her by God. For Matthew this dogma, implying the perpetual obduracy of Israel, is the sufficient explanation of the persecution.

Matthew's response to the persecution is reflected primarily in his theology of Israel and the Church. His pessimism concerning the possibility of the conversion of Israel is unrelieved by the eschatological hope found in Paul's treatment of the theme. Israel's rejection of the Gospel is for Matthew foreordained, but this motif is handled lightly in order to leave full responsibility for its refusal with the guilty nation. Because of obduracy, Israel has been rejected by God, permanently and completely. Her place in the history of salvation has been taken by another people, the Church. While composed of both Jews and Gentiles, the Church is neither Jewish nor Gentile but a new creation, a 'third race'. For Matthew there is no continuity between Israel and the Church; the Church is neither New Israel nor True Israel. Continuity between the two periods of *Heilsgeschichte* is located by Matthew not in the idea of a People of God but in the Messiah, who fulfils the hope of the old dispensation and builds the community which replaces Israel in the new. While much of Matthew's theology of the Church and its relation to Israel may have developed independently of the persecution, there can be little doubt that the bitterness of the conflict has left its mark in the pessimism with which he treats Israel's place in the divine plan. Indeed, were it not for the persecution it would be difficult to avoid ascribing the First Gospel to a Gentile simply on the basis of its view of Israel. The bitterness of the persecution and the frustration of a fruitless mission are sufficient, however, to account for so pessimistic a view of Israel on the part of a Jewish Christian author.

Despite his hostility toward the synagogue and its Pharisaic leadership, Matthew strives to be loyal to Jesus' insistence on loving one's enemies, although this love can now be manifested only in prayers for the persecutors. The mission to the synagogues and the attendant persecution of missionaries belong for Matthew essentially to the past. Since Matthew has de-eschatologized the persecution, associating it with the on-going life of the Church in the world, the failure and abandonment of the mission to Israel results not in a retreat into apocalypticism but in a redirecting of energy into the Gentile mission. The invitation which Israel has refused so rudely is now to be offered exclusively to the Gentiles. The closing words of the Gospel testify to this radical change in the vocation of Jewish Christian missionaries in the last two decades of the century: 'Go, then, and make disciples of all the Gentiles... And, behold, my presence will strengthen you in this mission all the days that remain until the completion of the age.'[1]

[1] Matt. 28: 18, 20, paraphrased.

USE OF THE TERM ΑΘΕΟΣ

ON the basis of Justin's use of the phrase αἵρεσιν ἄθεον in *Dial.*
17 (rendered 'godless heresy' by Reith; see above, p. 66),
Frend maintains that the Jews accused Christians of atheism.[1]
In similar fashion, Huidekoper suggests as the English equivalent 'an atheistic sect'.[2] This rendering is not impossible, but
ἄθεον can just as well be taken as meaning simply 'godless',
that is, 'wicked'. Huidekoper acknowledges that, were it not
for the evidence of this passage in Justin, he would be inclined
to regard ἄθεοι as a designation of Gentile monotheists
generally.[3] To the present writer it seems unlikely that Jews,
who were just as committed to the neglect of the State gods
as the Christians, would use ἄθεος in its narrower sense to attack
Gentile monotheists, whether Christian or not. It is therefore
better to understand the adjective in its broader connotation
as simply a term of strong disapproval. Such a use is clearly
indicated in Justin's *First Apology*, ch. 27, where the adjective
modifies μίξις, 'intercourse'. Philo, *De Fuga et Inventione* xxi (114),
employs ἄθεος as the equivalent of πολύθεος; that is, polytheism
is really atheism. If this is how hellenistic Jews employed ἄθεος
in its narrower sense, it is not likely that they applied the term
to Christians, who, despite their adoration of the Risen Christ,
were hesitant to refer to him as a δεύτερος θεός.

K. Lake, in the Loeb edition of Eusebius, translates this
phrase (cited by Eusebius from Justin) as 'a seditious sect'.[4]
This is an ingenious rendering, based on the notion that the
ἄθεοι who neglected the State gods were guilty of disloyalty to
the State. While such a charge could appropriately be made by
Gentiles, it would be poorly received by Gentiles when made
by Jews. It would be still less meaningful if addressed to Jews by
Jews. It is wise to remember that Jews were regarded by pagans
as ἄθεοι; cf. Jos. *Contra Apionem* ii. 14 (148).

[1] *J.E.H.* v, 156; *Mart.* p. 180, p. 202 n. 22, p. 260.
[2] *Judaism At Rome* (1877), p. 473 n. 53.
[3] *Ibid.*
[4] *Eccl. Hist.* IV, 18. 7; Loeb edition, I, 371.

THE ROMAN CHURCH IN THE FIRST CENTURY

THE present writer is firmly convinced that Paul wrote his Epistle to the Romans to a church that was predominantly Gentile, despite its 'Jewishness'. This is plain not only in the introduction (1: 1–15) and conclusion (15: 7–33), but also in the discussion concerning table fellowship (14: 1 — 15: 7). The men who are so weak in faith that they eat only vegetables are probably not Jews but Gentiles who were formerly synagogue-adherents. Paul's concern in 14: 15, 20 is for men whose faith is so weak that they may actually apostasize from Christ over the matter of food. This can hardly be a concern for Jewish believers. While many Jewish Christians of conservative persuasion were scandalized by neglect of the food laws on the part of Gentile Christians, they were more likely to withdraw into a separate fellowship than to apostasize; cf. Gal. 2: 12 ff. It must be remembered that Jews were accustomed to regarding Gentiles as unclean and would therefore not be deeply shocked at Gentile carelessness in matters of food. Doubtless there were many synagogue-adherents who accepted Jewish monotheism but did not observe the food laws; the behaviour of these 'God-fearers' is not likely to have threatened the faith of Jewish members of the synagogue!

The translations of Rom. 11: 13 found in the R.S.V. and the N.E.B. reflect the conviction that Paul had previously been addressing either Jews alone or Jews and Gentiles together. The Greek text does not imply a change of address. Moffatt's rendering is to be preferred: 'I tell you this, you Gentiles...'.

A COMMON 'VORLAGE' FOR
MATT. 5: 12c AND LUKE 6: 23c?

In his *Evangelium Lucae*, Wellhausen translates the Matthean τούς πρὸ ὑμῶν and the Lucan οἱ πατέρες αὐτῶν as 'your ancestors' and 'their ancestors' respectively, but offers no justification for these renderings. E. Lohmeyer, *Das Evangelium des Matthäus*, second edition edited by W. Schmauch (1958), p. 96, accepts Wellhausen's conjecture (Lohmeyer's transliteration is inaccurate). Black, p. 275, likewise follows Wellhausen, but omits the prefixed ד. Although the ד would be required in the *Vorlage* of Matthew's version (cf. Dan. 7: 7; Black's omission of the ד here is inexplicable), Wellhausen's דקדמיהון is impossible as the subject of the clause in Luke's *Vorlage*; G. Dalman, *Grammatik des jüdisch-palästinischen Aramäisch*, second edition (Leipzig: J. C. Heinrichs'sche Buchhandlung, 1905), p. 117, cites examples in which ד is used determinatively, but gives no instance in which ד with a substantive functions as the subject of a clause without any antecedent. Black, omitting the ד, apparently takes קדמיהון as the adjective קַדְמָי with 3 m. pl. suffix; cf. M. Jastrow, *A Dictionary of the Targumim, the Talmud Babli and Yerushalmi, and the Midrashic Literature* (New York/Berlin, Verlag Choreb, and London: Shapiro, Vallentine and Company, 1926), p. 1317. This could be translated 'their ancestors', or, in Greek, οἱ πατέρες αὐτῶν. Although it is very unusual for the subject to follow the object in Semitic syntax, it is not impossible for the Lucan *Vorlage* proposed by Black to be taken in this way.

To derive the two variants from the same *Vorlage* as Wellhausen does (Black's reconstruction includes both forms!) three difficulties must be surmounted. (1) The unusual word order implied by the Lucan rendering must have been the original, as the more difficult reading. (2) The transmitters of the Matthean *Vorlage* (or the translator of Q^Mt), finding the word order difficult, decided that the word modified the preceding noun, and added a ד. (3) The phrase so construed still made little sense ('the prophets which were before them') and so the suffix was changed to the second person. Is this process really credible? It presumes that the transmitters (or translator) of the Matthean *Vorlage* were seriously deficient in their knowledge of the language. Mistranslation in such cases is a far less probable hypothesis than intentional change. The mistranslation hypothesis further requires that we regard the beatitude as having been added independently to Q^{Mt} and Q^{Lk} after the bifurcation of the Greek Q.[1] This is improbable.

In the treatment of this question the writer has been helped greatly by a private communication from Dr William Lane, author of *A Handbook of Phoenician Inscriptions*, unpublished Ph.D. dissertation, Johns Hopkins University (1963).

[1] See above, p. 115 n. 5.

TWO TYPES OF SUFFERING

In the New Testament righteous (innocent) suffering is of two types. (1) General suffering is to be expected by all Christians, since it is the lot of the righteous to be persecuted by the wicked. This form of suffering is not necessarily brought upon Christians by their faith. Christian slaves, for example, may suffer ill-treatment from their masters, not because their masters hate Christians but simply because their masters are harsh and bad-tempered (1 Peter 2: 18–21). This kind of suffering is shared equally by Jewish and Gentile Christians and is inflicted by both Jewish and Gentile enemies. (2) The suffering of Jewish messengers to Israel belongs to a separate class, because it derives from a special form of wickedness which is peculiar to Israel.[1] Thus, the Maccabean martyrs provide prototypes for the suffering of the first category but not for that of the second. Confusion at this point vitiates the otherwise excellent study of H. A. Fischel.[2] While we may agree with Fischel, p. 382, that 'in the Tannaitic period, a far-reaching identification of the prophet with the martyr had taken place, i.e., every prophet had to suffer or die, and every martyr was in possession of prophetic powers, both being almost angelic figures', we must insist that identification of the two types in terms of the way the martyrdoms are narrated must not be confused with identification of the meaning of the suffering of the prophet with that of the non-prophetic martyr. The ordinary Jewish martyr suffers at the hands of foreigners, the prophet at the hands of his own people. It is a mistake, therefore, to suggest that the Maccabean martyr-tradition was the primary influence in the development of the motif of prophetic suffering as Fischel does, p. 270. Fischel is here followed by W. H. C. Frend.[3] The same confusion is found in Braun and Jas. M. Robinson.[4]

[1] See above, p. 140.

[2] 'Prophet and Martyr', *J.Q.R.* xxxvii (1946–7), 265–80, 363–86.

[3] 'The Persecutions: Some Links between Judaism and the Early Church', *J.E.H.* ix (1958–9), 145.

[4] Braun, ii, 100–8; Jas. M. Robinson, *The Problem of History in Mark* (1957), p. 58.

INTERPRETING MATTHEW 24

IN order to understand how apocalyptic materials are interpreted by a Synoptic author, it is necessary to determine, if possible, the point at which the author locates himself in the sequence of events predicted, that is, to discover which predictions are regarded by the author as already fulfilled in past events and which are for him still unfulfilled.

Because of the vagueness of the allusions in Matthew 24 this task is exceedingly difficult. Since the consensus is that the gospel was written after the destruction of Jerusalem, scholars are predisposed to find a reference to the desecration of the Temple in the 'abomination of desolation' of *v.* 15. Although this appears to have been Mark's understanding of the 'abomination of desolation', there is no positive evidence that Matthew understood it in this way. Thus it is possible for Marxsen, pp. 138 f., to maintain that the whole discourse, including even *vv.* 4–8, is a *Parusierede* concerned with the period *after* the destruction of Jersusalem.

Hummel, p. 160 n. 85, opposes Marxsen, maintaining that *vv.* 21 f. reflect the post-war period during which Christians were being persecuted. This is most improbable. The persecution as it is portrayed elsewhere by Matthew concerns missionaries only, and is not such as to be described as the greatest tribulation in the history of the world (*v.* 21); nor was it of short duration, as is the tribulation of *vv.* 21 f. In opposition to the view that *vv.* 15–20 are understood by Matthew as referring to the events of A.D. 70, we would point out that the Matthean addition, μηδὲ σαββάτῳ (*v.* 20), would be inappropriate and indeed meaningless as a supplement to a fulfilled prophecy. J. P. Brown, *N.T.S.* VIII, 30, suggests that the added phrase need not represent the point of view of the evangelist; it 'may be part of the remains of an M-apocalypse'. Even if the phrase were pre-Matthean, however, its retention by Matthew would be most improbable unless he regarded it as having reference to a future event. Indeed, on the basis of Matthew's editorial practice, we may suspect that the whole of *v.* 20 would have been dropped had Matthew regarded the prophecy as fulfilled, since the exhortation to prayer would be pointless after the event.

Another alternative to the traditional interpretation of Matthew 24 was proposed by A. Feuillet in the Dodd Fest-schrift.[1] Feuillet accepts the traditional view which sees three phases in Matthew's eschatology: (1) signs preceding the End, (2) the destruction of Jerusalem, (3) the final coming of the Son of man. Feuillet departs from the traditional view, however, with respect to the material he associates with the second phase. He maintains that in each use of the word παρουσία in this chapter (vv. 3, 27, 37, 39) the reference is not to the final coming of the Son of man with the clouds but to the historical judgment effected by the Son of man by means of Rome's armies. The phrase συντελείας τοῦ αἰῶνος (24: 3), he claims, likewise refers to the events of A.D. 70; the words indicate that the destruction of the Temple was regarded as the end of the old dispensation.

While many of Feuillet's arguments are attractive, the premise from which he starts is mistaken. He begins his case by asking: How could an author writing after A.D. 70 dare to report a pre-diction of Jesus which the facts had proved false, since this prediction combined the destruction of Jerusalem with the end of the world? He therefore finds it necessary to take the whole of v. 3 as referring to the destruction of Jerusalem; reference to the end of the world must be excluded. This is not necessary. Marxsen, p. 136, has shown how Matthew has carefully re-structured Mark 13: 4 with this very problem in mind, so as to separate the destruction of Jerusalem from the end of the world. If it is objected that in Marxsen's interpretation no answer is given to the disciples' first question (concerning the destruction of Jerusalem), it may be pointed out that this is not out of character for Matthew; after the long discourse giving mission-ary instruction (ch. 10), no mention is made of the mission itself.

Matthew's purpose in this last great discourse (chs. 24 f.) is not to show how Jesus' predictions have been fulfilled in the events of A.D. 70 but to prepare Christians for enduring faithful-ness during the indefinite period that remains. Matthew there-

[1] A. Feuillet, 'Le Sens du Mot Parousie dans l'Evangile de Matthieu: Comparaison entre Matth. 24 et Jac. 5: 1–11', *The Background of the New Testament and its Eschatology*, ed. W. D. Davies and D. Daube (1956), pp. 261–80.

fore totally ignores the first question, which for his generation is no longer vital, and makes the discourse as a whole an answer to the second, viz. 'What is the sign of your final coming and the consummation of history?'[1] In this way Matthew can retain the close relationship between the eschatological flight (*vv.* 15–28) and the final coming of the Son of man (*vv.* 29–31) which is found in Mark. In attempting to separate these two phases, Feuillet ignores the force of εὐθέως, 'immediately', in *v.* 29. There is no separation for Matthew, who adds this word to his Marcan material!

---

[1] Feuillet's efforts to de-eschatologize συντελείας τοῦ αἰῶνος are unconvincing. The meaning of the phrase here is surely the same as in its other occurrences in the gospel (13: 39, 40, 49; 28: 20), where the reference is clearly to the end of history, as Feuillet concedes (p. 270).

BIBLIOGRAPHY

ANCIENT SOURCES

The Babylonian Talmud. English translation edited by I. Epstein. 35 vols. London: Soncino Press, 1935–52.

Blackman, P. *Mishnayoth*. 7 vols. New York, 1963–4.

Brownlee, W. H. 'The Dead Sea Manual of Discipline', *Bulletin of the American Schools of Oriental Research*, Supplementary Studies nos. 10–12. New Haven, 1951.

Charles, R. H. *The Apocrypha and Pseudepigrapha of the Old Testament*. 2 vols. Oxford, 1913.

Danby, Herbert. *The Mishnah*. London, 1933.

—— *Tractate Sanhedrin: Mishnah and Tosefta*. London, 1919.

Eusebius. *The Ecclesiastical History*. English translation by K. Lake and J. E. L. Oulton. 2 vols. Loeb Classical Library. London and Cambridge, Mass., 1953.

—— *The Ecclesiastical History and the Martyrs of Palestine*. Translated with introduction and notes by H. J. Lawlor and J. E. L. Oulton. 2 vols. London, 1927.

Falls, Thomas B. *The Writings of Saint Justin Martyr*. New York, 1948.

Gaster, T. H. *The Dead Sea Scriptures*. Garden City, 1956.

Goldin, J. *The Fathers According to Rabbi Nathan*. New Haven, 1955.

James, M. R. *The Apocryphal New Testament*. Oxford, 1924.

Josephus. With an English Translation by H. St J. Thackeray, R. Marcus and A. Wikgren. 8 vols. Loeb Classical Library. London, New York and Cambridge, Mass., 1926–63.

Lake, K. *The Apostolic Fathers*. 2 vols. Loeb Classical Library. Cambridge, Mass., 1952.

Origen. *The Writings of Origen*. Translated by F. Crombie. 2 vols. Ante-Nicene Christian Library, vol. XXIII. Edinburgh, 1871.

Philo. English translation by F. H. Colson and G. H. Whitaker. 10 vols. Loeb Classical Library. London, New York and Cambridge, Mass., 1929–62.

Philo. *Supplement*. Translated by R. Marcus. 2 vols. Loeb Classical Library. London and Cambridge, Mass., 1953.

Philo Judaeus. *Works*. Translated by C. D. Yonge. 4 vols. London, 1854–5.

Philonis Alexandrini. *Opera quae supersunt*. Edited by L. Cohn and P. Wendland. 6 vols. Berlin, 1896–1915.

Rabin, Chaim. *The Zadokite Documents*. Oxford, 1954.

Reinach, Théodore. *Textes d'auteurs grecs et romains relatifs au judaïsme*. Paris, 1895.

Smallwood, E. Mary. *Philonis Alexandrini Legatio ad Gaium*. Leiden, 1961.

Stenning, J. F. *The Targum of Isaiah*. Oxford, 1949.

Strack, H. L. *Jesus, die Häretiker und die Christen nach den ältesten jüdischen Angaben*. Leipzig, 1910.

—— and Billerbeck, P. *Kommentar zum Neuen Testament aus Talmud und Midrasch*. 5 vols. Munich, 1922–8.

Suetonius. With an English translation by J. C. Rolfe. 2 vols. Loeb Classical Library. London and Cambridge, Mass., 1951.

Tacitus, Cornelius. *The Histories and the Annals*. Translated by C. H. Moore and J. Jackson. 4 vols. Loeb Classical Library. London and Cambridge, Mass., 1937–52.

Le Talmud de Jérusalem. Translated by Moïse Schwab. 12 vols. in 6. Paris, 1871–90.

Tertullian. *Works* in the Ante-Nicene Fathers, edited by F. Roberts and J. Donaldson, vols. III–IV. American reprint of the Edinburgh edition. Buffalo, 1885.

Whiston, William. *The Complete Works of Flavius Josephus*. Chicago, n.d.

The Writings of Justin Martyr and Athenagoras. Translated by George Reith. Ante-Nicene Christian Library, vol. II. Edinburgh, 1874.

STUDIES DEVOTED TO THE GOSPEL ACCORDING TO ST MATTHEW

Allen, W. C. *A Critical and Exegetical Commentary on the Gospel according to St Matthew*. Third edition. Edinburgh, 1912.

Bacon, B. W. *Studies in Matthew*. New York, 1930.

Barth, G. 'Matthew's Understanding of the Law', in G. Bornkamm, G. Barth and H. J. Held, *Tradition and Interpretation in Matthew*, pp. 58–164. Translated by Percy Scott. Philadelphia, 1963.

Blair, E. P. *Jesus in the Gospel of Matthew*. New York and Nashville, 1960.

Bonnard, P. *L'Evangile selon S. Matthieu*. Neuchâtel, 1963.

Bornkamm, G. 'End-Expectation and Church in Matthew', in G. Bornkamm, G. Barth and H. J. Held, *Tradition and Interpretation in Matthew*, pp. 15–51. Translated by Percy Scott. Philadelphia, 1963.

—— 'Matthäus als Interpret der Herrenworte', *T.L.* LXXIX (1954), cols. 341–6.

Brown, John Pairman. 'The Form of "Q" Known to Matthew', *N.T.S.* VIII (1961–2), 27–42.

Clark, Kenneth W. 'The Gentile Bias in Matthew', *J.B.L.* LXVI (1947), 165–72.

Dahl, N. A. 'Die Passionsgeschichte bei Matthäus', *N.T.S.* II (1955–6), 17–32.

Davies, W. D. *The Setting of the Sermon on the Mount.* Cambridge, 1964.

Dupont, Dom J. 'Vous n'aurez pas achevé les villes d'Israël avant que le Fils de l'Homme ne vienne (Mat. x. 23)', *Novum Testamentum*, II (1958), 228–44.

Feuillet, A. 'Le Sens du Mot Parousie dans l'Evangile de Matthieu: Comparison entre Matth. 24 et Jac. 5: 1–11', *The Background of the New Testament and Its Eschatology*, pp. 261–80. Edited by W. D. Davies and D. Daube. Cambridge, 1956.

Filson, F. V. 'Broken Patterns in the Gospel of Matthew', *J.B.L.* LXXV (1956), 227–31.

—— *A Commentary on the Gospel according to St Matthew.* London, 1960.

Glasson, T. F. 'Anti-Pharisaism in St Matthew', *J.Q.R.* LI (1961), 316–20.

Grant, F. C. *The Gospel of Matthew.* Harper's Annotated Bible Series, vol. I. New York, 1955.

Haenchen, Ernst. 'Matthäus 23', *Z.T.K.* XLVIII (1951), 38–63.

Hummel, Reinhart. *Die Auseinandersetzung zwischen Kirche und Judentum im Matthäusevangelium.* Munich, 1963.

Johnson, S. E. 'The Gospel according to St Matthew: Introduction and Exegesis', *The Interpreter's Bible*, vol. VII, pp. 231–625. Edited by G. A. Buttrick. New York and Nashville, 1951–7.

Kilpatrick, G. D. *The Origins of the Gospel According to St Matthew.* Oxford, 1946.

Klostermann, Erich. *Matthäus.* Tübingen, 1909.

Legg, S. C. E. *Novum Testamentum Graece: Evangelium secundum Matthaeum.* Oxford, 1940.

Lohmeyer, E. *Das Evangelium des Matthäus.* Second edition edited by W. Schmauch. Göttingen, 1958.

McNeile, A. H. *The Gospel according to St Matthew.* London, 1915.

Meyer, H. A. W. *A Critical and Exegetical Commentary on the New Testament.* Part I, *The Gospel according to St Matthew.* 2 vols. Edinburgh, 1880–1.

Michaelis, W. *Das Evangelium nach Matthäus.* Zürich, 1948.

Montefiore, H. 'Jesus and the Temple Tax', *N.T.S.* X (1964–5), 60–71.

Nepper-Christensen, P. *Das Matthäusevangelium: ein judenchristliches Evangelium?* Aarhus, 1958.

Plummer, A. *An Exegetical Commentary on the Gospel according to St Matthew.* Second edition. London and New York, 1910.

Schlatter, A. *Der Evangelist Matthäus.* Stuttgart, 1929. Sixth edition, Stuttgart, 1963.

—— *Die Kirche des Matthäus*. Gütersloh, 1929.

Schniewind, J. *Das Evangelium nach Matthäus*. Göttingen, 1962.

Schubert, K. 'The Sermon on the Mount and the Qumran Texts', in *The Scrolls and the New Testament*, pp. 118–28. Edited by K. Stendahl. New York, 1957.

Schweizer, E. 'Mt. 5: 17–20—Anmerkungen zum Gesetzverständnis des Matthäus', *T.L.* LXXVII (1952), cols. 479–84.

Smith, C. W. F. 'The Mixed State of the Church in Matthew's Gospel', *J.B.L.* LXXXII (1963), 149–68.

Stendahl, K. *The School of St Matthew*. London, 1954.

Strecker, Georg. *Der Weg der Gerechtigkeit: Untersuchung zur Theologie des Matthäus*. Göttingen, 1962.

Trilling, W. *Das wahre Israel: Studien zur Theologie des Matthäus-Evangeliums*. Leipzig, 1959.

OTHER STUDIES

Abrahams, Israel. *Studies in Pharisaism and the Gospels*. Second Series. Cambridge, 1924.

Albertz, M. *Die synoptischen Streitgespräche*. Berlin, 1921.

Allard, P. *Le Christianisme et l'Empire romain de Néron à Théodose*. Tenth edition. Paris, 1925.

—— *Histoire des persécutions pendant les deux premiers siècles*. Paris, 1903.

Bamberger, B. J. *Proselytism in the Talmudic Period*. Cincinnati, 1939.

Barnikol, E. *Die vorchristliche und frühchristliche Zeit des Paulus*. Kiel, 1929.

Baum, G. *The Jews and the Gospel*. Westminster, Maryland, 1961.

Beare, F. W. 'Thessalonians, First', *The Interpreter's Dictionary of the Bible*, vol. IV, pp. 621–5. Edited by G. A. Buttrick. New York and Nashville, 1962.

Beasley-Murray, G. R. *A Commentary on Mark Thirteen*. London, 1957.

Belkin, Samuel. *Philo and the Oral Law*. Cambridge, Mass., 1940.

Bell, H. I. *Jews and Christians in Egypt*. London, 1924.

Black, M. *An Aramaic Approach to the Gospels and Acts*. Second edition. Oxford, 1954.

Blinzler, J. 'Rechtsgeschichtliches zur Hinrichtung des Zebedäiden Jakobus (Apg xii. 2)', *Novum Testamentum*, V (1962), 191–206.

—— 'Das Synedrium von Jerusalem und die Strafprozessordnung der Mischna', *Z.N.W.* LII (1961), 54–65.

—— *The Trial of Jesus*. Translated from the second revised and enlarged edition by Isabel and Florence McHugh. Westminster, Maryland, 1959.

Bonsirven, Joseph. *Le Judaïsme palestinien au temps de Jésus-Christ.* 2 vols. Paris, 1934–5.

Bornkamm, G. 'Evangelien, synoptische', *Religion in Geschichte und Gegenwart.* Third edition, vol. II, cols. 753–66.

Brandon, S. G. F. *The Fall of Jerusalem and the Christian Church.* London, 1951.

Braun, Herbert. *Spätjüdisch-häretischer und frühchristlicher Radikalismus.* 2 vols. Tübingen, 1957.

Brown, R. E. *The Gospel according to St John (i–xii).* Garden City, 1966.

Bruce, A. B. 'The Synoptic Gospels', *E.G.T.* vol. I, pp. 1–651. Edited by W. R. Nicoll (Reprint). Grand Rapids, Mich., 1961.

Büchler, A. *The Economic Conditions of Judea after the Destruction of the Second Temple.* London, 1912.

—— 'The Minim of Sepphoris and Tiberias in the Second and Third Centuries', *Studies in Jewish History* (Adolph Büchler Memorial Volume), pp. 245–74. London, 1956.

—— *The Political and Social Leaders of the Jewish Community of Sepphoris in the Second and Third Centuries.* London, n.d.

Büchsel, F. 'Die Blutgerichtsbarkeit des Synhedriums', *Z.N.W.* XXX (1931), 202–10, and *Z.N.W.* XXXIII (1934), 84–7.

Bultmann, R. *The History of the Synoptic Tradition.* Translated by John Marsh. Oxford, 1963.

—— *Theology of the New Testament.* Translated by K. Grobel. 2 vols. New York, 1951–5.

Burkill, T. A. 'The Competence of the Sanhedrin', *Vigiliae Christianae*, X (1956), 80–96.

Canfield, L. H. *The Early Persecutions of the Christians.* New York, 1913.

Charles, R. H. *A Critical and Exegetical Commentary on the Revelation of St John.* 2 vols. Edinburgh, 1920.

Colwell, E. C. 'A Definite Rule for the Use of the Article in the Greek New Testament', *J.B.L.* LII (1933), 12–21.

Conzelmann, H. *The Theology of St Luke.* Translated by Geoffrey Buswell. New York, 1960.

Cranfield, C. E. B. *The Gospel according to St Mark.* Cambridge, 1963.

Cullmann, Oscar. *Peter: Disciple—Apostle—Martyr.* Translated by F. V. Filson. Philadelphia, 1953.

—— *The State in the New Testament.* New York, 1956.

Dalman, G. *Grammatik des jüdisch-palästinischen Aramäisch.* Second edition. Leipzig, 1905.

—— *Jesus-Jeschua. Studies in the Gospels.* Authorized translation by P. P. Levertoff. New York, 1929.

—— *Die Worte Jesu.* Leipzig, 1898.

—— *The Words of Jesus.* Translated by D. M. Kay. Edinburgh, 1902.

Daube, D. *The New Testament and Rabbinic Judaism.* London, 1956.

Davies, W. D. *Christian Origins and Judaism.* Philadelphia, 1962.

—— *Paul and Rabbinic Judaism.* London, 1948.

—— *Torah in the Messianic Age and/or the Age to Come.* Philadelphia, 1952.

Deever, Philip H. *The Anti-Judaism of the New Testament in the Light of its Biblical and Hellenistic Context.* Unpublished Th.D. dissertation, Union Theological Seminary, New York, 1958.

Descamps, A. *Les Justes et la Justice dans les évangiles et le christianisme primitif, hormis la doctrine proprement paulinienne.* Louvain, 1950.

Dibelius, M. *Der Brief des Jakobus.* Göttingen, 1921.

—— *From Tradition to Gospel.* Translated by Bertram Lee Wolf. London, 1934.

—— *Studies in the Acts of the Apostles.* Edited by H. Greeven. Translated by Mary Ling and Paul Schubert. New York, 1956.

Dix, Dom Gregory. *Jew and Greek: A Study in the Primitive Church.* London, 1953.

Dobschütz, E. von. *Die urchristlichen Gemeinden.* Leipzig, 1902.

Dodd, C. H. *New Testament Studies.* Manchester, 1953.

—— *Parables of the Kingdom.* Revised edition. New York, 1961.

Dugmore, C. W. *The Influence of the Synagogue on the Divine Office.* London, 1944.

Dupont, J. *Les Béatitudes.* Brussels, 1954.

Easton, B. S. *Christ in the Gospels.* New York, 1930.

Farmer, W. R. *Maccabees, Zealots and Josephus.* New York, 1956.

Fischel, H. A. 'Prophet and Martyr', *J.Q.R.* xxxvii (1946–7), 265–80, 363–86.

Frame, J. E. *A Critical and Exegetical Commentary on the Epistles of St Paul to the Thessalonians.* Edinburgh, 1912.

Frend, W. H. C. 'The Gnostic Sects and the Roman Empire', *J.E.H.* v (1954–5), 25–37.

—— *Martyrdom and Persecution in the Early Church.* Oxford, 1965.

—— 'The Persecutions: Some Links between Judaism and the Early Church', *J.E.H.* ix (1958–9), 141–58.

Fuchs, Harald. 'Tacitus über die Christen', *Vigiliae Christianae,* iv (1950), 65–93.

Goguel, M. *The Birth of Christianity.* Translated from the French by H. C. Snape. London, 1953.

Goodenough, E. R. *Jewish Symbols in the Greco-Roman Period.* 3 vols. New York, 1953.

Goppelt, L. *Christentum und Judentum im ersten und zweiten Jahrhundert.* Gütersloh, 1954.

Grant, F. C. *The Economic Background of the Gospels*. London, 1926.

—— 'Modern Study of the Jewish Liturgy', *Z.A.W.* LXVI (1953), 59–77.

Guignebert, Charles. *Jesus*. Translated by S. H. Hooke. New York, 1956.

Haenchen, Ernst. *Die Apostelgeschichte*. Göttingen, 1959.

Harnack, Adolf. *The Expansion of Christianity in the First Three Centuries*. Translated and edited by James Moffatt. New York, 1904.

—— *Die Mission und Ausbreitung des Christentum*. Leipzig, 1902.

—— *New Testament Studies II: The Sayings of Jesus: The Second Source of St Matthew and St Luke*. Translated by J. R. Wilkinson. New York and London, 1908.

Hawkins, J. C. *Horae Synopticae*. Oxford, 1899.

Herford, R. T. *Christianity in Talmud and Midrash*. London, 1903.

—— *The Pharisees*. New York, 1924.

Hirsch, E. *Frühgeschichte des Evangeliums*. 2 vols. Tübingen, 1941.

Holzmeister, U. 'Zur Frage der Blutgerichtsbarkeit des Synhedriums', *Biblica*, XIX (1938), 43–59, 151–74.

Huidekoper, Frederic. *Judaism at Rome: B.C. 76 to A.D. 140*. Second edition. New York, 1877.

Hunzinger, Claus-Hunno. *Die jüdische Bannpraxis im neutestamentlichen Zeitalter*. Göttingen dissertation 1954 as reported in *T.L.* LXXX (1955), cols. 114–15.

Husband, R. W. *The Prosecution of Jesus*. Princeton, 1916.

Jackson, F. J. Foakes and Kirsopp Lake. *The Beginnings of Christianity*. Part I. 5 vols. London, 1920–33.

Jeremias, Joachim. *Heiligengräber in Jesu Umwelt*. Göttingen, 1958.

—— *Jesus' Promise to the Nations*. Translated by S. H. Hooke. Naperville, Ill., 1958.

—— *The Parables of Jesus*. Revised edition, translated by S. H. Hooke from the sixth German edition. New York, 1963.

—— 'Zur Geschichtlichkeit des Verhörs Jesu vor dem Hohen Rat', *Z.N.W.* XLIII (1950–1), 145–50.

Jocz, Jacob. *The Jewish People and Jesus Christ*. London, 1949.

Johnston, George. *The Doctrine of the Church in the New Testament*. Cambridge, 1943.

Juster, Jean. *Les Juifs dans l'Empire romain*. 2 vols. Paris, 1914.

Kilpatrick, G. D. *The Trial of Jesus*. Oxford, 1953.

Kittel, G. 'Die Stellung des Jakobus zu Judentum und Heidenchristentum', *Z.N.W.* XXX (1931), 145–57.

Knowling, R. J. 'The Acts of the Apostles', *E.G.T.* vol. II, pp. 1–544. Edited by W. R. Nicoll. Reprint. Grand Rapids, Mich., 1961,

Knox, John. *Chapters in a Life of Paul*. New York and Nashville, 1950.

Knox, W. L. *The Acts of the Apostles.* Cambridge, 1948.

—— *The Sources of the Synoptic Gospels.* Vol. II, *St Luke and St Matthew.* Cambridge, 1957.

Kohler, K. 'Synagogue', *Dictionary of the Apostolic Church,* vol. II, pp. 541–5. Edited by J. Hastings. New York, 1918.

Kuhn, K. G. 'Giljonim und sifre minim', *Judentum, Urchristentum, Kirche,* pp. 24–61. Edited by W. Eltester. Berlin, 1960.

Kümmel, W. G. *Promise and Fulfilment.* Second English edition, translated by Dorothea M. Barton. London, 1961.

Lieberman, Saul. *Greek in Jewish Palestine.* New York, 1942.

Lietzmann, Hans. 'Bemerkungen zum Prozess Jesu, II', *Z.N.W.* XXXI (1932), 78–84.

—— *Der Prozess Jesu.* Berlin, 1931.

Loisy, A. *Les Actes des Apôtres.* Paris, 1920.

Mantel, Hugo. *Studies in the History of the Sanhedrin.* Cambridge, Mass., 1961.

Marcus, R. 'Pharisees, Essenes and Gnostics', *J.B.L.* LXXIII (1954), 157–61.

Marxsen, Willi. *Der Evangelist Markus: Studien zur Redaktionsgeschichte des Evangeliums.* Second edition. Göttingen, 1959.

Merrill, E. T. *Essays in Early Christian History.* London, 1924.

Montefiore, C. G. *The Synoptic Gospels.* Second edition. 2 vols. London, 1927.

Moore, G. F. *Judaism in the First Centuries of the Christian Era: The Age of the Tannaim.* 3 vols. Cambridge, Mass., 1927.

Moule, C. F. D. *The Birth of the New Testament.* New York, 1962.

Munck, J. 'Israel and the Gentiles in the New Testament', *Bulletin of the Studiorum Novi Testamenti Societas,* no. 1, pp. 26–38. Cambridge, 1950.

—— *Paul and the Salvation of Mankind.* Translated by Frank Clarke. Richmond, Va., 1959.

Parkes, James. *The Conflict of the Church and the Synagogue.* London, 1934.

—— *The Foundations of Judaism and Christianity.* London, 1960.

Percy, Ernst. *Die Botschaft Jesu. Eine Traditionskritische und exegetische Untersuchung.* Lund, 1953.

Ramsay, H. L. *The Place of Galatians in the Career of Paul.* Unpublished Ph.D. dissertation, Columbia University, 1960.

Riddle, D. W. *Jesus and the Pharisees: A Study in Christian Tradition.* Chicago, 1928.

—— 'Die Verfolgungslogien in formgeschichtlicher und soziologischer Beleuchtung', *Z.N.W.* XXXIII (1934), 271–89.

Robinson, J. A. T. *Jesus and His Coming.* New York and Nashville, 1957.

Robinson, James M. *The Problem of History in Mark*. London, 1957.

Rosché, T. R. 'The Words of Jesus and the Future of the "Q" Hypothesis', *J.B.L.* LXXIX (1960), 210–20.

Roth, Cecil. 'An Ordinance against Images in Jerusalem, A.D. 66', *H.T.R.* XLIX (1956), 169–77.

Schoeps, H. J. *Aus frühchristlicher Zeit*. Tübingen, 1950.

—— *The Jewish–Christian Argument: a History of Theologies in Conflict*. Translated by D. E. Green. New York, 1963.

—— *Die jüdischen Prophetenmorde*. Supplementhäften till Svensk Exegetisk Årsbok 2. Uppsala, 1943.

—— *Paul: The Theology of the Apostle in the Light of Jewish Religious History*. Translated by Harold Knight. London, 1961.

—— *Theologie und Geschichte des Judenchristentums*. Tübingen, 1949.

—— *Urgemeinde, Judenchristentum, Gnosis*. Tübingen, 1956.

Schürer, Emil. *Geschichte des jüdischen Volkes im Zeitalter Jesu Christi*. Fourth edition. 3 vols. Leipzig, 1901–9.

—— *A History of the Jewish People in the time of Jesus Christ*. Edinburgh, 1897–8.

Schwartz, E. 'Noch einmal der Tod der Söhne Zebedaei', *Z.N.W.* XI (1910), 89–104.

Simkhovitch, V. G. *Toward the Understanding of Jesus*. Unabridged edition with new preface. New York, 1947.

Simon, Marcel. 'Retour de Christ et reconstruction du Temple dans la pensée chrétienne primitive', *Aux sources de la tradition chrétienne: Mélanges offerts à M. Maurice Goguel*, pp. 247–57. Neuchâtel and Paris, 1950.

—— *Verus Israel*. Paris, 1948.

Smalley, S. S. 'The Delay of the Parousia', *J.B.L.* LXXXIII (1964), 41–54.

Smallwood, E. Mary. 'High Priests and Politics in Roman Palestine', *J.T.S.* XIII (n.s. 1962), 14–34.

Smith, Morton. 'The Dead Sea Sect in Relation to Ancient Judaism', *N.T.S.* VII (1960–1), 347–60.

—— 'The Jewish Elements in the Gospels', *J.B.R.* XXIV (1956), 90–6.

Stauffer, E. *Jerusalem und Rom im Zeitalter Jesu Christi*. Bern and Munich, 1957.

Streeter, B. H. *The Four Gospels*. London, 1924.

Studies in the Synoptic Problem. By Members of the University of Oxford. Edited by W. Sanday. Oxford, 1911.

Surkau, Hans-Werner. *Martyrium in jüdischer und frühchristlicher Zeit*. Göttingen, 1938.

Turner, C. H. 'The Gospel according to St Mark', *A New Commentary on Holy Scripture*, pp. 42–124. Edited by Charles Gore, H. L. Goudge and Alfred Guillaume. New York, 1928.

BIBLIOGRAPHY

Tyson, J. B. *The Execution of Jesus*. Unpublished Th.D. dissertation, Union Theological Seminary, New York, 1959.

Van Unnik, W. C. 'Corpus Hellenisticum Novi Testamenti', *J.B.L.* LXXXIII (1964), 17–33.

Wellhausen, J. *Einleitung in die drei ersten Evangelien*. First edition, Berlin, 1905. Second edition, 1911.

—— *Das Evangelium Marci*. Berlin, 1903.

—— *Evangelium Lucae*. Berlin, 1904.

Wilckens, Ulrich. *Die Missionsreden der Apostelgeschichte*. Neukirchen, 1961.

Winter, Paul. *On the Trial of Jesus*. Berlin, 1961.

Workman, H. B. *Persecution in the Early Church*. London, 1906.

Zahn, Theodor. *Forschungen zur Geschichte des neutestamentlichen Kanons und der altkirchlichen Literatur*. VI. Teil. Leipzig, 1900.

Zeitlin, Solomon. *Who Crucified Jesus?* New York and London, 1942. Second edition, 1947.

Ziegler, Ignaz. *Der Kampf zwischen Judentum und Christentum*. Berlin, 1907.

Zucker, Hans. *Studien zur jüdischen Selbstverwaltung im Altertum*. Berlin, 1936.

INDEX

I. INDEX OF PASSAGES QUOTED

A. OLD TESTAMENT

13-2

C. APOCRYPHA AND PSEUDEPIGRAPHA OF THE OLD TESTAMENT AND THE DEAD SEA SCROLLS

II. INDEX OF GREEK WORDS
(selected)

III. INDEX OF AUTHORS

IV. INDEX OF SUBJECTS